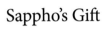

Sappho's Gift

Sappho's Gift

The Poet and Her Community

Franco Ferrari

translated by Benjamin Acosta-Hughes
and Lucia Prauscello

Michigan Classical Press
www.michiganclassicalpress.com

Ann Arbor

Published in the United States of America by Michigan Classical Press
www.michiganclassicalpress.com

Manufactured in the United States of America

2013   2012   2011   2010   4   3   2   1

∞ Printed on acid-free paper and bound by Thomson-Shore, Inc., Dexter, MI
www.thomsonshore.com

Library of Congress Cataloging-in-Publication Data

Ferrari, Franco.

[Una mitra per Kleis. English]

Sappho's gift : the poet and her community / Franco Ferrari ; translated by Benjamin Acosta-Hughes and Lucia Prauscello.

  p. cm.

"Originally published in Italian in 2007 as Una mitra per Kleis. Saffo e il suo pubblico. Biblioteca di "materiali e discussioni per l'analisi dei testi classici" 19, by Giardini editori e stampatori in Pisa, www.libraweb.net."-T.p. verso.

Includes bibliographical references and index.

ISBN 978-0-9799713-3-4 (hardcover : alk. paper)

1. Sappho—Criticism and interpretation. 2. Sappho—Translations into English. 3. Alcaeus—Criticism and interpretation. 4. Alcaeus—Translations into English. 5. Love poetry, Greek—Translations into English. I. Title.

PA4409.F4713 2010

884'.01--dc22   2009053549

Preface

This book is a journey through Sappho's texts, those long known and those recently discovered. The journey's goal is an attempt, inasmuch as this is possible, to capture the political, anthropological, and discursive realms in which these songs were conceived and composed.

In this respect the question of public or audience whom the Mytilenean poet addressed, whether through her own voice or that of a young girls' chorus, one she had herself taken care to instruct in singing and dancing, takes on a particular emphasis.

The characterization of this group as an association of committed loyalties, in competition with other circles under the direction of other adult women, in an educative course that covered the onset of adolescence until marriage, takes on a decisive role in our comprehension of this poetry. In doing so we must however acknowledge a distinction between such a private sphere (a dimension of "interiors") and the sphere of poetic performance, oriented rather to a public space ("externals") and tied to cult and celebratory occasions of a variety of types.

The conception of Sappho as an "intimate" voice confiding her own emotions to a few friends or followers, though one that obstinately persists even among authoritative modern scholars, has no basis since it is compatible neither with our extant texts nor with literary and iconographic evidence.

This study depends in large part on the textual reconstruction and the interpretation of fragments, whether from papyrus, ostraka, or worn parchment, and citations taken for the most varied reasons and interests by rhetoricians, grammarians, metricians, and antiquarians of different epochs. Our analysis will thus inevitably engage with clues, conjectures, supplementations, hypotheses, pseudo-facts. Without the constant effort at philological recovery this could result in an easier and smoother discussion, but would come down to cheating the reader. For this reason I have not hesitated to explore the possible import to our knowledge of even the smallest fragments and scraps—and there are not a few of these—that are usually disregarded. Little by little I have tried to unravel the boundaries, indistinct though these may be, between sure facts, conjectures, and inferences.

I am thankful to all who have read part or the whole of this work and who have provided me with observations, hints, objections. To name all would take too long, yet I cannot avoid mentioning two scholars, and I do so with pleasure, without whom this book would not exist. Lucia Prauscello has followed the unfolding of all the stages of this book and debated with me many individual problems, giving freely from the wealth of her acumen and learning. Enzo Puglia with ever increasing participation has joined in the examination of papyrus finds, sharing with me his original contributions and brilliant intuition and saving me, with his papyrological expertise, from several over-hasty hypotheses.

Where not otherwise specified the texts of Sappho and Alcaeus are cited, preceded with the sign "F," following the numeration of Eva-Maria Voigt's 1971 edition; on the other hand, I have used the abbreviation "fr." for the papyrus fragments as edited in their respective original editions. The concise apparatus that accompanies citations has the sole purpose of integrating information given in Voigt's edition and of indicating differences in respect to her text.

This book is dedicated to my granddaughter Matilde.

Table of Contents

Translators' Preface

We undertook to translate Franco Ferrari's book *Una mitra per Cleis* a year after its original publication (2007). As is generally the case with rendering Italian scholarship into English, we have tried to remain as faithful as possible to the Italian original while at the same time conveying its essence in idiomatic English prose. We have also occasionally corrected minor errata in the original text and incorporated into the text some bibliographical addenda suggested by the author. We have also replaced citations from French or Italian works with citations from their English translations, particularly in those instances where the English version is considerably better known to the Anglo-American audience (e.g., G. Gentili's *Poetry and Its Public in Ancient Greece*).

Coming to the conclusion, after long consideration, that rendering Italian translations of original Greek and Latin texts into English would put the English-speaking reader at one further remove from the original, we have translated all of the Greek and Latin texts in the volume into English ourselves, keeping, however, always an eye on the Italian translation, whether this was by the author or cited from another source.

We are grateful to the following institutions for providing the illustrations used in this volume: the Ruhr-Universität Kunstsammlungen in Bochum, the Staatliche Antikensammlungen und Glyptothek in Munich, the National Museum in Warsaw, and the National Archaeological Museum in Athens.

Our deepest debt of gratitude goes to the author, who has supported and advised our endeavor throughout, and especially to Ellen Bauerle, who took on this project for the Michigan Classical Press, and who has been a model of patience and understanding for what has often been a quite complex undertaking.

Benjamin Acosta-Hughes and Lucia Prauscello

I Song of the Headband

§1 Between Copenhagen and Milan

At the end of August 1941, at the publishing house Ariel, in Milan, Achille Vogliano published two small fragments of what appeared to be a single poem of Sappho.[1]

The first piece was preserved at Copenhagen, but had been entrusted to Vogliano, not without a certain reluctance, by Carsten Hoeg, professor at the University of Copenhagen. The second he had acquired together with other fragments in the spring of 1937 from the scholar and trader Carl Schmidt (who had himself procured it from the antiquities market in Cairo), without initially realizing that he had gotten his hands on a fragment of Sappho;[2] he first made it known in *Philologus* 93 (1938). Vertically juxtaposing the two fragments Edgar Lobel realized, between Vogliano's first and second publications, that these must have belonged to the same column of writing and were originally placed not far apart from one another.

The papyrus dated to the Ptolemaic period, between the third and second centuries BC, and at the moment of its discovery it represented, together with an ostrakon published by Medea Norsa in 1937, the oldest known example of Aeolic poetry: it was several centuries earlier than previously known papyri, principally from Oxyrhynchus and dating from the first century of the common era.

---

1 Vogliano 1941.
2 On the entire episode see Canfora 2005: 354–74.

Precisely because it is of such a comparatively ancient date, the text Vogliano published is earlier than, or in any event independent of, the edition of Sappho in eight or nine books produced at Alexandria, probably by Aristophanes of Byzantium, in the first half of the second century BC and destined to become canonical for the rest of antiquity.

The Alexandrian edition was put together also with an eye to the reader, and in fact the most recent papyri are furnished with a series of indications, such as accents, breathings, elisions, signs of syllable quantity, etc., that aided, and continue to aid, the reader in orienting himself among the difficult dialect forms and within a system of accentuation and aspiration different from that in use in other Greek dialects. Documents prior to this standard edition, on the other hand, have no such annotation; they appear to the eye, other than being in verse and stanza divisions (in this case three-line stanzas), as unadorned successions of signs from which the reader had to extract both the single words and their pronunciation.

There is, however, one exception: a horizontal stroke in the left margin accompanies each of the last three verses in the column of writing. Paul Maas immediately suggested that the three verses in question had been accidentally omitted by the scribe where they ought to have been transcribed, and were then successively added at the bottom of the column. The horizontal lines added in the margins served to mark this circumstance and ought to have been accompanied by some other sign (perhaps a similar line) in the margin of the area (now a lacuna) where the verses had been omitted.[3]

This is why things are presented in this order in the current editions of Sappho (i.e., the 1955 edition by Edgar Lobel and Denys Page published at Oxford and the 1971 edition by Eva-Maria Voigt published in Amsterdam):

- the lines that come from the Copenhagen fragment
- a lacuna of imprecise size
- the three verses at the bottom of the Milan fragment
- a further lacuna of imprecise size
- the other verses of the Milan fragment

3 See Page 1995: 98. The same type of explanation does not work for the horizontal strokes placed in the left margin of lines 1–7 in P.Köln 59, col. II = Alc. F 298.25–31. Perhaps here we should follow the first editor (Merkelbach) in understanding these as oboloi meant to athetize the relevant verses (and also col. I, line 24 = verse 24) as an alternative version of lines 32–39 (see the apparatus of Voigt to lines 25–31 and Liberman 1999: II.100 n. 1).

Actually, only in the case of the second verse of these three-line strophes can we be sure that it was the same (a glyconic) in both fragments. For the other two verses, for neither of which there is a complete line, there can be no certainty that the type of stanza employed throughout the whole column was a single one, and that we aren't rather dealing with two different poems. Nothing on the other hand clashes with the possibility of only one type of stanza of the shape gl || gl || cr gl, and the contents we can derive from the text seem in accord with a single composition.

§2   The Advice of Grandmother Cleis

In the twelve verses originating from the Copenhagen fragment (F 98a) Sappho recalls first that her mother, at the time of her own youth, was quite happy to be able to adorn her hair with a scarlet ribbon; however, for one who is blonde, a garland of flowers would be more appropriate.

Sappho turns to her daughter, who was named Cleis after her grandmother[4] and, from what we can tell from F 132, was a blonde, and speaks to her showing implicit understanding for her aspirations to elegance and taste. As she recalls the grandmother, Sappho reconstructs a piece of female tradition on how to bind one's hair (on the basis of other fragments we can also imagine with which flowers such a garland might be entwined: violets, roses, crocuses, dill).

Here is F 98a:

_..].θος· ἀ γάρ μ' ἐγέννα[τ
σ]φᾶς ἐπ' ἀλικίας μέγ[αν
κ]όσμον αἴ τις ἔχη φόβα<ι>ς [
_πορφύρωι κατελιξαμέ[να πλόκωι   4
ἔμμεναι μάλα τοῦτο δ[ή,
ἀλλ' ἀ ξανθοτέρα<ι>ς ἔχη [
_τα<ὶ>ς κόμα<ι>ς δάιδος προφ[7
σ]τεφάνοισιν ἐπαρτία[ις
ἀνθέων ἐριθαλέων· [
_μ]ιτράναν δ' ἀρτίως κλ[10

---

4 Cf. P.Oxy. 1800 fr. 1 = Sapph. T 252 V.: θυγατέρα δ' ἔσχε Κλεῖν ὁμώνυμον τῆι ἑαυτῆς μητρί.

ποικίλαν ἀπὺ Σαρδίω[ν
πρὸ]ς Ἰαονίας πόλ{ε}ις [

4 κατελιξαμέ[να πλόκωι Vogliano   5 fin. δ[ή Page   6 ἀλλ᾽ ἀ Vogliano   7 προ-
φ[έρει Page (an προφ[έρην?)   10   fin. κλ[έος Kamerbeek   12   πρὸ]ς supplevi Ἰαονίας
Diehl

... she who bore me [she told me once]

that at the time of her youth it was truly a great
adornment if a girl held her hair
bound with a purple [ribbon]   4

but that it was better
that she who had hair blonder
than a torch's fire   7

wore it adorned with garlands
of bright flowers [...]
but recently a headband [...]   10

of varied colors from Sardis
[towards] Ionia's[5] cities ...

In comparison with the purple band and the garlands of flowers, simple and
traditional adornments, the mention of the diffusion among the cities of Ionia of the Lydian mitra—an embroidered head-piece that covered the hair like
a veil but left the ears visible[6]—represented a small but perceptible cultural
breach.

Headgear had been in use for centuries in the Greek world—bands, nets,
and ribbons—but that a head-piece made, or any rate invented, in neigh-

---

5   From the photograph]οι seems to me the best of the possible readings for the beginning
of line 12.]μ (]Μαονίας Vogliano) seems to me on the contrary impossible, and also]χ or]ψ of
Lobel and Page is scarcely plausible.

6   Good examples of such a "mitra" (but there are already attestations on relief work from the
seventh century BC, from the Spartan acropolis) can be seen on the so-called Anacreontic vases,
e.g., on an Attic red-figure cup dating to 480/70 BC, preserved at the Getty Museum (86.AE.392)
and reproduced in Kurke 1992: 115 (note particularly the two aulos players).

boring Lydia could command attention as an object capable of disquieting the dreams of a young aristocratic girl is one of the signs of a process of acculturation that was spreading among the Aeolian and Ionian cities of Asia Minor and the nearby islands.[7]

A Lydian headband was not then so very different from a traditional head-covering, but with the fine character of its fabric and embroidery it might represent a status symbol. It might also suggest, within the political tensions that divided Mytilene, an expression of sympathy for that clan or those clans that had promoted and sustained the opening of microasiatic trade and of a style of life of an "orientalizing" type.

Even Sparta of that period, though it would soon be closed to external influences, was in the seventh century BC at the forefront of commercial contacts and in taste for novelty in fashion and in art. Alcman, perhaps a native of Sardis, in order to extol the beauty of the chorus-leader Hagesichora, had had the girls' chorus he himself instructed say that no other beautiful thing and no other female figure could distract their minds from the erotic obsession that seized them regarding their chorus-leader. Among the "beautiful things" we find, alongside a superabundance of purple and a bracelet engraved in gold, just such a "Lydian headband, adornment of lovely-lidded girls" (fr. 1.67–69 PMGF μίτρα | Λυδία, νεανίδων | ἰανογ[λ]-εφάρων ἄγαλμα).

Pindar was to transform the headband into one of the symbols of the scintillating polymorphism of his own art (N. 8.14–15), Posidippus of Pella (46 A.-B.) was to have the aged Battis say that she grew old "teaching how to handle wool and the yarn for headbands / of many colors,"[8] and Vergil was to show the king Iarbas venting his jealousy of Aeneas as a *semivir* who draws back his perfumed hair with a Maeonian mitra (*Aen.* 4.216–17).[9]

As for Lydian fashion, Sappho herself (F 39) says, though we don't know whether of a man or a woman, that "gaudy footwear, splendid Lydian work, en-

---

7   If, as Battezzato* suggests, ἀρτίως of F 98a10 is still part of the discourse relating to the grandmother Cleis, the first diffusion of the mitra in Anatolia would go back to that time in which Sappho's mother held this discourse with her daughter, so around 625; this would agree both with the testimony of Alcm. fr. 1.67–69 mentioned below and with the rule of the Cleanactids at Mytilene. Hence my preference for the infinitive προφ[έρην rather than for προφ[έρει at line 7.

8   Lines 3 ff.: εἴρια παιδεύουσα κομεῖν καὶ νήματα μίτραις | παιπαλέαις (παιπαλέαις Livrea 2002: 62 ff.: ποιπαλεαι pap.).

9   Cf. also Eur. *Ba.* 833, 929, and 1115, *Hec.* 924, Aristoph. *Th.* 162–63 and 257, and Men. *Per.* 823.

velops the feet."[10] Also of Lydian origin are the pektis, the harp Sappho herself uses (F 22.11 and 156),[11] as well as the barbitos, a type of lyre used at symposia, which as Pindar mentions (fr. 125 M.) was imported to Greece by Terpander of Lesbos:

τόν ῥα Τέρπανδρός ποθ᾽ ὁ Λέσβιος εὗρεν
πρῶτος, ἐν δείπνοισι Λυδῶν
ψαλμὸν ἀντίφθογγον ὑψηλᾶς ἀκούων πακτίδος.

This Terpander from Lesbos once conceived,
on hearing at the Lydians' banquets
the sound that accompanied the high-pitched pektis.

§3   The Mytilenean

The reason Sappho was not in a position to procure the ornament for her daughter (whom she calls by name) that the latter so desired seems to have been the subject of the three verses that ended up being placed at the bottom of the column but which were presumably part, as we have seen, of an area between the two pieces from Copenhagen and Milan, i.e., F 98b.1–3:

σοὶ δ᾽ ἔγω Κλέι ποικίλαν [
οὐκ ἔχω πόθεν ἔσσεται [
_μιτράν\<αν\>· ἀλλὰ τῶι Μυτιληνάωι [

But I, Cleis, the headband
of varied colors, I don't know whence I can get it,[12]
[but take it up] with the Mytilenean...

---

10   The word used here, μάσλης (Aeolic form of μάσθλης), which in itself signifies a strip of leather, recurs also at Alc. F 143.12 (and cf. also Hesych. M 332 ... μάσλης ... ὑπόδημα φοινικοῦν).

11   On the characteristics of this instrument see West 1992: 71.

12   Voigt follows Snell in considering πόθεν ἔσσεται a parenthetic interrogative, but the detached progression that results seems foreign to Sappho's mode of expression. It is better to think of it, with Page 1955: 101, as the contamination of two constructions: οὐκ ἔχω μιτράναν and οὐκ ἔχω πόθεν ἔσσεταί σοι μιτράνα.

For us the period does not come to a conclusion because of the accompanying lacuna, but the train of thought is clear—if I am not in a position to procure for you this bonnet for which you ask me, don't fault your mother, for whom it would not seem to be possible to make her daughter content in this, but take it up with him who is truly responsible for this block on the import of luxury objects, i.e., "the Mytilenean."

Within the framework of a discursive mode that mimics the tone of family discussions is introduced a political reference of general import. But who is "the Mytilenean"? Already close upon the publication of the papyrus Vogliano and others[13] identified this man as Pittacus, whose sumptuary laws would have prevented Sappho from access to articles of Lydian origin (we know from Theophrastus, fr. 97 Wimmer, that as a result of a politics of austerity Pittacus raised the penalties for excesses in drink and regulated funeral ceremonies).[14] Consequently the poem would have been composed during the rule of Pittacus, who was elected aesimnetes among the wrestling factions and ruled the city for a decade beginning from c. 597 BC.[15]

Alcaeus mentions this election with enraged bitterness (F 348):

...τὸν κακοπατρίδαν
Φίττακον πόλιος τὰς ἀχόλω καὶ βαρυδαίμονος
ἐστάσαντο τύραννον, μέγ᾽ ἐπαίνεντες ἀόλλεες.

...that man of lowest birth,
Pittacus, him they elected tyrant of this weakened and
unhappy city, all together according him their favor.

---

13 See Mazzarino 1943: 57–61; Treu 1954: 215–19; Page 1955: 102–3 is skeptical.

14 Cf. also Aristot. *Pol.* 1274b19–23 and *EN* 1113b30–33, D.L. 1.76.

15 According to the manuscript tradition of D.L. 1.79 Pittacus, whose *floruit* is placed in the forty-second Olympiad (612–9), died when Aristomenes was eponymous archon at Athens in the third year of the fifty-second Olympiad (i.e., in 570/69), ten years after having given up power of his own will and when he was already more than seventy. There is thus a contradiction between the numbers "fifty-second" (Olympiad) and "70" (years of life). Further, the *Suda* (Π 1659) places Pittacus' birth in the thirty-second Olympiad (652–49). The simplest solution is, with Jacoby, that of correcting into ν′ (= 50) the νβ′ (= 52) of the tradition, very likely arising from the influence of the preceding μβ′ (= 42) relative to Pittacus' *floruit*. A confirmation of this chronology comes from the fact that, according to Plut. *Sol.* 14.7, Pittacus had already been elected aesimnetes when Solon became archon at Athens (594/93 BC).

And Aristotle, in the third book of his *Politics* (3.14, p. 1285b), after having mentioned that there existed various forms of "monarchy" and having discussed the Spartan type (a sort of autocratic and life-long supreme military command) and also that type, characteristic of certain foreign kingdoms, which seems very similar to tyranny but is founded on legal right and on hereditary transmission, so defines the role of aesimnetes specifically in relationship to Pittacus :

> These are two types of monarchies, but there was still a third, which was in force among the ancient Greeks, practiced by those sovereigns called "aesimnetai." At issue, so to speak, is a kind of elective tyranny, which differs from that common among the barbarians not because it had no legal basis, but only because it was not founded on hereditary right. Some of these sovereigns governed for life, others for a definite period of time or with a view to a particular action: for example the Mytileneans chose Pittacus to combat the exiles led by Antimenidas and the poet Alcaeus.

An objection has been raised, not without reason, against identifying Pitta-cus as "the Mytilenean": according to the traditional chronology, Sappho was born around 650 BC and so around 595 she would have been 55,

> an age hardly consistent with the existence of so young a daughter, prob-ably an adolescent. Her young age is not explicitly stated, but can be de-rived from the emphasis on the young age of the grandmother, from the sense of instruction of one younger by one older that pervades the frag-ment, and finally from the fact that the ornaments mentioned appear for the most part associated in songs dedicated or performed by girls.[16]

There can be no doubt about Cleis' young age: the young woman would have claimed her headband when she first came of an age to wear it in public, in a celebration in which, as the girls of Alcman's parthenion, she could dance and sing as a member of a chorus. But the text gives no indication of the grand-mother's age; rather she seems to have been dead for some time ("your grand-mother once told me..."), and one has the impression that Sappho is referring to what her mother told her regarding her own youth.

As for the age of the poet, we cannot be too precise. Among the ancient sources one placed her acme around 612-09 (thus born around 650); another

16 Aloni 1997: lxix.

placed it in 600–599 (thus born in 640–39).[17] If we follow the first chronology, the hypothesis of a Cleis who was an adolescent around 595 is not impossible but unlikely (Sappho would have had to give birth to her in her 40s); if we follow the second there are no problems.

§4 Exile of the Cleanactids

"The Mytilenean" is a vague definition, with the article (used very sporadically in Aeolic) marking the adjective emphatically, and we cannot even say whether "the Mytilenean" is itself a self-contained reference or was followed by a substantive with which it agrees (e.g., βασίλευς as in Alc. F 5.14, or τύραννος, as in Alc. F 348.3).

We can on the other hand ask ourselves what relationship might exist between "the Mytilenean" and the "exile of the Cleanactids" to which F 98b.5–9 refers:

> παι.α.ειον ἔχην πο.[
> _αἰκε.η ποικιλασκ...(.)[6
> ταῦτα τὰς Κλεανακτιδα[
> φύγας †..ισαπολισεχει †
> _μνάματ᾽· οἴδε γὰρ αἶνα διέρρυε[ν   9

6 αἰ κέλη<ι> vel αἴ κεν ἦ<ι> Vogliano, αἴ κ᾽ ἔχη<ι> Srebrny   7 Κλεανακτίδα[ν Vogliano   8 αλισα leg. Vogliano fort. ἄλιθ᾽ (Grassi) ἔχει πόλις (Vogliano)   9 οἴδε vel αἴδε

---

17 The first is the *Suda* (Σ 107), the second is Jerome's *Chronicon* (from Eusebius), p. 99b H, in relation to the first year of the forty-fifth Olympiad: *Sappho et Alcaeus poetae clari habebantur* (but the Armenian version, p. 187 K, refers to the second year of the forty-sixth Olympiad, i.e., to 595/94). Strabo (13.2.3) underlines generically that Sappho and Alcaeus were contemporaries of Pittacus (the *Suda* adds Stesichorus), while Athenaeus (13.599c) places Sappho's life in the reign of Alyactes (c. 610–560 BC). Beloch's reconstruction, accepted by Mazzarino 1943: 73–78, is decidedly eccentric. According to this, Pittacus, Alcaeus, and Sappho would have been contemporaries of Croesus, whose reign begins around 560. This is based on an anecdote of Herodotus (1.27.2) in relation to a meeting between Pittacus and Croesus. Against this reconstruction see Liberman 1999: I.xv n. 23.

...daughter, [...] to have [...]
if [...] varied- [...]   6

these memories the city has in abundance[18]
about the exile of the Cleanactids:
in fact they were terribly scattered.   9

Even in a text that appears in pretty bad shape (whether because of the difficulty in deciphering some letters, especially at the upper edge of the fragment,
or because of the certain corruption at line 8), we glimpse that, in relation to
something of elaborate artistic fashioning, the poet declares that "our city has
in abundance these memories of the exile of the Cleanactids" (or, with a different reading, "of the Cleanactid") and shortly after she remembers that they
(or these goods) were terribly scattered. Consistent with the presence of ταῦτα
at the beginning of line 7, the effects or "memories" of such a group should be
bound up with the subject of the preceding stanzas (the headband and perhaps
something else of the kind).

We know something of the Cleanactids thanks to a marginal note to Alcaeus F
112.23, where Κλεανακτίδαν, i.e., "the Cleanactid" or, less likely, "some Cleanactids," appears accompanied in the right margin with the gloss τ(ὸν) Μυρσίλον.

Further Strabo (13.2.3), in mentioning that Pittacus had put an end to domestic feuds at Mytilene, adds that Alcaeus had insulted the tyrants who succeeded each other before Pittacus, i.e., in a nonchronological order, "Myrsilus
and Melanchros, Cleanactids, and still others."[19]

Myrsilus, whose father bore a name that in its first part coincides with
Κλεανάκτιδαις (this is Cleanor, as we know from S 263.11 *SLG* = Alc. F 306B.11
Liberman), was initially a follower of the tyrant Melanchros (who in turn had
overthrown the Penthilid monarchy)[20] and after this man's death (which oc-

---

18   For ἄλιθα, an unpublished conjecture of Carlo Grassi (but Grassi suggested ἄλιθα πόλλ'
ἔχει, with ἔχει intransitive; I am inclined rather to accept the inversion ἔχει πόλις proposed by
Vogliano), cf. Hom. *Il.* 11.677 ληῖδα δ᾽ ἐκ πεδίου συνελάσσαμεν ἤλιθα πολλήν, *Od.* 5.483 and,
without the combination with a form of πολύς, A. R. 2.283.

19   Nevertheless, the assumption that Melanchros and Myrsilus were both part of the Cleanactid *genos* presupposes eliminating, in Strabo's textual tradition, on the suggestion of Wilamowitz
1907, the καί between Μελάγχρωι and τοῖς Κλεανακτίδαις, but this deletion is inevitable if Myrsilus is a Cleanactid (see Mazzarino 1943: 56–57 and Liberman 1999: I.2 n. 4).

20   Melanchros is also mentioned in Alc. F 331 Μέλαγχρος αἴδως ἄξιος ἐς πόλιν ("worthy of respect"
ironically) and in relation to his death by Pittacus and the *genos* of Alcaeus at D.L. 1.74 and *Sud.* Π 1659.

curred between 612 and 609) was sent into exile. On his return to Mytilene (Alcaeus F 305a.15–19 makes mention of the "return of Myrsilus" and of one Mnamon who to this end had provided him with a boat: ll. 17–18 ἀκάτιον παρέστησεν εἰς τὴν Μυρσίλου κάθοδον), he imposed himself on the city as tyrant.

Thereupon Pittacus and the Alcaeids, who were pursued into exile in their turn, took a solemn oath to overthrow his power, as we read in Alc. F 129, but Pittacus betrayed the alliance he had made with the Alcaeids and gained power just as a follower of Myrsilus (cf. also Alc. F 70.7): hence a new exile for Alcaeus. Finally, at the death of Myrsilus, Pittacus was elected aesimnetes, taking advantage of an alliance, sanctioned by a marriage, with the Penthilid clan.[21]

§5 Lydian Fashion

The archaeological digs conducted on the site of ancient Sardis have brought to light an impressive series of discoveries that document the constant growth of Greek commerce with Lydia from the time of Gyges to that of Alyactes and Croesus. Notwithstanding the repeated attacks of Lydian sovereigns against the Greek cities of Anatolia—Miletus and Priene were attacked by Ardys, Miletus suffered incursions first by Sadyactes and then by Alyactes, who also moved against Clazomenae and Smyrna—there was, stretching across the seventh and sixth centuries, a period of friendly relations. This was so much the case that in Sappho Lydian men-at-arms do not appear as objects of fear or hatred, but as one of the most beautiful things in the world: for the poet declares that she prefers the radiance of Anactoria's face to the spectacle of "Lydian chariots" (F 16.17–19) and, to extol her own affection for her daughter, she can say that she would not take all of Lydia in exchange for Cleis (F 132.3).

And the Lydians, without having received any benefit from them, indeed without even knowing them, provided to the Alcaeids the enormous sum of two thousand staters to help them reach the "sacred city," perhaps Mytilene (Alc. F 69.3 ff. ἴρ[αν] | ἐς πόλιν ἔλθην).[22]

---

21 On the biographical tradition relating to this marriage (and in particular the anecdote told at Plut. De tranq. an. 471b) see Lapini 2007.

22 The context of this aid escapes us, but we read that a "clever fox" (Pittacus?) hoped to get away with prophesying an easy task for the sum's recipients (lines 6–8). It however seems likely that the collocation ἴραν πόλιν, with no other determination, refers to Mytilene (on this question see Page 1955: 226–33; Liberman 1999: I.48 and II.209). It should be added that all the other

Lydian fashion—what Laevius, fr. 18 Morel was to call *Lydium decus*—must have spread also to Lesbos in the second half of the seventh century, at the time of the tyranny of the Cleanactids, and then also in the first half of the sixth, through the reign of Croesus until the fall of Sardis (around 547 BC), but after the period of austerity marked by the decade of Pittacus' government.

But if this is the historical framework, what is the specific context of the ode? In other words, where was Sappho at the moment that she composed the poem?

Page suggested the following reconstruction:

> Sappho tells her daughter that she cannot provide her with fashion-
> able attire; such things are indeed obtainable in Mytilene, but there the
> Cleanactidae are in power—they are reminders of the time when our
> enemies were in exile and we were in the city; now *they* are in the city
> and we are in exile; our fine clothes are all worn out, and we have no
> means of obtaining more [...] Sappho might call the inaccessible shops
> in Mytilene "memorials of happier days," because they remind her of
> the time when the party in exile was not her own but her opponents'.[23]

We shall not digress here in repudiating this reconstruction since nothing suggests that Sappho speaks of her own exile and not the Cleanactids', nor that she mourns for Mytilenean shops, nor that the memories are those of happier days, nor that Sappho's faction was opposed to that of the Cleanactids. What we must underline here is what this ode has become in Page's view: a private discourse between mother and daughter, something that Sappho might have said to Cleis, who was intent on going out walking.

With the greatest brevity let us recall that, on the contrary, there is no indication of the existence of poetic compositions from archaic or classical Greece, at least from Homer to Euripides, that were not composed with a view to a specific context, for a conventional oral situation and for a definite audience—public religious celebration (*panegyris*), symposium, temple, marriage, funeral, theater, etc.

For this and for many other odes, many have imagined that Sappho was the exception, that her audience was informal and private, a restricted circle (even-

---

passages commented upon in P.Oxy. 2307 (=Alc. F 306a-i) seem to pertain to the government of Pittacus (see Porro 1994: 110-11).

23   Page 1955: 102.

tually called a thiasos);[24] there is even one scholar who has considered the occasional possibility of poetry in the form of "notes" sent to specific recipients.[25]
As will become gradually clear in the course of this study, Sappho was not the
exception to the rule. There are many indications of performances in the context of festivals and ceremonies that articulated the cultural calendar of the island of Lesbos,[26] and on the contrary there are none at all of performances for
a closed circle. There are also no signs of symposiastic performances that would
have made a female equivalent to Alcaeus' poems.[27] Only one viable working hypothesis remains: Sappho's compositions had a public, festive purpose, and were
meant to be performed by Sappho herself (or by some other solo performer) or
by a duly instructed chorus. It is true that her poems contain—and to a large
extent—subjective moments, personal messages, amorous declarations, didactic statements, but these are no different from what we encounter in the rest of
Greek lyric poetry from the seventh century to the fifth.[28]

If then Sappho says to Cleis that she cannot procure a Lydian headband for
her, this is not a matter of an embarrassed confession uttered *sotto voce*, but a
statement that had a precise pragmatic function. In this perspective the headband becomes a *deixis* of absence. Cleis' head is not covered by a headband
that would have been exactly appropriate for the situation; there is on the other
hand a garland of flowers such as the grandmother suggested for blonde girls,
while the other girls each wear a scarlet ribbon.

We are unable to determine exactly which occasion was of concern, since the
relative documentation—by which should be understood not only the whole

---

24 Cf., e.g., Fränkel 1969: 198, Page 1955: 119 (Sappho was accustomed to offer her own poems "informally to her companions"), Merkelbach 1957: 6, West 1970: 324-25 ("music and song
for public as well as private performance"), Gentili 1988: 77-78, Di Benedetto 1987: 76 ("l'ipotesi
più probabile è che queste poesie fossero destinate in prima istanza alla stessa comunità entro
la quale nascevano, perché esse fossero eseguite e cantate con accompagnamento musicale in
occasione dei riti che si svolgevano all'interno della comunità [...] si può parlare di autocommit-
tenza"), Williamson 1995: 130 and 147, Aloni 1998: 200, Hutchinson 2001: 146.

25 Stehle 1997: 288-318, esp. 311.

26 Certainly there could also be celebrations whose participants were exclusively women,
such as the *Adonia*, or those that were reserved for small groups, celebrations that are "not state-
sponsored and community-wide" (Stehle 1997: 262): but these are distinctions that remain uncertain for Sappho's Lesbos through lack of documentary evidence. In general, for performances
of female choruses see the first volume of Calame 1977 and Stehle 1997: 71-118.

27 For the symposiastic revival of extracts from Sappho cf. however Plut. *Quaest. Conv.* 71d,
Aelian. *ap.* Stob. 3.29.58.

28 There are good observations on this point in Parker 1993 (who however thinks primarily,
without any textual support, of symposiastic contexts).

composition or whole production of Sappho, but also a range of documentary information useful for defining moments and aspects of local Lesbian festivals—is completely lost, but in general terms it is obvious to think of a female chorus that Cleis herself leads in the role of chorus-leader. Regarding this choral spectacle Sappho's poem could be offered as a monodic prelude—almost an expected justification, in times of austerity, of the simplicity in dress and hair arrangement of chorus leader and chorus dancer.

Some confirmation of this comes from F 81.4–7, where the same perspective is underlined also in the form of instruction (an infinitive with jussive function) with which the poet, who here takes on the role of chorus teacher, addresses Dika in order that she bind her head with a crown of dill:[29]

σὺ δὲ στεφάνοις, ὦ Δίκα, πέρθεσθ᾽ ἐράταις φόβαισιν
ὄρπακας ἀνήτω συναέρραισ᾽ ἀπάλαισι χέρσιν·   5
εὐάνθεα †γὰρ πέλεται† καὶ Χάριτες μάκαιρα<ι>
μᾶλλον †προτερην†, ἀστεφανώτοισι δ᾽ ἀπυστρέφονται.

4 ἐράτοις Fick   7 προσόρην Ahrens

And you, Dika, place garlands around your lovely hair
interlacing boughs of dill with your delicate hands.   5
She who adorns herself with flowers, to her the Graces turn more
their eyes, but divert their gaze from her who wears no crown.

The very fragmentary F 62 (+ F 71.8) hints at a situation in some ways comparable:[30]

Ἐπτάξατε [- - ◡ ◡ - -] δροσ[ό]εσσα[ν - -
_δάφνας ὄτᾳ [- - ◡ ◡ - - - - ◡ - ◡ -]αι,   2
πὰν δ᾽ ἄδιον[

---

29 Bartol 1997 correctly thought of a "preparation for a ritual ceremony at which participate both the speaker of the message, i.e., Sappho herself surely, and Dika." For the connection between crowns and choral dance cf. Pind. *Parth.* 2.11–12 M., where the chorus states: ὑμνήσω στεφάνοισι θάλ-|λοισα παρθένιον κάρα.

30 For the combination of the two fragments (and also F 87(14).3–14 LP) see Puglia 2007: 8–31.

```
_ἢ κῆνον ἐλο[                                        4
 καὶ ταῖσι μὲν ἀ̣[
_ὀδοίπορος ἄν[                                        6
 μύγις δέ ποτ' εἰσάιον· ἐκλ̣[
_ψύχα δ' ἀγαπάτασυ.['.                                8
 τέαυτα δὲ νῦν ἔμμ̣[ατα
_ἴκεσθ' ἀγανα[                                        10
 ἔφθατε· κάλαν [
_τά τ' ἔμματα κα̣[                                    12
```

1 [μέν, παῖδες Puglia   ὑπ' ἔρνη]? fin. [ν ἄγνας Puglia   2 fin. e.g. ἄητ]αι   4 ἐλο[ίμαν Puglia   5 ἄ[λλαισι? ἄ[κτισι Puglia   6 ἄν[θρωπος Puglia   8   fort. σὺν̣ [ἔμοι   9 ἔμμ[ατα Diehl ἔμμ[ατ' ἔχοισαι?   12 κα̣[ὶ Diehl


```
you crouched, [girls, below] the wet [branches of a sacred
laurel when [...]                                                    2
but everything is sweeter [... not]
would I prefer [anyone] to him [...]                                 4
and to these [...]
a passer-by [...]                                                    6
and once I hardly paid heed to [...]
but you, beloved soul, together with me [...]                        8
and now [wearing] such clothes [...]
you came [...] before [...]                                          10
delicate- [...] the beautiful [...]
and the clothes and [...]                                            12
```

At line 8 Cleis should be the object of address (cf. F 132.2 Κλέις ἀγαπάτα, and Alc. F 44.8 ἀγαπάτ[ω τέκεος μᾶνιν)[31] in relation to clothes (ἔμματα at lines 9 and 12) that, we might imagine, a group of girls (παῖδες in the lacuna at line 1?), of whom Cleis herself was a member, were to wear on the occasion of a celebration or rite after which, for some reason,[32] they had been compelled to

---

31 Already in Homer this verbal adjective refers constantly to a sole descendant, and in fact is used only of the only sons Astyanax (*Il.* 6.401) and Telemachus (*Od.* 2.365, 4.727 and 817, 5.18). For ψύχα used as an apostrophe cf. Pind. *P.* 3.61, Eur. *Ion* 859 and *IT* 839.

32 Because of the midday heat (Puglia)?

crouch below the damp leaves of a laurel.[33] Now however the girls had suc-
ceeded in reaching (ἴκεσθ'... | ἔφθατε 10-11) a predetermined spot (a dancing
ground?) wearing clothing appropriate for the occasion (τέαυτα 9).

It seems however clear that νῦν ἔμμ[ατα at line 9 signals with a temporal
deixis an imminent event, to which this poem articulated in six distichs was to
stand for the introduction.

---

33 The figure of the wayfarer should have been introduced not in a censorious function (see
Treu 1954: 204: "die üble Nachrede eines ὁδοίπορος"), but rather in relation to that same motif
of shelter from the midday heat and from thirst that was to become a topos of Hellenistic poetry
(cf. e.g. Anyt. 18 G.-P., Leon. *AP* 9.326.5, Sat. *AP* 10.13, Antiph. *AP* 11.71).

II Exile

§1 Sappho a Cleanactid?

The presence of Cleis, both grandmother and granddaughter, arouses a suspicion: that together with Sappho (whose name is encountered elsewhere in Greek only in one word of Semitic origin: σάπφειρος, "lapis lazuli") they belonged to the family of the Cleanactids[1] whose etymon (κλεϝ) of the first part of the name they repeat;[2] we have also seen that the father of Myrsilus is called Cleanor. If this were true, the exile mentioned would be that of "the Cleanactids," not of "the Cleanactid," Myrsilus having already died.

But there is additional evidence:

- Sappho, as we shall see again, is a supporter of that "refinement" (ἁβροσύνη) that in the archaic period designated orientalizing taste, and of that openness regarding fashion and articles of Lydian origin that at Lesbos ought to have coincided with the Cleanactid tyranny.[3]

---

1 Battezzato rightly emphasizes the presence of both the daughter Cleis and the grandmother Cleis in an ode that mentions the Cleanactids.

2 The name Κλέϊς is in fact derived from the root *klew on the line of Homeric or archaic names like Κλέϊτος, Κλύτιος, Κλύμενος, and Κλυμένη, Κλέεια, Κλειώ, and also the Athenian Ὀνυμακλέης of Alc. F 130b.9 (see Schulze 1892: 66). As this phenomenon does not occur on the male side (the brothers are Charaxos and Eurygius or Erigius; in the case of the father the *Suda* mentions all of eight possibilities, but Scamandronimus occurs, as an alternative to Scamandrus, also at P.Oxy. 1800 fr. 1), membership in the *genus* of the Cleanactids may have been connected to the female line.

3 As Kurke 1992: 96 observes: "Sappho's declaration 'I love *habrosune*' is a programmatic political statement. It means, I align myself with an aristocratic elite that has strong ties with the East."

- The name Myrsilus itself shows the close contacts of this family group with Lydia. "Myrsilus" was an alternative name for Myrsus, son of Candaules, the last Lydian sovereign of the Heraclid dynasty,[4] and Myrsus is also the name of a Lydian nobleman who died in 497 BC.[5] In honor of Myrsilus, the mythical equerry of Lydian Pelops, a *heroon* named the Μυρσίληον may have been erected at Lesbos,[6] in which, according to Alc. F 383, Dinomenes son of Tyrrakus deposited his arms.
- Sappho opposed both Pittacus and figures associated with him in Mytilene in the education of young aristocratic girls and in choruses for the island's religious festivals; as we will see, of these figures one (Andromeda) apparently belonged to the Penthilids, one (Gorgo) to the Polyanactids.

§2   At Syracuse

There is only one reliable witness on Sappho's exile, the *Marmor Parium* (*FGrHist* 239 A 36 = Sapph. T 251 Voigt), which with reference to 264/63 BC states that a certain number of years have passed "from the time when Sappho went to sea in exile [...] when the first Critias was archon at Athens and the *geomoroi* retained power at Syracuse."[7]

The number of the year mentioned has been swallowed by a lacuna, but because the chronological indication immediately preceding refers to 605/4 and

---

4 Cf. Hdt. 1.7.2 ἦν Κανδαύλης, τὸν οἱ Ἕλληνες Μυρσίλον ὀνομάζουσι, τύραννος Σαρδίων with Asheri's note *ad loc.*, who observes that Myrsilus (a name of Hittite origin) would have been his own name, Candaules a sacred title (perhaps connected with the Carian cult of the dog, whom the Greeks identified with Hermes), and that "Myrsus and Myrsilus are common names in Lydia, although Herodotus considered them as Hellenized forms."

5 Cf. Hdt. 3.122 and 5.121.

6 In Alcaeus' text Μυρσιλήω is Seidler's 1829 correction: Μυρσίννωι is given at Hephaist. 15.10, p. 58 C. (cod. A; Μυρσινήωι *deteriores*). Voigt accepts Μυρσινήωι, but, as Liberman 1999: II.248–49 notes, a suffix in -νηον / -νειον for a forest of myrtle would be surprising (cf. ῥοδεών).

7 In general the term γεωμόροι or γαμόροι came into use to indicate great landowners (Thuc. 8.21, Plat. *Lg.* 737e), but at Syracuse this referred specifically to the property owners who were descendants of the first Corinthian colonists, who settled there around 733 BC. In 7.155.2 Herodotus speaks of the return of the "geomoroi" from Casmene (Monte Casale?) where they had taken refuge when hunted "by the people and by their slaves, called Killyrioi," immediately before Gelon, tryant of Gela, conquered Syracuse in 485/84 BC. His mention of these however provides only a very vague chronological indication.

that following to 591/90, and because the reference to Critias' archonship at Athens allows the exclusion of the years between 595 and 591 (we know the names of the archons for these years), this departure for exile has to be situated between 604/3 and 596/95. An easy if not certain inference is that this date coincides with Pittacus' accession to power in the course of 597: this would give a coherent logic to Sappho's hostility to Pittacus and to her distress at the sorrowful exile of the Cleanactids, which shows itself clearly in the song for Cleis.

We have no other indications of Sappho's forced stay in Sicily except that of Cicero in his second *Verrine Oration* (*Ver.* 4.57), when he mentions a statue of the poet that was the work of the Athenian sculptor Silanion (active around the mid fourth century BC), which was placed in the agora of the Sicilian city.

§3   Memories

A further gleam appears if we put under closer scrutiny a papyrus (P.Oxy. 1787) that dates from the end of the second century AD[8] and was published in 1922 by A.S. Hunt in *Oxyrhynchus Papyri* XV.[9]

Many of the forty remaining fragments of this book roll were correctly matched by Hunt and then by Lobel, but new matchings and new combinations are still possible. All the extant fragments of this roll are odes belonging to the fourth book of the Alexandrian edition, laid out in distichs[10] (a *paragraphos* systematically marks the division of one poem from another) of verses that may be defined as acephalic hipponacteans with a double choriambic expansion (^hipp^{2ch}: x-⏑⏑--⏑⏑--⏑⏑--).

---

8   For the dating not to the third century AD but to the last quarter of the second, see Funghi-Messeri 1992 (but on the whole group of papyri to which P.Oxy. 1787 is related see, in partial disagreement with Funghi-Messeri, also Johnson 2004: 26–27 and 63).

9   But a fragment of the same papyrus had already been published in 1913 as P.Halle 3, and new pieces were joined subsequently and were edited by Lobel in 1925 in his edition of Sappho and in 1941 and 1951 respectively in vols. XVIII and XXI of the *Oxyrhynchus Papyri*.

10   Voigt (p. 97 of her edition) admits some exceptions, hypothesizing for some fragments an articulation in three-line stanzas, but F 88 comes from a separate roll (P.Oxy. 2290), and we don't know to which book this belonged, while F 65 and F 86 are certainly in distichs (see Ferrari 2005b: 19 n. 14). On the implications of articulation in distichs see Fassino-Prauscello 2001, and Prauscello 2006: 185–213.

One of these combinations concerns the matching of fr. 13 (= F 70) with both fr. 7 (= F 68a) and, following a suggestion of E. Puglia,[11] fr. 29 (= F 75a): further, the conjunction of fr. 19 (= F 68b) with fr. 32 (= F 69) seems to me certain (they also share a letter in common).

Because, as Lobel sees, fr. 19 (= F 68b) comes from the same area as F 68a, aligned vertically and not at a great distance, we are in a position to reconstruct a whole (F 68a + F 70 + F 68b + F 69 + F 75a) that constitutes one or two poems of Book IV and from which also emerges a reference on the poet's part to her own exile:

A

]..[.].. γάρ μ' ἀπὺ τὰς ἔμ[ας γᾶς

ἄμι[λ]λ' ἀ[πεκίν]ησ' ἀδο[κητ - - ˇ ὔ]μως δ' ἔγεν[το
μ]νᾶμ[   ]λα[   ] ἴσαν θέοισιν,
νῦ]ν δ' εἶμ' ἐ[πὶ - - ὀ]νίαν [- ˇ] ἄσαν ἀλίτραν
ἐπο]ρσομέν[α, σὺν δ' ὀ]δύγ[αισ' Ἀν]δρομέδαν [ὐ]πάξ[ει   5
ἀπά]λικ' ὑπ' ἄ[ρμ' ὑψ]ιμέδο[ισ'] Ἄρ[τεμι]ς ἀ μάκα[ιρ]α,
ἀ δ'] οὐκ [ἀ]βά[κην] μὰν στέ[ρ]εον δὲ τρόπον α[ἰσ]χύνη[ται·
οὔτι]ς γὰρ ἔπαυ[σ'   ].κ[   ] κόρον οὐ κατίσχει.
ἦ] μάν κ' ἀπύθυσ' [ὤ]κ' ἀ[γέλα]ν Τυνδαρίδαι[σιν ἄρνων
χ] ἀρμονίας δ' ἀσυ[χ]ία[ι] κὰ[τ] χαρίεντ' ἀ.[- -   10
γ]άθην χόρον, ἆ, α[ἴ] κ' ἄδολον [μ]ηκέτι συν[- - -
πᾶκτιν] δὲ λίγηαν Μεγάραν [τὰ]ν ἀ[κάλ]α[ν λάβοισαν
- - δύν]ατόν σφι[
χ - ˇ ˇ] πάντεσσι [
        ]επ[.].[

*

B

]....φ[

].[.] 'θύραμ[εν - ˇ - -
]μοι χάλεπ[- ˇ - -
]δε κύ[
ἰ]σοπάλην ὄλ[- -   5

11 See Puglia 2007: 22–23.

] ἐπε[ὶ σ]τέγα μ[ε
]ας ἀλίτρα[
]έτ᾽ αὐ[-

A 1 ἔμ[ας Treu fin. γᾶς supplevi   2 ὔ]μως Hunt ἔγεν[το Lobel cetera supplevi   3 μ]νᾶμ[(α) supplevi (μ]νᾶμ[᾽ οὐ?) ἀλ]λὰ?   4 ὀ]νίαν Prauscello cetera supplevi   5 Ἀν]δρομέδαν Hunt cetera supplevi · 6 μάκα[ιρ]ᾱ Diehl cetera supplevi   7 μᾱ ante corr.: μᾶν post corr. στέ[ρ]εον Puglia cetera supplevi ("α[ἰσ]χύνη[(fut.)?" iam Voigt)   8–10 supplevi   10 init. fort ἦς fin. ἀρ[ήσκοι Puglia   11 [μ]ηκέτι Hunt cetera supplevi   12 "ακαλαν in αβακην corr.?" (Lobel) cetera supplevi   13 supplevi

B 2 (ἀ)θύραμ[εν Voigt   3 χαλέ ante corr.: χάλε post corr. e.g. χάλεπ[αι μέριμναι   4 Κύ[πρ-?   5 ἰ]σοπάλην supplevi   ὄλ[οιτο?   6 ἐπε[ὶ σ]τέγα μ[ε legi et supplevi

A

[...] and indeed away from my [country]
strife [unexpectedly banished me...] and yet
the memory was [not...] like the gods.
But [now] I'll turn to attack the one responsible [for these] torments
[and of these] worries, [and with] sorrow blessed Artemis   5
who rules from on high will all alone drive Andromeda [under] her
     chariot
[so that she] will be ashamed of her character, one not soft, but hard.
[No one] in truth has put down [her pride] nor reined in her greed.
Surely [it would be possible] immediately to sacrifice [a flock of lambs]
to the Tyndarids and [it would be good] to enjoy the quiet of a song 10
in a pleasant dancing place, ah if truly no longer [...]
And gentle Megara, [having taken the harp] resounding,
could [...]
... to all ...

*

B

...

... we took pleasure...
...to me hard- [...

> ...Cy[pris...]
> ...equivalent to [...]
> ... since a roof me
> ...culprit...

At the end of A 1 the genitive γᾶς is given as a supplement, but in fact it represents the sole possibility since we in any case need a monosyllabic feminine in the genitive. The subject of the sentence, "strife" (ἄμιλλα), therefore concerns the banishment of the subject from her country following upon a contrast that, in the case of Mytilene of this period, must have concerned divisions of aristocratic factions. If Pittacus was responsible for her exile, among those exiled would have been both the heads of the Cleanactids after Myrsilus' death and the Alcaeids.

As a matter of fact we know that, after his first exile to Pirra at the time of Myrsilus' tyranny,[12] Alcaeus suffered a second exile concomitant with the accession of Pittacus: as we have seen, Aristotle, in the *Politics* (3.14), states that the Mytilenean *demos* elected Pittacus aesimnetes precisely "to combat the exiles led by Antimenidas and the poet Alcaeus," and Alcaeus himself refers to a "second exile" (which was to be followed by yet another) in his own poems (cf. F 306Ae, lines 4–5).

It is thus very likely that Alcaeus' first exile ended with Myrsilus' death (celebrated with a burst of joy in F 332: "now we must get drunk and drink deeply, for Myrsilus is dead") and the second coincided with the election of Pittacus as aesimnetes or shortly preceded it.[13]

With an irony typical of papyri there is a lacuna just between the words "second" and "exile": hence, our only source about the place where Alcaeus and his companions spent their "second" exile is a commentator to F 306Ae, according to whom this place was a *polis* that has the two final letters (in the Attic form of the accusative) -ας (possibly Athens or Thebes).[14] Considering the size of the lacuna, it cannot be Syracuse, nor are there any indications in Alcaeus or in the sources on Alcaeus that refer to Sicily. It would seem that Sappho and Alcaeus followed different routes into exile.

---

12 Cf. Schol. Alc. F 114.1–8.
13 See Gentili 1988: 208–9 and Liberman 1999: I.xx–xxi.
14 F 306 line 5: [εἰς Ἀθή]ναϲ Barner, [εἰς Θή]βαϲ Liberman.

Then, at the beginning of A3, we find, in the singular, the same substantive (μνᾶμα) that we met in relation to the Cleanactids' exile in the ode to Cleis (F 98b.9). If these "memories" were concerned with restriction from access to Lydian finery, what was said here (from what we can extract from the overall turn of phrase) must have been that the memory is not of an exile of any length or excessively painful, so that Sappho was able subsequently, perhaps at the moment of her return home, to feel or be said by others to be "equal to the gods."

But behold from A4 the *persona loquens* takes on the posture of a warrior moving to assault his enemy: "but now I'll turn to attack..." (forms of the verb ἐπόρνυμι often occur in Homer denoting martial attack[15]) even though the target here is not an armed combatant, but rather a woman, and the weapon used by the assailant is not the spear, but the word.

§4   What Andromeda Did

As follows immediately, the main culprit is Andromeda, director of a competing group or "school" and in some way responsible, it appears, also for Sappho's exile. The details of the circumstance do not become clear in what remains, but we can get a glimpse of the relations between the forces at play if we attempt to understand to which group Andromeda belonged.

This identification is possible if, purely in a conjectural way, we take into account a passage from Maximus of Tyre (18.9 = Sapph. T 219), in which he names Gorgo and Andromeda as Sappho's "artistic rivals" (ἀντίτεχνοι), in the same way that Prodicus, Gorgias, and Thrasymachus are Socrates', each time censured, challenged, or made the object of irony.

Maximus gives only three briefest hints as to these antagonists of Sappho. These are F 155 (many greetings to the Polyanactid's daughter), F 49.2 (on Atthis,[16] who deserted to Andromeda, as we know from F 130.3–4), and F 57.2 (on the same Andromeda's rustic dress).[17] Since two examples concern An-

---

15   Cf. *Il.* 21.324 ἐπῶρτ᾽ Ἀχιλῆι, 23.689 ἐπὶ δ᾽ ὄρνυτο δῖος Ἐπειός and also A. *Supp.* 187 τῶνδ᾽ ἐπόρνυται στόλος.

16   Provided that, naturally, we accept with Lobel-Page and with Voigt the hypothesis Bergk proposed on the basis of a passage of *De metris* of Terentianus Maurus (6.390.4–5 Keil), that lines 1 and 2 belong to the same composition (on this see IV, § 4).

17   On the relationship among the verses assigned by Lobel-Page and by Voigt to F 57 see IV, § 1.

dromeda, if the "daughter of the Polyanactid" of F 155 were the same Andromeda, it follows that the neo-Sophist, while he meant to illustrate Sappho's mode of attack against both figures, made no citation that involved Gorgo.[18]

In that case, given that Sappho (F 71) names another group, the Penthilids, in regard to a young woman whose name (or nickname) is dear to her—Mika who has just chosen "the friendship of the Penthilid ladies"—Andromeda must have been a member of this fallen family. Until a few decades prior, this family had represented the ruling house of Mytilene and had traced their name to one mythical Penthilus, son of Orestes and Erigone (who was in turn daughter of Aegisthus). Following Lesbian tradition, Penthilus as *oikistes* had led—together with a Boeotian contingent—the Aeolic colonization of the island and of the opposite Anatolian coastline (cf. Ephor. *FGrHist* 70 fr. 119.5).

Proud and violent, the Penthilids had ruled until their power was overthrown, at an unknown date, by a faction led by Megacles; from here began the tyranny of Melanchros, which was in turn overthrown by Pittacus and by the Alcaeids c. 612.

As Aristotle again states (*Pol.* 5.10, 1311b23–30), when discussing those who rebel against the arrogance of authoritarian monarchy:

> And many, outraged at having even endured physical blows to their bodies, kill or attempt to kill both magistrates and royal dynasts on the grounds that they have been done physical wrong. So in Mytilene Megacles, setting against them with his friends, killed the Penthilids, who had beaten the citizens with clubs. And later Smerdis, who had taken blows and been dragged apart from his own wife, killed Penthilus.

The Penthilus Smerdis killed was probably the father of the Dracon whose sister Pittacus married (cf. D.L. 1.81), and anyhow Alcaeus refers with sarcastic emphasis to a "political" marriage Pittacus contracted with the representative of a *genos* that, even after the overthrow of the monarchy, continued to retain a degree of power worth the attention of one who aspired to leadership. Indeed in F 70 we find the prophecy that Pittacus will "devour" the city as he had already done with Myrsilus "now that he has become related with the line of the Atreids,"[19] and in

---

18 Williamson's alternative proposition (1995: 88), that Andromeda and Gorgo both belonged to the Polyanactids, seems unlikely.

19 Alc. F 70.6 παώθεις (Ἀτρεῖδα[.].[Ατρεῖδα[ν] γ[ένει Bowra, Ἀτρεῖδα[ι]σ᾽ [ὄλαν) Page.

F 5 a snapshot of Pittacus who "weds accompanied by spearmen,"[20] a variation of that body of mace-bearers that Aristotle mentions as the armed escort of the Penthilids. In the same fragment the title βασίλευς used of Pittacus seems to delineate Pittacus' ambition to put himself forward, through the alliance with the Penthilids, as the heir of the ancient sovereigns of Mytilene.

Thus the poet takes up the attack against the Penthilid Andromeda,[21] declaring herself assured of the cooperation of Artemis, the goddess who, as an Attic drinking song has it, "has great power over women,"[22] and to whom seems to have been attributed an epithet (ὐψιμέδοισα) that in its masculine form is traditional of Zeus,[23] and that in its second part ironically echoes the name "Andromeda."

Aphrodite was not the only goddess close to Sappho's heart: F 17 alludes to a prayer to Hera, a fragment such as F 44 Aa belonged to a sort of rhapsodic hymn dedicated to Artemis, and the same goddess must have been invoked for someone's protection at F 84.6–7.[24]

Here it seems possible to understand that Artemis whom Homer defines as "of golden reins" (Il. 6.205 χρυσήνιος Ἄρτεμις) will drive her chariot over this arrogant woman, an image of order and rectitude as in Simon. fr. 11.12 W.² (= 3b.8 G-P²) ἄρμα ... Δίκης.[25]

So Andromeda should be ashamed that her character is not mild and gentle, but rather harsh and obstinate.[26] To be gentle, mild, willing to converse were the merits of social life, and all the more so for a woman who presented herself as leader of a group of adolescents. It is no accident that we find the same Sappho (or rather her *persona loquens*) protesting her own mildness, clearly

---

20 Alc. F 5.11–12 γάμει |]κε ξυστοφο[ρή]με[νος.

21 The conjecture ἀπά]λικ' at the beginning of line 6 finds a parallel at Hom. Il. 22.490 παναφήλικα ("deprived of all companions"), H.Cer. 140 γυναικὸς ἀφήλικος, Hdt. 3.14.7, Cratin. fr. 385 K.-A. The Iliadic reminiscence further suggests that Andromeda is not to draw the chariot as part of a pair, but, with the greater physical exertion, alone.

22 Fr. 886.4 PMG Ἄρτεμιν, ἃ γυναικῶν μέγ' ἔχει κράτος.

23 Cf. Hes. Th. 529, Pind. N. 2.19, B. 15.51, Aristoph. Nu. 563.

24]αν Ἄρτεμι[|]ναβλ[(i.e., I would think of something like]ν ἀβλ[αβ-, cf. F 5.1–2).

25 For [ὐ]πᾱ́ξ[ει |... ὐπ' ἄ[ρμ' cf. Sapph. F 44.13–14. Ἰλιάδαι σατίναι[ς] ὐπ' εὐτρόχοις | ἆγον αἰμιόνοις and 17 ἵ]πποις δ᾽ ἄνδρες ὔπαγον ὐπ' ἄρ[ματα, Hom. Il. 16.148 ὔπαγε ζυγὸν ὠκέας ἵππους etc., for Artemis' chariot Hom. Hymn. 9.4, Call. Dian. 106, A. R. 3.878, Nonn. Dion. 48.304 and the numerous vase representations collected by L. Kahil, in LIMC 2.1: 1196–1225.

26 For στέ[ρ]εον (Puglia's supplement) cf. Hom. Il. 12.267 στερεοῖς ἐπέεσσι, A. Pr. 173–74 στερεὰς ... ἀπειλάς, Soph. Aj. 926 στερεόφρων, Plat. Plt. 309b στερεὸν ἦθος.

in the context of a polemic exchange, surviving in the one extant fragment in which we find the precious adjective ἀβάκης[27] (F 120):

> ἀλλά τις οὐκ ἔμμι παλιγκότων
> ὄργαν, ἀλλ᾽ ἀβάκην τὰν φρέν᾽ ἔχω ...

> I am not a person of recurring
> rages, but have a gentle spirit...

An ideology of society and of good manners finds a convinced defender in Anacreon, active a few decades later at the court of the tyrants of Samos, as we see in a fragment (fr. 416 *PMG*). Here, the same type of antithesis between harshness (obstinacy) and gentleness (malleability) recurs in a very similar turn of phrase and with the use, in the second term of the antithesis, of a verb formed from the root ἀβακ-:

> ἐγὼ δὲ μισέω
> πάντας ὅσοι χθονίους ἔχουσι ῥυσμοὺς
> καὶ χαλεπούς· μεμάθηκά σ᾽, ὦ Μεγιστῆ,
> τῶν ἀβακιζομένων.

> but I hate
> those who have hard and gloomy
> characters: I have learned, Megistes, that you
> are among those who have a gentle spirit.

After all it is only too clear that, in Sappho's case, it is a question of a rhetorical gesture: accusing her rival of hardness of character just at the moment in which she actually attacks her puts the responsibility of the attack upon her rival. She further expresses this with a contradictory formulation—she will be ashamed of a character not at all (οὐ μάν) "mild" but (δέ) "hard"— which seems to allude to an earlier claim of the contrary on the part of Andromeda.

---

27   The adjective does not recur elsewhere except for being entered in the lexicography of late antiquity (Hesychius, Photius), but ἀβακέω appears, with the sense of "remain silent," in Hom. *Od.* 4.249 (and we find ἀβακίζω in Anacr. fr. 416.4 *PMG*, on which see immediately below).

§5   Between Lesbos and Athens

Sappho justifies her own attack (line 8): "[No one] in truth has put down [her pride] nor reined in her greed." If, as has been noted, the condemnation of greed and excess is an important and ubiquitous theme of Greek wisdom literature that appears other times also in the context of Greek lyric,[28] there is in particular a passage that shows a very close affinity with this denunciation.

Born like Sappho around 640 and dead by 560/59, Solon was a controversial protagonist of Athenian political life and a leader of Athenian symposia with his own poetic compositions. In his elegy *Eunomia*, after stating that Athena will never allow her city to fall into ruin, Solon complains of the behavior of his fellow citizens and "the minds of those at the head of the people," and he adds (fr. 4.9–10 W.[2]):

οὐ γὰρ ἐπίστανται κατέχειν κόρον οὐδὲ παρούσας
εὐφροσύνας κοσμεῖν δαιτὸς ἐν ἡσυχίηι.

they do not know in fact how to contain their insolence, nor even
to manage the joys of the symposium before them.

As M. Noussia observes,[29] "the order of the symposium appears already in Homer to be a metaphor/manifestation of a stable community, serene and well-ordered, based on the principle that knowing how to organize a symposium lacking excess and the knowledge that opened the way to good government of a city were of the same kind."

Just as he sings in a *symposion*, in the way he is accustomed, Solon contrasts the *hetaireia* joined around him with the heads of other groups (it is possible that he is thinking primarily of Pisistratus and his ambitions to impose himself as "tyrant" of Athens). These are the ones, as he comes to say further on (lines 21–22), who plot to harm the city "in secret meetings[30] dear to the unjust."

As Solon contrasts greed (κόρος) for other riches with the serene enjoyment of symposiastic pleasures (wine, music, song, games), Sappho seems to suggest

---

28   For κόρος, in particular, cf. Pind. *I.* 3.2 κατέχει φρασὶν αἰανῆ κόρον.

29   Noussia 2001: 241.

30   But σύνοδοι, as well as "secret meetings," can denote *tout court*, as in Aristoph. *Eq.* 477 and Thuc. 3.82.6, aristocratic associations.

that the arrogance of her rival, her perverse greed, stands in the way of a peaceful relationship with other groups and so prevents the possibility of what would be an ideal situation: a sacrifice to the Tyndarids (venerated at Lesbos as tutelary divinities of navigation),[31] which would have been followed for her group as well as for Andromeda's, by a public banquet and the enjoyment of music[32] in a pleasant dancing space. And this would have happened with the company of Megara, mentioned by the *Suda* (Σ 107) as "companion and friend" of Sappho together with Atthis and Telesippa, entrusted with taking up the resounding harp: Megara who, in contrast with the hard and asocial Andromeda, comes to be defined, following a likely supplement of Lobel, with the synonym of ἀβάκην at line 7, i.e., ἀκάλην.[33]

If then Solōn's text belongs to the realm of the symposium where the performance of elegy had a part, Sappho's words point, for the *mise en scène* of the song, to a dancing space (χόρος).[34]

The reference to a song produced by Megara with a harp in a dancing course would make little sense if a dancing performance on the part of a more or less numerous group of young girls were not meant. On the other hand, a dance does not necessarily presuppose a song, and in any case, where dance and song occur together, it is not a given that the performance concerns the song currently being sung and not a composition to be sung soon afterwards. Finally one should consider that the canonical, if exclusively modern, distinction[35] between monodic and choral lyric was anything other than neat and binding: not only could a single poet compose for solo and choral performance, but many compositions were able to be interpreted in both ways.[36]

---

31   On the Tyndarids (originally distinct from the Dioscuri) as divinities propitious to navigation cf. Alc. F 34, Eur. *Hel.* 1495 ff. and 1663 ff.; for sacrifices of lambs (white) in their honor cf. Hom. *Hymn* (to the Dioscuri) 33.8–10.

32   It seems clear from the context that the genitive ἁρμονίας here has the force not of "pact," "accord" as in Hom. *Il.* 22.255, but already of "melodic line," "musical performance" (based on knowledge of accords or intervals in the musical scale, on which see West 1992: 177–89), as in Eur. fr. 773.23–25 K. μέλπει λεπτὰν | ἀηδὼν ἁρμονίαν | ὀρθρευομένα γόοις and in Aristoph. *Eq.* 994.

33   Cf. F 43.5 ἄκαλα κλόνει (perhaps in connection with the breeze), Hes. fr. 339 M.-W. ἀκαλὰ προρέων.

34   For χόρος / χορός as "dancing space (course)" cf. Hom. *Il.*18.590 and 603 ἱμερόεντα χορόν, *Od.* 8.260 and 264, 12.4 and 318.

35   A passage in Plato's *Laws* (764d-e) appears to be the only place in which the terms μονωιδία and χορωιδία are applied to lyric song and are opposed the one to the other; for the rest, in this context dedicated to a discussion of musical performance, Plato dwells not on poetic "genres" but on the different practice of songs sung *solo* and those sung in a chorus.

36   On this issue see Davies 1988.

A different but related question is that of identifying the speaker of the "I." This kind of question can be resolved, if ever, only with reference to the specific contextual occasion.

What is certain is that this "I" that mentions the time of its own exile and the sufferings endured in the past and the present, and that decides to attack a well-defined figure, one explicitly named, does not present itself as a collective "I." It evidently leads back to Sappho in the depth of her existential experience and her polemical feeling, even if one cannot deny to such expressions a traditional value (or perhaps a conventional one) within a genre (the "foil") of which the outlines and constants for this era largely escape us, and also if in principle it is always opportune to distinguish among Sappho the actual person, Sappho the poet, and Sappho the literary persona put into play by the poet Sappho.

Finally as regards section B, there is some reason to question whether this was part of the same composition as section A.

The coincidence of the end of B 7 ἀλίτρα[and the end of A 4 ἀλίτραν̣ can, in truth, be explained as much as internal repetition as the result of the juxtaposition, the latter the work of Alexandrian editors, of two poems relating to the same or to an analogous target of polemic. Yet there are two possible indications favoring one poem:

- The (ἀ)θύραμ̣[εν of B 2 can be interpreted as a reference to a time, prior to the tensions connected to the exile, in which both women took pleasure in playing and singing in the context of the same festivals and on the same occasions.[37]
- The end of B 6 ἐπε̣[ὶ σ]τέγα μ̣[ε could allude to Sappho's return home.

---

37 For ἀθύρω in the sense of "to sing" cf. Hom. *Hymn.* 19.15, Pind. *I.* 4.39, in that of "to play" Alc. F 70.3 and [Anacr.] fr. 43.10.

III   Sappho's School

§1   "Even You It Pleased to Sing"

That (ἀ)θύραμ[εν of B 2 refers to a time when Sappho and Andromeda had participated in friendship at the island's festivals can only remain, given our documentation, a simple hypothesis, but that Sappho occasionally returns in her memory to the times of her youth to bring these memories to the addressee of her lyric discourse emerges clearly from a fragment of Book 1 (F 27.4–11):

> ...]. καὶ γὰρ δὴ σὺ πάις ποτ᾽ [ἦσθα   4
> κάφ]ίλης μέλπεσθ᾽· ἄγι ταῦτα [
> σοὶ] ζάλεξαι κἄμμ᾽ ἀπὺ τῶδε κ[
>   ἄ]δρα χάρισσαι·   7
> σ]τείχομεν γὰρ ἐς γάμον, εὖ δε[
> κα]ὶ σὺ τοῦτ᾽, ἀλλ᾽ ὄττι τάχιστα [
> πα]ρ[θ]ένοις ἄπ[π]εμπε, θέοι [
>   ]εν ἔχοιεν.   11

4 [ἦσθα Voigt   5 κάφ]ίλης Di Benedetto;]ίκης Lobel-Page, Voigt   6 σοὶ] Treu   8 δὲ [δέρκηι Di Benedetto   9 fin. [ταίσδε?

> ... at one time you too [were] a girl   4
> [and] loved to sing. Come, [all] these things […]
> discuss [with yourself] and to us from this […]
>   grant generous delights,   7

since we go to a wedding celebration, and this [see]
also you. And as soon as possible [send]
[these] girls, [and] the gods [...]
    may they have [...]   11

What remains of the poem (which would have concluded with line 11)[1] allows us to assume an appeal to someone—a mature woman who ought to be persuaded with a recollection of a youth made cheerful with song and dance—in order that she may reason with herself, and decide as soon as possible to send the girls who are part of her circle to a wedding celebration to which the *persona loquens*, or a collective "we" (the first person plural of line 8 and the pronoun ἄμμ(ι) at line 6), is going. What emerges here—as Di Benedetto has observed[2]—is "a glimpse of everyday life: we could imagine that the scene takes place on the street, with the other 'teacher' before her door who [i.e., the teacher] looks at the procession of Sappho and her pupils" in the wake of Hom. *Il.* 18.490–96.

The lyric dialogue, where the imperatives ζάλεξαι and χάρισσαι at lines 6–7 and ἄπ[π]εμπε at line 10 stand out, involves two groups identified respectively with the "we" of line 6 and the girls of line 10: actually the speaker seems to impart stage directions for organizing the program of the wedding celebration according to its canonical ways and stages.

It has been hypothesized that this is a message from the chorus, and that this chorus addresses the bride in an attempt to "convince the addressee to leave her companions and set out to the wedding without showing sadness but instead herself being a cause of joy for her companions."[3] However, the phrase "at one time you too [were] a girl / [and] loved to sing" assumes that this addressee is not a young woman on the day of her wedding but rather a mature woman, presumably one of her rivals standing in front of the door of the house where the group pauses on its way to the wedding celebration; a woman, in any case, whose attention the poet tries to capture by making her glance at the possibility of reviving her own past through the youth of the girls who are part of Sappho's entourage.

---

  1 In fact it is probable that line 12] ὅδος μ[έ]γαν εἰς Ὀλ[υμπον signals, with a didactic pre-amble, the beginning of a new poem.
  2 Di Benedetto 1987: 51–52.
  3 Aloni 1997: 57.

A revival of the past also arises in the very lacunose F 24:

>]ανάγα[
>   ].[   ]εμνάσεσθ᾽ ἀ[
> κ]αὶ γὰρ ἄμμες ἐν νεό[τατι
> _ ταῦτ᾽ [ἐ]πόημμεν.   4
> πό̣λ̣λ̣α̣ [μ]ὲν γὰρ καὶ κά[λα
> ...η.[ ]μεν, πολι[
> .μμε.[.] ὀ[ξ]είαις δ[

2]ε μνάσεσθ(ε) vel -σθ(αι) Hunt   7 ὀ[ξ]είαις Maas (ὀξήαις Voigt)

> ...
> ... you will remember...
> and in truth even we in our youth
> did this,   4
>
> for many beautiful things
> ...
> [...] sharp [...]

§2   Sappho Schoolmistress?

We cannot prove that the woman addressed in F 27 is Andromeda: however, what is clear is a pattern of communal participation at local festivals.

Thus, now that we have seen a fragment in which "we" occurs as the focus of poetic discourse, we can approach the old question whether Sappho directed a school or group or circle or *hetaireia,* or whatever we wish to call[4] an association in which young girls of the island or other areas learned music, song, dance, and elegance while awaiting a marriage that would have concluded an experience that we should not hesitate to define as educative.

---

4 But the widely used term "thiasos" is, in relation to Sappho's circle, a modern invention that seems to go back to W. Schmid (1908): see Lasserre 1989: 114–15.

The digression is necessary also because the idea of a "school" has become the subject of discussion at various times in recent decades, in particular in the work of Holt Parker and of Eva Stehle.[5]

These scholars have denied that Sappho habitually addressed adolescent girls and that these girls came together around the poet as a teacher of art and life. A suppression of "Sappho Schoolmistress," so the forceful title of Parker's article, inevitably raises the question of the contextualization of this poetic production and of its intended audience.

If Parker's contestation of this second point, a vulgate based on an idea of a restricted and private audience, turns out, as we have already begun to observe, to be fully justified, the negation of an enduring, intense, organic relation with young adolescents is, apart from single problematic aspects, to a large degree refutable.[6]

Without dwelling at length on the details (some will arise in what follows), we may confidently state that Sappho was concerned with the education of young girls in the role of χοροδιδάσκαλος[7] and that she often referred to them with strongly subjective overtones; this obviously does not mean that she could not also address herself occasionally to her own age-mates who were not adolescents, as we just observed in the case of F 27.

Let us try lining up a series of internal evidence from the extant fragments:

- In F 58.11 (as we shall see, the beginning of a poem) we find an apostrophe to παῖδες, i.e., adolescents who have just been urged to demonstrate their skill in dance while the poet, now old, is inhibited in her ability to move on agile knees (same vocative also in *Inc. Auct.* 18.2]σα φύγοιμι, παῖδες, ἄβα....).

---

5 Parker 1993, Stehle 1997: 262–318. Both bring to far-reaching conclusions a hypercritical orientation in evaluating the biographical testimony, a stance promoted especially by Lefkowitz 1981.

6 Lardinois 1994 and Tsomis 2001: 22–37 raised objections to this critical approach, but a correct recognition of the fact that "several poems specify that the status of the female figures mentioned is that of a parthenos" may be found in Williamson 1995: 80–84 (and see also Tedeschi 2005: 13–15).

7 On Sappho as a teacher of μουσική see in particular Dover 1985: 181–87. The Spartans had assigned to Alcman the job of διδάσκαλος of traditional choruses of girls and ephebes, according to an anonymous author of a commentary to the lyric poets (P.Oxy. 2506, fr. 1 col. II = Alcm. T A2 *PMGF*). Plato enlarges on the χορεία (combination of dance and song) as a fundamental qualification of the education of youths in the second book of the *Laws* (654a–661d); there also is a reference to χοροδιδάσκαλοι (cf. 812e).

- In F 140.2 the dancers who are invited, in the context of a ritual "dialogue," to lament the death of Adonis are apostrophized as κόραι.
- In F 94.22–23 the preeminent figure of the poem (a young woman who has just taken leave of the group) is said to satisfy her desire of figures defined as ἄπαλαι.[8]
- Complementary to these indications regarding adolescent girls is the fact that in F 96.6–7 the Lydian wives, among whom Atthis' friend now lives at Sardis after leaving Sappho's circle, are termed γυναίκεσσιν. And the same epithet ἄπαλος—an adjective that also elsewhere appears constantly to refer to very young persons (or parts of their body)[9]—is attributed to Gyrinno (F 82a: εὐμορφοτέρα Μνασιδίκα τὰς ἀπάλας Γυρίννως), to the neck of the girl who has now left the group in F 94.16, and to a "companion" on the breast of whom another girl sleeps (or would like to sleep) in F 126.
- At F 16.18 the face of Anactoria, now distant, is referred to as bright by way of a substantive (ἀμάρυχμα) that, as instances of the application of the epic formula Χαρίτων ἀμαρύγματ' ἔχουσα(ν) show,[10] denotes the grace characteristic of a nubile girl.

These are internal indications that are consistent with external testimony of a variety of periods and trustworthiness that outline a lacunose but coherent picture, and that we record here with the minimum objective of considering Sappho—as much as her rivals Andromeda and Gorgo—as engaged in directing educative allegiances fully recognized as such in Lesbian society.

- Vase representations from the fifth century BC, with which we shall be concerned more elsewhere, show Sappho (indicated by name) in the company of young women. On the Bochum krater, the figure that follows Sappho on the vase's other face is explicitly indicated as ἡ παῖς.
- The anonymous compiler of a commentary of which a few lines remain in a second-century AD papyrus published in 1974 (P.Köln II 61 fr. a = 261a.7 ff. SLG), contrasts Sappho's life with that of Alcaeus, and affirms that she passed her life educating peacefully not only the best girls of the island but also those who came from Ionia. It also states that she was

8 For the text and interpretation of the passage see XI, § 1 and § 3.
9 Cf. e.g. Hom. Od. 13.222–23, Alcm. fr. 39a.5 and 45.6, Thgn. 1341.
10 Cf. Hes. fr. 43(a).4, 70.38, 196.6 M.-W. and see Brown 1989: 14. Likewise, we have βάλλεν ... ἀμαρύγματα of the virgin Medea in her first contact with Jason in A. R. 3.288.

held in such favor by her fellow-citizens that, as Callias the Mytilenean says, she received the front seat at festivals in honor of Aphrodite (... ἡ δ᾽ ἐφ᾽ ἡσυχία[ς] παιδεύουσα τὰς ἀρίστας οὐ μόνον τῶν ἐγχωρίων ἀλλὰ καὶ τῶν ἀπ᾽ Ἰωνίας· καὶ ἐν τοσαύτηι παρὰ τοῖς πολίταις ἀποδοχῆι, ὥστ᾽ ἔφη Καλλίας ὁ Μυτιληναῖος, ἐν Μυτ[ιλήν]ηι Ἀφροδι[σίων τὴν προε]δρ[ίαν λαβεῖν[11]). So at Mytilene in the second/third century BC (the period in which the grammarian Callias, author of, among other things, an erudite small tract on gastronomical aspects in Alcaeus, was active), there circulated a tradition that recorded public recognition of Sappho in the context of public festivals.[12]

- In the letter of Sappho to Phaon (*Ep.* 15.15–16) Ovid shows a Sappho surrounded by a *turba* of *puellae*:[13]

> *nec me Pyrrhiades Methymniadesve puellae*
> *nec me Lesbiadum cetera turba iuvant.*

Neither the girls from Pyrrha nor those from Methymna
Nor do the other crowds of Lesbian girls please me.

- Philostratus, in the *Life of Apollonius of Tyana* (1.30 = Sapph. T 223), mentions that a Pamphylian woman named Damophila had gathered around her, with Sappho as model, girls for whom she composed hymns and love poems.[14]
- As we have already mentioned, Maximus of Tyre (*Or.* 18.9 = Sapph. T 219) says that the ἀντίτεχνοι of Sappho, on par with Prodicus, Gorgias, and Thrasymachus in their relations with Socrates, were Gorgo and Andromeda, and that the objects of Sappho's affections were Gyrinno, Atthis, and Anactoria, as those of Socrates were Alcibiades, Charmides, and Phaedrus.
- The orator Himerius (*Or.* 28.2 = Sapph. T 221) affirms that all of Sappho's poetic production was occasioned by "maidens and Graces."[15]

---

11   For the supplement τὴν προε]δρ[ίαν λαβεῖν see Lasserre 1989: 113 n. 3.

12   For a full appreciation of this *testimonium* see Lasserre 1989: 114–18. Even Parker has no alternative interpretation and limits himself to an appeal to the fact that "we have no idea of the commentator's sources or accuracy."

13   That *puella* in the Roman erotic lexicon means "girlfriend" (Stehle 1997: 266) is something quite different from the use of the word in the plural.

14   That this cannot be, as Parker objects, a "formal school" (a notion that would require some qualification) does not change the substance of the educative model Philostratus recalls.

15   In saying ὅλην ... τὴν ποίησιν Himerius cannot have had in mind, as Stehle 1997: 266 sug-

- The *Suda* (Σ 107 = T 253) mentions in relation to Sappho three "companions and friends" (ἑταῖραι ... καὶ φίλαι)—Atthis, Telesippa, Megara —and three "pupils" (μαθήτριαι)—Anactoria of Miletus,[16] Gongyla of Colophon, Eunica of Salamina. To disentangle oneself from the forest of facts and pseudo-facts that have come together in this erudite jungle is, as everyone knows, a desperate undertaking, and Parker may be right to observe that the distinction between "friends" and "pupils" is an illusory one. The fact remains that all these names, with the exception of Eunica, are recognizable or at least plausibly supplemented in Sappho (for Megara cf. F 68a.12, for Telesippa F 87f.5). This case is then quite different from that which Parker invokes, of Erinna and Nossis being named companions of Sappho in the *Suda* as well.[17] And even if the sources of Hesychius' *Onomatologos*, on which the *Suda* depends, had invented a discipleship of girls at Lesbos to justify the presence of female figures of foreign origin in Sappho's poems, it would be hard to think that this could have happened without the support of a related tradition of Sappho's educative role convergent with that in the biography of the Cologne papyrus mentioned above.

§3   Two Colleagues?

It may be possible also to find outside of Lesbos, in archaic or late archaic Greek poetry, two chorus teachers comparable to Sappho.

In the *Louvre Partheneion* of Alcman the chorus members, in saying that the attraction of their leader conquers all opposition, declare (lines 73–75):

οὐδ᾽ ἐς Αἰνησιμβρ[ό]τας ἐνθοῖσα φασεῖς·
Ἀσταφίς [τ]έ μοι γένοιτο
καὶ ποτιγλέποι Φίλυλλα   75
Δαμαρ[έ]τα τ᾽ ἐρατά τε ϝιανθεμίς·

---

gests, only the wedding compositions.

16   Actually the manuscript tradition of the *Suda* has Ἀναγόρα, but Neue's correction Ἀριγνώτα has in its favor also the importance of this name in Milesian onomastics (see Cavallini 2006: 148–50).

17   The case of Erinna seems to depend on Adesp. *A.P.* 9.190 (see Neri 2003: 212–13).

... nor arrived at Aenesimbrota's house will you say:
"Oh if only Astaphis were with me
and Philylla were looking at me   75
and Damareta and lovely Vianthemis!"

While μοι γένοιτο and ποτιγλέποι are erotic expressions that the girls mention as vague recollection of frustrated yearnings, even before taking form, for
Hagesichora's beauty, M. West has hypothesized that the figure of Aenesimbrota
is a sorceress capable of making love potions and dictating magic formulas.[18]
However, the whole lyric discourse that takes up the stanza of lines 64–77 refers
to the group that is actually singing: Astaphis, Philylla, Damareta, Vianthemis
are girls of the chorus just as Nanno, Areta, Sylakis, and Kleesisera named just
before, just as purple, gold bracelets, and the headband are the ornaments with
which these girls adorn themselves. To insert their names involved, for Alcman, honoring their presence in obedience to presumed requests of the participants in question, just as mentioning their ornaments was meant to draw the
gaze of the audience to their elegance.

    If Aenesimbrota was the teacher of the chorus members, then the mention of her
name would serve the same strategy; on the contrary, the reference to a given sorceress would not have had any relationship with the context of the performance.

    We encounter the second figure in another "parthenion," namely in Pin-
dar's second *Parthenion* (lines 71–72). Here the chorus members—after
saying that Damaena, who is the daughter of the client Pagondas who com-
missioned the song and the sister of Agasicles, will lead them with her quiet
rhythmical step in the *Daphnephoria* in the direction of the sanctuary situated near the river Ismenus—specify that Damaena has been trained by
Andaesistrota. These lines are rather lacunose and we cannot exclude the
possibility that Andaesistrota is Damaena's mother, as even Maehler assumes in the genealogical tree of the family of Pagondas that appears at the
end of the poem in the Teubner edition (1989). However, the verb that occurs here (ἐπάσκησε) suits a teacher rather better than a mother.

---

18 West 1965: 200.

IV   Tales of Abandonment

§1   A True Peasant

Let us turn then to Andromeda and the attacks Sappho directs against her. In F 57 Sappho emphasizes Andromeda's "rustic nature":

τίς δ᾽ ἀγροΐωτις θέλγει νόον ...
τίς δ᾽ ἀγροΐωτιν ἐπεμμένα σπόλαν ...
οὐκ ἐπισταμένα τὰ βράκε᾽ ἔλκην ἐπὶ τῶν σφύρων;

2   τίς δ᾽ secl. Blomfield fort. τίς δέ <σ᾽> ἀγροΐωτιν <‿ ˘ - - - ˘ > ἐπεμμένα | σπόλαν

What uncouth woman charms your mind?[...]
and who, dressed in a rustic dress [...]
doesn't know to let her dress fall over her ankles?

That these three lines, assigned to F 57 in most recent editions (not however in Bergk's) belong originally to the same poem,[1] as J. Casaubon first proposed, is not entirely certain.[2] It is true that the two citations (of lines 1 + 3 and of line 2) both have the adjective ἀγροΐωτις (not found elsewhere before Dioscorides *A.P.* 7.411.1)[3] and the presence, in lines 2 and 3, of clothing as a theme.[4]

---

1   Athenaeus (1.21b-c) cites lines 1 and 3, with the specification that Sappho mocks Andromeda; verse 2 is taken from Maximus of Tyre.
2   See Di Benedetto 1982: 13–16.
3   But in Homer we find ἀγρωιότης, in Alc. F 130b.2 ἀγροΐώτικος.
4   Further, if we take the text of line 2 as transmitted in Maximus of Tyre (with the initial τίς δ᾽,

In and of itself "rusticity" could not be appropriate to a woman who belonged to an ancient royal family, even if Sappho might exploit, in an ironic way, the contrast between the noble background and contrasting appearance of her rival. But there is some reason to suspect another, less immediate explanation.

If the importing of goods of Lydian origin and familiarity with Anatolian culture had been strengthened in the decades of the Cleanactid tyranny (first under Melanchros, then Myrsilus), the Penthilids might have continued sustaining the taste of the former good times. Hence the accusation of "rusticity" is all the more forceful if directed against a woman who not only had the means to buy elegant things but who also appeared greedy for wealth (but indifferent to the artistic quality of the work involved in transforming raw materials into consumer goods). Therefore, "rusticity" seems to complete the profile: a rich but greedy woman yet, at the same time, boorish and ignorant.

It is significant here that the word used in line 2 as "clothing" (σπόλαν) is value-neutral, whereas that in line 3 (βράκε᾿), an ensemble of "rags" or "scraps," is decidedly negative. It is true that Theocritus at line 11 of his *Distaff* (*Id.* 28)— an *Idyll* composed in Aeolic dialect and in the same meter—picks up just the Sapphic form βράκη to indicate the "supple garments,"[5] evidently expensive, for which the distaff will spin the material. It is also true that Hesychius (B 1047) glosses the same form in the singular as "expensive cloak."[6] However, since elsewhere, and particularly in a series of passages from the *Odyssey* (6.178, 14.342 and 349, 14.512, 18.67 and 74, etc.), ῥάκος always means "rag," it is likely that both Theocritus and Hesychius may have depended on a wrong interpretation of Sappho's text.[7]

But for what reason does Andromeda's rusticity center, other than on her "rags," also on her inability to let her gown fall above her ankles? Recalling the delicate ankles of the young girls who, together with a group of women, take part in the marriage celebration in the *Epithalamium of Hector and Andromache*,[8] Marzullo observes that such a trait "is included in that canon of refine-

deleted by Blomfield, before ἀγροΐωτιν) and insert a pronoun (σ᾿) between τίς δ᾿ and ἀγροΐωτιν, we obtain a sequence that, through a single conjectured lacuna, can be brought into agreement with the scansion of line 3, that is, a gl[2cho], the meter characteristic of the third book of the Alexandrian edition: τίς δέ <σ᾿> ἀγροΐωτιν <‿–‿‿‿–> ἐπεμμένα | σπόλαν. Naturally in this case it would be necessary to assume a rather large-scale alteration of line 1 in the textual tradition of Athenaeus.

5 Theocr. 28.11 ὑδάτινα βράκη.
6 Hesych. B 1047 βράκος· ... ἱμάτιον πολυτελές.
7 See Burzacchini 1977: 156; Gianotti 1981; Andrisano 1997–2000.
8 Sapph. F 44.15 παρθενίκα[ν] τ᾿ ἀπ[αλ]οσφύρων (suppl. Pfeiffer).

ment, in which the ankle receives particular attention."[9] More precisely, how and when it is important to let the gown fall above the ankle we can see in an image of a pupil of Sappho in a vase illustration that adorns an Attic krater from 480/470 BC now at Bochum (Inv. S 508).

An adolescent, indicated in writing above her head as "the girl"[10] (Fig. 2), from a distance follows Sappho (also indicated by name), who, on the other side of the vase (Fig. 1), holds a long lyre (barbitos) with her left arm. As she goes forward she turns her head back and stretches out her right arm, pressing a plectrum in her hand. The girl, wearing a long cloak, moves forward in the same direction, raising her right heel (but without taking her foot completely off the ground) and holds the edge of her cloak lightly raised with either hand. The gesture is graceful and aims at facilitating the girl's walking (one thinks of the "graceful step of Anactoria"[11]). As the thickness of the cloak indicates, the scene is imagined as being outside and recalls the standard images of young men who, after having made a komos outside with a player of aulos or lyre, go from one symposiastic gathering to another.

A precise parallel for the gesture of the *pais* comes from the figure of a young man, in a scene of "komasts on their way" on an Attic stamnos by the Cleophontes painter of 440/430, now at Munich (stamnos 2414), where again the two figures on two sides of the vase can be read as in succession. On the first side three komasts and a flute-player move to the right, with the young man who proceeds behind the woman holding in his hand a torch to shed light into the night's darkness. On the other side come forth, toward another symposion or homeward, another three komasts, of whom one has a torch in his hand and another a skyphos, while the one at the center proceeds as he holds his cloak with the borders raised.[12]

This suggests that Andromeda is accused of not knowing how to raise her cloak above her ankles not so much in everyday life or on some unspecified occasion, but rather with regard to a festive celebration in which the woman carried out the role of leader of the procession. Here too it seems that we ought

9   Marzullo 1958: 163 n. 1. On praise of a wife's ankles see Lyghounis 1991: 170. Literary parallels for the manner of holding a gown in relation to the ankles occur at Eur. *Ba.* 935–36 and at Theocr. 15.134: ἐπὶ σφυρὰ κόλπον ἀνεῖσαι (see Andrisano 1997–2000).

10   The inscription Η ΠΑΙΣ above the girl's head has been clearly identified by Yatromanolakis 2005. We will return in Ch. VIII to this and other images relative to Sappho and her circle, and their interpretation.

11   F 16.17 ἔρατον ... βᾶμα.

12   See Gossel-Raeck 1992: 296–97.

to understand not a private dimension but a public one of showing both herself
and her group to a festive audience.

§2   "You Fly to Andromeda"

Nevertheless, though rustic and arrogant (or perhaps exactly because of this),
Andromeda is in a position to attract to herself various followers of the most
refined Sappho: Atthis, Gyrinno, and Mika leave for Andromeda's circle.

In F 130.3–4 (= 131 LP) we read:

> Ἄτθι, σοὶ δ᾽ ἔμεθεν μὲν ἀπήχθετο
> φροντίσδην, ἐπὶ δ᾽ Ἀνδρομέδαν πότη<ι>.

> Atthis, for you it has become hateful
> to think of me, and you fly to Andromeda.

So Atthis, as a result of a sudden change, not only "flies" to Andromeda
(a not-infrequent hyperbole; one might compare Hector at *Il.* 13.755 who
"flies" among the allies and the Trojans, or Aristoph. *Lys.* 321: πέτου πέτου,
Νικοδίκη), but nurtures hostile feelings toward Sappho. The deep tie that she
maintained with her teacher and that is underlined by the immediate juxtaposition, as in F 49.1, of personal pronouns (*lit.* "for you ... of me") has been erased.

§3   Economic Questions

In what form could these acts of abandonment have arisen? In the absence of
more precise evidence, it seems possible to infer that a young woman entrusted
by her family to the guidance of one teacher might be able to opt for another
source of guidance.

On the base of a commentary to texts of Sappho preserved in P.Oxy. 2506
(and in particular of fr. 48 col. II, lines 12–13 = Sapph. T 213 Ag.12–13), Treu[13]

---

13   Treu 1966, and see also Gentili 1988: 264 n. 77.

suspected that Sappho's activity had an economic implication in the form of
the compensation she received from her pupils for the educative role she held,
and the reality of this seems hinted at in a passage in which the poet says of the
Muses (F 32):

αἴ με τιμίαν ἐπόησαν ἔργα
τὰ σφὰ δοῖσαι

these who have made me honored
in giving me their works

This is all the more true if Aelius Aristides, *Or.* 28.51 (2.158 K.), as Bergk first
suspected,[14] is referring to this ode when he says that Sappho "addressing some
ladies thought fortunate (εὐδαιμόνων)," would have boasted that the Muses
had made her "rich and envied" (ὀλβίαν τε καὶ ζηλωτήν) and that not even after
her death would oblivion fall upon her.

The education of a Greek woman began at a very early age and could be
considered completed at the end of adolescence. Considering that the girls
whom Sappho and her rivals educated did not necessarily come only from
Mytilene and the other cities of Lesbos but also from far lands, it comes inevitably to mind that these *parthenoi* would have lived in close contact with
their teacher and there would be a need either for a place to house them or
means to guarantee that elegance that was to be an integral part of their education.

Consequently their families of origin must have had to provide, in the most
varied forms, for substantial contributions to the administration of such an
institution (gifts, in particular, will have been sent or brought with a new pupil
at the time of her entry into the community).

A fragment belonging to a hymn to Aphrodite from Book V (F 101), for all
its textual problems, appears interesting in this regard:

---

14 See Voigt on F 32 (p. 60). The connection has been taken up by Di Benedetto 2005: 17 and
2006: 11–12. However, the passage of Aelius Aristides is referred by Lobel-Page to F 147 (where
however there is a mention of some recollection "of us") and by Fränkel 1928: 269, followed by
Voigt, to F 55 (where however the reference is to the oblivion that will come to a woman against
whom Sappho polemicizes).

χερρόμακτρα δὲ †καγγόνων†
πορφύρα κὰτ ἀύτμενα
τά τοι Μ<ν>ᾶσις ἔπεμψ᾽ ἀπὺ Φωκάας,
δῶρα τίμια †καγγόνων†

1 πορφύρα Ahrens: πορφύραι Athen. 9.410d-f cod. A   fin. Μαιόνων vel Ἰαόνων Lobel   2 κὰτ ἀύτμενα Lobel: καταυταμενά- A   3 τά τοι Μ<ν>ᾶσις Wilamowitz: τατιμάσεις A

... and purple veils
of the Ionians(?) that with the wind's breath
Mnasis sent you from Phocea,
precious gifts [...].

Whether Mnasis had sent these gifts from her native Phocea for the goddess most venerated by the group before arrival at Lesbos, or as a gesture of gratitude after her sojourn on the island, this elegant object[15] would have also represented, as well as a cultural offering, the confirmation of the link between the family of the young woman and her poet-teacher.

The abandonment of one circle in favor of another circle could therefore signify a crack in more complex relations; a break between Sappho and a single student could bring about crises and readjustments in the changeable distribution of power and prestige among the leading families of the island.

§4   Questions of Age

Distribution by age groups is characteristic of all educative associations in archaic Greece, from Athenian ephebes and Spartan youths to the female *agelai* of Sparta and Crete,[16] and in Sappho herself the group of young friends of the

15 Etymologically a χειρόμακτρον is a tablecloth or napkin for wiping the hands, but cf. Hdt. 2.122.1 χειρόμακτρον χρύσεον in reference to golden cloth, corresponding to "*nms*, the golden headdress with blue stripes worn by the Egyptian kings" (Lloyd 1989: 342), which has been brought from Hades as a gift offered by Demeter to the king Rhampsinitus.
16 For a survey of the theme see Lardinois 1994: 71–74; Williamson 1995: 119–25.

bridegroom are defined as "coevals,"[17] just as in Theocr. *Id.* 18 (an epithalamium inspired by Sappho) the young girls who sing the song and who form a "young group" (νεολαία) are identified as "coeval" among themselves and with respect to Helen.

A fragment (F 49) suggests that Sappho may have begun her own educative activity very early, perhaps following in the footsteps of her mother:

ἠράμαν μὲν ἔγω σέθεν, Ἄτθι, πάλαι ποτά

*

σμίκρα μοι πάις ἔμμεν᾽ ἐφαίνεο κἄχαρις.

I was in love with you, Atthis, once …

*

To me you seemed a little and graceless girl.

These two verses are cited in different sources, the first in Hephaistion among others, the second in Maximus of Tyre, and therefore, even though they are composed in the same meter—that of all of Book II of the Alexandrian edition (glyconics with double dactylic expansion, gl^{2da})—they might derive from different compositions. Except that, as Bergk saw, a passage from Terentianus Maurus (*Gramm. Lat.* 6.390.4–5 K.) shows, if not their immediate contiguity, that they at least come from within the same poem:

Cordi quando fuisse sibi canit Atthida
parvam, florea virginitas sua cum foret.

So a Sappho in the bloom of youth (*sua* can only refer to the main subject) had shown tenderness and love for an Atthis still *parva*; no more than a small and graceless *pais*, what must have been the typical condition of one who entered the group on one day to come out of it a young woman full of charm and ready for marriage.

It has been objected that, if at the time recalled in the poem the one was *parva* and the other was in the bloom of her *virginitas*, Atthis cannot have been

---

17 F 30.7 ὑμάλικ[ας and 103.11 ἄσαροι γὰρ ὑμάλικ[ες. And cf. also, though the context is uncertain, F 64a.4 α]λίκεσσι[and 76.7]αλίκ[.

much younger than Sappho and that therefore, if the necessary weight is given to the temporal adverb πάλαι, one ought to suppose that Atthis and Sappho were both adults at the time of the poem's composition.[18]

There is no evidence from the passage of when the poem was composed, but we can make two observations. First of all, there isn't actually a need to emphasize the sense of πάλαι given that this adverb has a very vague connotation: it can mean "very long ago" but also "a little while ago." Actually what matters is not the chronological duration of the time passed (a time measurable in days, months, years), but rather the use of the term πάλαι to mark a period as a phase now surpassed. So, to limit ourselves to two passages prior to Sappho, at Hom. *Il.* 9.105 Nestor says to Agamemnon that he has thought πάλαι of the idea that the Atreid restore Briseis to Achilles, even back to when Agamemnon sent heralds to take the woman from Achilles' tent (in fact a few days earlier), and at *Il.* 22.301–33 Hector, noticing that Deiphobus is not next to him, understands that the gods had turned their backs on him πάλαι, even if "earlier" (πάρος), that is up to the preceding battle, they had protected him.

So in our passage the poet could well have said that she loved Atthis πάλαι, i.e., when the latter was still in a phase of youthful immaturity that has now definitely passed.

Secondly, the *florea virginitas* to which Terentianus Maurus alludes in reference to Sappho sounds antithetical to the "smallness" and lack of grace of Atthis at the time when Sappho was in love with her. If the poem had been directed from one adult woman to another adult woman, this type of contrast would have had very little point.

If on the other hand the composition goes back to the time when Atthis "flew" or gave signs of getting ready to "fly" to Andromeda, the play in the antithesis becomes more forceful in a *do ut des* logic of gratitude or ingratitude. When you were little and insignificant I was in the flower of my youth (at the height of my value as a woman) and I was in love with you (I transmitted to you a value that you did not possess) and showed you my affection and my interest. Now that, thanks to me (to the formation you've had at my hands) you are worth more than ever before (now that you have the power of your charm as a young woman ready for marriage), look! you don't return the debt of gratitude that you contracted with me, rather you betray me and give honor to my odious rival.[19]

18 Stehle 1997: 268–69.

19 A strong sense of sorrow at another's ingratitude arises at lines 2–4 of the very lacunose F 26, which was part of a poem directed at a "you" (sing., cf. line 9) that we are not in a position

§5   Atthis' Romance

Aloni has rightly ironically treated the "sort of romance of Atthis, that from the eighteenth century, and in particular from Bergk onwards, philology has gone on to construct, not without a great effort of imagination." He has rather claimed the presence, in Sappho, of "conventional, recursive themes" which "enable the names of those mentioned in the poems, without the actual existence of these people being at issue, or the reality of the events or sentiments described or alluded to—elements about which the poetry says nothing—to indicate also (and for us especially) personalities of a world whose reality is its poetic realization. They are a necessary structure for a process of communication that is not exclusively personal and idiosyncratic, but paradigmatic and repeatable."[20]

On the other hand, if we succeed at avoiding the risk of biographism and take into account the exemplary dimension that events like that of Atthis would have assumed within Sappho's community, we can glimpse with a certain transparency snapshots of a story, or at least of a "collection of lyrics." [21]

We have already glanced at the beginning of this love parable, with a rough, immature, and tiny Atthis coming into contact with her teacher and her new environment, and its sad conclusion, where Atthis flees to other shores, but we can supplement the unfolding of the event with two other contributions.

In a fragment from Cologne, usually overlooked—whether because it is extensively damaged or because it was published [22] after Voigt's edition (P.Köln II 60

---

to identify: ὄ͵ττινα͵ς γὰρ | εὖ θέω, κῆνοί με μά͵λιστα πά[ντων | σίνοντα͵]! "[...] in truth those to whom / I do well, are those who most of all / [...] do me wrong." Also significant is the occurrence, at lines 11–12 of the same fragment, of the phrase ἔγω δ᾽ ἔμ᾽ [αὔται | τοῦτο σύνοιδα, first formulation of the notion of *conscientia* (a dimension that seems then to arise in a state of tension in relation to others, see Gentili 1988: 257 n. 39).

20   Aloni 1997: xiv.

21   Even if for us, as far as the extant literary production goes, only with Meleager's *Heliodora* is there for the first time an impulse for the creation of a "song-book" as a mirror of a love story with its beginnings, its curve of jealousy, infidelity, broken promises, separations, new flames and their undoing, marked by the death of the woman and the dialogue with her from beyond, we can postulate a hypertextual reception already among the first audiences of archaic lyric: other than in Sappho, in Archilochus (Neobule) and in the "true" Theognis (Cyrnus).

22   See Merkelbach 1974.

= S476 *SLG*)—we find referring specifically to Atthis the adjective ἀγέρωχος[23] —which we find again used to refer to certain arrogant women in the context of a commentary (P.Oxy. 2293, fr. 1 a + b = F 90a. col. III) in which the subject is Gyrinno's abandonment, again, for Andromeda:[24]

```
[
.[                          ἀγε-]
ρώχου[ς            ἄγαν ἐχού-]
_σας γερας: .[
  καὶ Γυρινν[                                    15
_τας τοιαύτας. .[.]..[        ἔ-]
γω τὸ κάλλος ἐπετ.[
μέ<σ>δον· τί γὰρ ἠνεμ[
εἶναι καὶ ἀρετῆς πο[      ἀλ-]
λὰ μήποτε λέγει ὅτι ο[                           20
_καλλι  εὐφήμεισθα[      ἔ-]
μοι ζεφύρω π̣νευμα[
σοὶ δ᾽ ἀν̣[εμ]οφόρητο[
  ]νονδεκα.[
  ]ς̣ πάϊ τασμ̣ [          πρὸς]                 25
Ἀνδρομέ]δην γέγρα̣[πται
  ] ὑπὸ Ἀνδ[ρομέδης
  ]τι οὐκευν[
  ]ωαρρε.[
  ]χητισ[                                        30
```

... [12–18] ... arrogant ... who have too much privilege ... Gyrinno ... such women ... "never have I reproved beauty ... greater": what in fact ... she means to say that in beauty there is also a large part of virtue, but perhaps she means to say that she herself was once very beautiful..., [22] "but to me the breath of Zephyrus. [23] but to you...borne by the wind" [25–26] "... daughter of the ..." ... is written against Andromeda [27] ... by Andromeda ...

---

23 Line 3 ἀ]γέρωχος Ἀτ̣[θις (Page's supplement).
24 On this part of the commentary see Cavallini 1990: 109–16.

We do not know what occasion inspired this poem, commented upon by the anonymous scholar of our commentary. That the subject, as one scholar has suggested,[25] is a *propemptikon* due to the reference to Zephyr and the winds more generally is anything but certain, considering how frequently the winds appear in Greek poetry to denote the instability of the human condition.

Certainly the poem, as the commentator explicitly states, was composed against Andromeda and the case of Gyrinno—the girl whom we met as "delicate Gyrinno" in F 82a in the context of a confrontation with Mnasidika and who was to be herself involved in a case of abandonment—provided the cue for an attack on arrogant and privileged[26] women who had accused Sappho of devaluing physical beauty.

From the commentator's paraphrase we can deduce that the poet must have replied to an accusation by maintaining that she did love beauty, and indeed she did not recognize any greater value provided that beauty included part of virtue (cf. line 19). What followed then was the wish of good for herself and ill for her rival: to me may Zephyr's breath (the wind tied to spring and to the reopening of the seas to marine traffic) bring joy and serenity, to you waves (?) raised from stormy squalls bring turbulence and ruin!

That Atthis, so loved until puberty, is assigned an adjective that brands her as an evil sort of lady like Andromeda seems the sign, after the desertion, of a condemnation without appeal, a break that cannot be repaired.

§6   The Sorrows of Atthis' Friend

In F 96.1–20 Atthis appears on the contrary as one of those presences who enliven a situation in which an anonymous "I" (individual or choral) speaks to a "you" (identified precisely as Atthis) with reference to the fragment's preeminent figure, i.e., a young girl who has left to go to Sardis, presumably to become the wife of an aristocratic Lydian:

$$] \, \sigma\alpha\rho\delta.[..]$$
$$\pi\acute{o}\lambda]\lambda\alpha\kappa\iota \, \tau\upsilon\acute{\iota}\delta\underset{.}{\epsilon} \, [.]\tilde{\omega}\nu \, \check{\epsilon}\chi o\iota\sigma\alpha \qquad\qquad 2$$

---

25 See Treu 1954: 167.

26 For ἀγέρωχος cf. also F 7.4 ὀφλισ]κάνην ἀγερωχία[ν (in relation to Doricha), Alc. F 402, Archil. fr. 261 W.², Alcm. fr. 10 (b).15 *PMGF*.

ὠσπ.[...].ὠομεν.[...]..χ[..]
σε †θεασικελαν ἀρι-
_γνωτα†, σᾶι δὲ μάλιστ᾽ ἔχαιρε μόλπαι·   5
νῦν δὲ Λύδαισιν ἐμπρέπεται γυναί-
κεσσιν ὥς ποτ᾽ ἀελίω
_δύντος ἀ βροδοδάκτυλος <σελάννα>   8
πάντα περ<ρ>έχοισ᾽ ἄστρα· φάος δ᾽ ἐπί-
σχει θάλασσαν ἐπ᾽ ἀλμύραν
_ἴσως καὶ πολυανθέμοις ἀρούραις·   11
ἀ δ᾽ <ἐ>έρσα κάλα κέχυται τεθά-
λαισι δὲ βρόδα κἄπαλ᾽ ἄν-
_θρυσκα καὶ μελίλωτος ἀνθεμώδης·   14
πόλλα δὲ ζαφοίταισ᾽ ἀγάνας ἐπι-
μνάσθεισ᾽ Ἄτθιδος ἰμέρωι
_λέπταν ποι φρένα κ.ρ... βόρηται·   17
κῆθι δ᾽ ἔλθην ἀμμ.[..]..ισα τόδ᾽ οὐ
νῶντ᾽ ἀ[..]υστονυμ[..(.)] πόλυς
γαρύει [..(.)]αλον[.....(.)]τ̣ο̣ μέσσον.   20

---

1 ἀπὺ] Σαρδ[ίων Blass. ἐνὶ] Σάρδ[εσιν Edmonds   2 [ν]ῶν Blass   3 ὡς πε[δε]ζώομεν Wilamowitz   4–5 θέα<ι> σ᾽ ἰκέλαν ἀριγνώτα<ι> Lobel (θεα<ι> iam Blass, ἀριγνώτα<ι> iam Edmonds)   17 καρτέρωι Kamerbeek, καρχάρωι Bonanno   19 ὔμ̣[ως] Theander   20 ὀν] τ̣ὸ̣ Lobel

[... from] Sardis
[...] your mind often turning here   2

to how we lived together [...]
like a goddess easily recognized[27] you [...]
and so highly enjoyed your song,   5

but now among the Lydian ladies she is resplendent
as then, when the sun has set,
_____ the rosy-fingered moon,   8

27 Above all on the basis of Hom. *Od.* 6.108 ῥεῖά τ᾽ ἀριγνώτη πέλεται (Artemis) the interpretation of ἀρι-|γνώτα as an adjective is superior to that according to which this is a proper name (see Marzullo 1970: 266–67).

who surpasses all the stars, and her light
is on the salt sea
as on the fields of flowers,   11

and lovely dew is sprinkled
and the roses bloom and the gentle
chervil and flowering mellilot,   14

and she often wanders with memory
of gentle Atthis and, I believe, her heart
is devoured by powerful desire,   17

and there [...] to go we [...]
[...] still much
resounds [...] in the midst.   20

Atthis' friend lives in Lydia and thinks back to the group she has left. The relationship the text recalls is a preferential relation that one of Sappho's pupils might harbor for another pupil, and it focuses on the pleasure of hearing her sing. It has thus been inferred that Atthis must have been the leader of songs that her friend once performed[28] and that also the present song must be of a choral nature. But neither of these two inferences is compelling and at least in relation to the second one might suspect that the two modalities of performance, monodic and choral, were equally possible and feasible from the very beginning since there are no indications that favor one or the other (there is no "I" to which we can ascribe feelings or personal experiences and there is no "we" that appears tied to an actual ongoing performance, but rather at line 18 we find a "we" that can refer as much to Sappho and Atthis as to Sappho's circle in its entirety).

The subject of the lyric discourse seeks to assure Atthis that her friend has nostalgic memories of her, even wanders disquieted absorbed in the memory of the past, and her intense desire for Atthis eats at her gentle spirit. There is an evident agreement between the delicacy (λέπταν) of the spirit of Atthis' friend and the sweetness of the same Atthis (ἀγάνας 15) just as there is an evident contrast between these two ideas and, if Kamerbeek's (1956) reading καρτέρωι is right, the intensity of the friend's desire.

---

28 See Aloni 1997: xvii n. 3.

Therefore the song, offering to Atthis' ear and imagination the certainty of such an emotional profile, is meant to soothe her from the crisis of a presence that must be in some way overcome. Even the representation of the moon's light upon the sea and the flowering fields in combination with the sprinkling of the dew and the blossoming of the roses has a consolatory function. In fact this same light that surpasses that of the nocturnal stars offers itself, following a pattern that we find also in the very famous F 34 ("The stars around the beautiful moon hide their faces..."), as a physical (and sensual) emblem of the figure that is resplendent among the Lydian women.

As a hyperbolic result of this effort to neutralize a traumatic separation occurs, in what was perhaps the final stanza of the poem,[29] the fantasy of a cry that invited friend and teacher (or the whole group) to come close to her (and this cry, from what can be gathered from the mutilated syllables, echoed several times over the sea[30]).

If with regard to Atthis we don't have a romance, the image of a gentle girl expert at song and capable of arousing a friend's passion appears to us, however, always as a temporally intermediate icon between the small and graceless Atthis, on her first entry to the group, and the proud Atthis departed to Andromeda's circle.

§7   The Little Fugitive

After Atthis and Gyrinno here is Mika, she who, after her name (in truth, nickname, as μίκα is an alternative form[31] for σμίκρα that we have seen referred to Atthis in F 49.2) has been defined as "the little fugitive."[32]

The fragment concerning her (F 71) also comes from P.Oxy. 1787. It is a strange fact that the text that Lobel and Page established and that Voigt almost

---

29 The first subsequent stanza (lines 21–23), which opens with the phrase "it is not easy for us to equal the gods in their pleasing form" (ε]ὔμαρ[ες μ]ὲν οὐκ ἄμμι θέαισι μόρ-|φαν ἐπή[ρατ] ον ἐξίσω-|σθαι), while it supposes something of the theme touched on at lines 4–5, seems to start on a new discourse with a sentence that functions as a "preamble."
30 The expression of line 20 seems equivalent, in relation to the sea, to that which the poet uses in relation to celestial space at F 1.11 f. ἀπ᾽ ὠράνω αἴθε-|ρος διὰ μέσσω.
31 For Μίκα cf. Aristoph. *Th.* 760 ταλαντάτη Μίκα, with μικκός (Doric and Boeotic) and Μίκκος, Aristoph. *Ach.* 909, Plat. *Ly.* 204a, Call. *Ep.* 48.1 Pfeiff., Posid. 94.3 f. A.-B., Philod. *A.P.* 5.121.1.
32 Schadewaldt 1950: 149.

exactly offered again[33] has been declared unsatisfactory by both editors, given that two supplements to lines 3 and 4 that are too short correspond to a supplement to line 5 that is too long.[34]

In truth it is possible to overcome these contradictions in the textual structure of the fragment if we modify the reconstruction of line 4 and if for the supplementation of line 3 we take into account the fact that, in the practice of this as of other scribes of the second/third centuries AD, the signs of punctuation (in this case the apostrophe) are often accompanied by a consistent spacing.[35]

We can thus advance the following reconstruction of F 71:[36]

$$
\begin{aligned}
&\text{x - ⏑ ⏑ - - - ⏑ - οὐδὲ θέ]μις σε, Μίκα,}\\
&\text{x - ⏑ ⏑ - - - ⏑ γ]έλα[ν, ἀλ]λά σ' ἔγωὐκ ἐάσω}\\
&\text{x - ⏑ ⏑ - -]. φιλότ[ατ'] ἤλεο Πενθιλήαν}\\
&\text{x - ⏑ ⏑ - - - ⏑ -] δάκυ[ε, πολύ]τροπ', ἄμμα[}\\
&\text{x - ⏑ ⏑ - - ⏑] μέλ[ος] τι γλύκερον ..[⏑ - -}\qquad 5\\
&\text{ἔγεντ.[⏑ ⏑ - - ⏑ ⏑]ᾱ μελλιχόφων[ον] ὤραν·}\\
&\text{οὐ γάρ κ[⏑ ⏑ - - ⏑ ⏑ -]δει, λίγυραι δ' ἄη[ται.}
\end{aligned}
$$

1 suppl. Treu. 2 γ]έλα[ν supplevi ἀλ]λά Hunt   3 suppl. Hunt   4 δάκυ[ε, πολύ]τροπ' supplevi]τροπε· pap.: corr. Hunt ἄμμα[ν Hunt, at fort. ἄμμα[ις | φρένας   5 μέλ[ος] Hunt   6 e.g. ἔγεντο [φέροισ' ἀσυχί]ᾱ μελλιχόφων[ον] Puglia   7 κ[άλαμος vel κ[ίθαρις Puglia fort. ταῦτα μελίσ]δει   ἄη[ται Lobel (ἄη[δοι Hunt)

[... and it is not] permitted, O Mika,
that you laugh [at us ...], but I will not allow you
[...] you have chosen the Penthilids' friendship,
[... and this ...] has bitten, you fickle one,[37] our

---

33   The only difference is the insertion of the supplement ἀλ]λά at line 2.

34   Hunt 1922: 43 already admitted for line 4: "κα[κό]τροπ' seems probable, though the letters ακο must have been rather spread out to fill the lacuna."

35   Also in our fragment: σ' at line 2, -πε· at line 4, δ' at line 7.

36   This takes into account the combination, as Puglia 2007: 28–31 has worked out, of P.Oxy. 1787 fr. 3 = F 61–63, fr. 6 = F 71 and fr. P.Oxy. 2166 (d)4 = F 87 (14) LP, from which can be deduced, among other things, that the composition addressed to Mika ended at line 7.

37   For πολύ]τροπ' in the sense of fickleness of character cf. [Phocyl.] 95 λαῶι μὴ πίστευε, πολύτροπός ἐστιν ὅμιλος, and the same sense occurs already at Theogn. 218 κρέσσων τοι σοφίη γίνεται ἀτροπίης.

[hearts...] some sweet melody [...]
has come [the calm of the sea bringing] the season of sweet songs,
since [these notes] not [the aulos modulates], but the melodious
    breezes.

With this reconstruction there also appears (l. 4) the image of the "bite" in-flicted on the heart or spirit that we have seen at F 96.16–17, for the anguish of her distant friend at the thought of Atthis, although here it expresses the pain caused to the whole of Sappho's circle. At lines 1–2 arises the well-known motif of enemies' laughter.[38]

Nothing could be more bitter and painful, says Sappho as mouthpiece for the whole group, than the possibility that Mika joined to the damage of her deser-tion the mockery of derision, showing disdain toward the community she has abandoned.

The "I" seeks to neutralize these bitter thoughts by proposing to the group—but in first place to Mika herself—that it listen to those sounds that oncoming nature modulates in the air. Though the text is in truth somewhat lacunose, the song seems to culminate in a comparison between the absence of notes produced by musical instruments and the presence of breezes enlivening the spring landscape with their sounds. Thus we have here a renewal of nature and of the voices that this spontaneously produces, which is complementary to overcoming the crisis that Mika's desertion has threatened to create.

---

38 Cf. Archil. fr. 172.3–4. W.² νῦν δὲ δὴ πολὺς | ἀστοῖσι φαίνεαι γέλως, Theogn. 59 ἀλλήλους δ᾽ ἀπατῶσιν ἐπ᾽ ἀλλήλοισι γελῶντες and 1041–42 παρὰ κλαίοντι γελῶντες | πίνωμεν, κείνου κήδεσι τερπόμενοι, A. *Ch.* 222, Soph. *Aj.* 79 and 961–62, *Ant.* 483, 647, and 838, Eur. *Cyc.* 687, *Med.* 285–86, 383, and 797.

V The Rendering of Accounts

§1 A Collage

Sappho's tension regarding Andromeda seems to come to a rendering of ac-
counts (certainly not final) in the context of a poem in which Aphrodite
herself comes to declare that Andromeda must be punished, and Sappho re-
warded, for their respective behavior and style of life.

Scattered fragments of this poem, which we shall call *Against Andromeda*,
have been known for decades, but only recently have they been joined together
to form a continuous sequence, using, in this case, as in that of the poem I dis-
cuss in II, § 3, scraps from P.Oxy. 1787:[1]

$$].\,\breve{\alpha}κάλα.[$$

_x - ˘ - - - Δίος ἐξ] αἰ γιόχω λά[χοισα	2
x - ˘ - - -] . Κυθέρη᾽, εὐχομ[˘ - ˘ - -	
_x - ˘ - - - - ˘ ˘ - πρόφρ]ον᾽ ἔχοισα θῦμο[ν	4
x - ˘ - κλ]ῦθί μ᾽ ἄρας αἴ π[οτα κάτέρωτα	
_x - ˘ ˘ - - - ˘ -]ας προλίποισα Κ[ύπρον	6
x - ˘ - - - ˘ ˘ ἦλθε]ς πεδ᾽ ἔμαν ἰώ[αν	
_x - ˘ ˘ - - - ˘ -].ν χαλέπαι μ[ερίμναι	8

desunt versus tres

---

1 In comparison with the reconstruction given in Ferrari 2005b, the text as given here takes
into account two contributions of Puglia: a) the combination of F 60 (= P.Halle 3) with fr. 3,
hence the necessity of postulating a five-line lacuna between F 86 and F 60 and of considering F
86.1, not F 86.2, as the initial line of the poem; b) the location of F 67 at the left and on line with
F 60.1. On this see Puglia 2007: 22–28.

```
 _                              ].ν
                                ]ạ
_θέ]ων μακ̣[άρων - ⌣ ⌣ - - - ⌣ -]τύχοισα                          14
  κ]αὶ τοῦτ᾽ ἐπίκει [ρ() - ⌣ - - - ⌣ ] θέλ᾽ ὦν τ᾽ ἀπαίσαν
_δ]αίμων ὀλόφ[ωι() - ⌣ - - - τέ]λ̣εσον νόημμα·                     16
  σὺ μὰν ἐφίλης [- ⌣ - - - ⌣ ]έτων κάλημ<μ>ι,
_νῦν δ᾽ ἔννεκα [- - ⌣ - - μοι] πεδὰ θῦμον αἶψα᾽.                   18
  ᾽τόδ᾽ αἴτιον οὔ τ᾽ [αἶσχρον᾽, ἔφα, ᾽κῶ]σσα τύχην θελήσηις
_οὐδὲν πόλυ̣ ..[                       γὰ]ρ ἔμοι μάχεσθαι          20
  ο]ὑδ᾽ Ἀ̣[νδ]ρομέ[δα - ⌣ ⌣ - - χ]λιδάναι πίθεισα
_x οὐ] λ̣ελάθ̣[ην ἀθανάτοις ἔστ]ι, σὺ δ᾽, εὖ γὰρ οἶσθα            22
  κρότην Νέμε[σιν κῆνον ὃς αἶσχρ᾽ οἶδε κρ]έτει τ᾽ ἀ[ο]λλέω̣ν̣ ...
_Ψάπφοι, σὲ φίλ[εισ᾽ ἀμφ᾽ ὀχέεσσ᾽ ἥρμοσε κύ]κλα σ[οί τε          24
  Κύπρω β[α]σίλ[η᾽ ἦλθ᾽ ἰκετεύοισα Δί᾽ αἶψα σέ]μνα,
_καί τοι μέγα δῶ̣[ρον Κρονίδαις  ϝο]ῖ̣ κατ̣έ̣ν̣[ευσ᾽ ὀπάσδην,     26
  ὄ]σσοις φαέθων̣ [᾽Αέλιος φέγγεσιν ἀμφιβ]ά̣σ̣κ[ει
_πάνται κλέος [- - ⌣ ⌣ - - ⌣ - ⌣ - -                              28
  καί σ᾽ ἐνν Ἀχέρ[οντος  ⌣ ⌣ - - ⌣ - ⌣ - -
_..[......]ν̣π̣[                                                   30
```

F 86 cum F 60 coniunxit E. Fraenkel, F 65 cum F 66c Lobel, Snell, West; F 65 cum F 60 coniunxi; F 67 et F 60 subiunxit Puglia

2 suppl. West 3 e.g. εὐχομ[έναι μ᾽ἄρηξον 4 suppl. Fraenkel 5 κλ]ῦθι Fraenkel π[οτα Lobel κὰτέρωτα Fraenkel 6 suppl. Fraenkel 7 ἦλθε]ς supplevi ἰώ[αν Gallavotti 8 μ[ερίμναι Fraenkel 14 suppl. Diehl 15 ἐπίκει[ρ(ε) Puglia fin.]θέλ᾽ὠντἄπάισᾶν pap. 16 ὀλόφ[ωι(α) supplevi τέ]λ̣εσον Hunt 17 init. σ̣υ legit Puglia (οὐ edd.) κάλημ<μ>ι Diehl 18 supplevi 19 οὔτ(οι) vel οὔ τ(οι) [αἶσχρον᾽, ἔφα, ᾽κῶ]σσα Puglia (ὄ]σσα iam Hunt) 20 πά[σασθ᾽? γὰ]ρ Snell; πὰ]ρ Puglia 21 ο]ὑδ᾽ Diehl Ἀ[νδ]ρομέ[δα Hunt χ]λιδάναι ed. pr. 22 supplevi (]λελάθ[iam Treu) 23 κρότην D'Alessio cetera supplevi 24 supplevi 25 κύπρωι pap.: corr. Lobel β[α]σίλ[η᾽ Snell σέ]μνα Snell, West cetera supplevi 26 καί τοι Fränkel: καίτοι Lobel-Page, Voigt δῶ̣[ρον Fränkel cetera supplevi 27 [᾽Αέλιος Fränkel φέγγεσιν ἀμφιβ]ά̣σ̣κ[ει West 29 Ἀχέρ[οντος Diehl

[You who from Zeus] armed with the aegis had as your lot
[...] the beautiful [...]   2
... Cytherea, [come to my aid] since I pray to you

... with [kind] heart   4
... hear my prayer if [ever at another time]
... upon leaving [Cyprus,]   6
... [you came] at my cry:
[...] with heavy [care]   8
                    (*lacuna of 3 verses*)

...

...

of the blessed gods [...] having obtained   14
and be willing to take away also this [misfortune ...] then, you
    who of all
[are] the goddess [who has thoughts the most] astute, fulfill
    my wish.   16
You surely were accustomed [to satisfy me in everything] for
    which I invoked you,
and now for this [purpose come to aid] straightway as my
    heart desires.   18
"This reason, [you said,] is surely not [shameful, and] what
    you wish to obtain
is truly not excessive [to have ... in truth cannot] contend
    with me   20
even Andromeda, [but what she has done] trusting in a
    luxurious
[lifestyle cannot] have escaped [the immortals], and you,
    since you know well   22
that Nemesis strikes [him who knows shameful things]
    and prevails over all ...
Sappho, since in love for you [she fastened] the wheels to
    her chariot [and for you   24
the venerated queen left Cyprus [and went straightway to
    supplicate Zeus,]
and [the son of Cronus] agreed [to allow] you a great gift: 26
and all whom [the Sun] shining surrounds [with his rays]
everywhere [may they be reached by your] fame [...]   28
and that you on the [banks] of Acheron ...
...   30

§2   Aphrodite's Journey

At the beginning Sappho turns to Aphrodite, as she recalls the power that the goddess received from her father Zeus, with a turn of phrase that may cause us to recall the start of Pindar's fourteenth *Olympian*:

Καφισίων ὑδάτων
λαχοῖσαι αἴτε ναίετε καλλίπωλον ἕδραν,
ὦ λιπαρᾶς ἀοίδιμοι βασίλειαι
Χάριτες Ἐρχομενοῦ, παλαιγόνων Μινυᾶν ἐπίσκοποι,
κλῦτ᾽, ἐπεὶ εὔχομαι.

You who received the waters of Kephisus as gift
And inhabit a land of lovely fillies
Graces friends of song, queens of rich Orchomenos,
Protectresses of ancient Minyan line,
Hear me, since I call upon you!

Just as Pindar says λαχοῖσαι to begin praise of the Graces and then concludes his apostrophe with κλῦτ᾽, so Sappho says λά[χοισα to recall Aphrodite's prerogatives and then asks that the goddess receive Sappho's own supplication, whose content she does not initially reveal, with favorable spirit. Then she repeats, following a model typical of prayer (αἴ π[οτα κἀτέρωτα),[2] the recollection of previous favors she has received from the goddess, and this evoking of particular aid received in the past takes up a considerable part of the song (in this case the rest that we have of it).

So, if Sappho initially addresses Aphrodite as "Cytherean," in that she was born on the island of Cythera, in this long analepsis she refers to her rather as "queen of Cyprus":[3] indeed at Cyprus, specifically at the city of Paphos, Aphrodite had her most famous and ancient temple, already mentioned at *Od.* 8.362–63.[4]

---

2 Cf. F 1.5, Alc. F 38 A.11 and 208A.3, Soph. *OT* 164, Aristoph. *Th.* 1157 ff.
3 Cf. F 90a col. II 5 and F 140.1.
4 Cf. also Hom. *H.Ven.* 58–59, Eur. *Ba.* 402–6, Hdt. 1.105.3, Paus. 1.14.7, Tac. *Hist.* 2.3.

Cypris[5] has then left her island (just as the Tyndarids are asked to leave the Peloponnese at the beginning of one of Alcaeus' poems: F 34.1 νᾶ]σον Πέλοπος λίποντε[ς) to respond to Sappho's cry for help. The content of the poet's plea in her heavy suffering is in a passage not without lacunae; then in a more reconstructable section (ll. 19 ff.) comes the response of the goddess, who in the past has accepted without condition each plea of her protégée.

After this preamble, which emphasizes the contact of mortal and immortal by confirming the link that binds them, now as before arises the question of Andromeda, whose ongoing arrogant conduct comes down to ostentation based on wealth. But Andromeda, says the goddess, will not be able to avoid the gods' recognition of what she has done. We are ignorant of the nature of the transgression itself because of the lacunae of the previous and following sections, but we can imagine what it is like. The transgression must have been one of the usual requests, whether unconscious or deliberate, to desert Sappho's circle.

The certainty of divine sanction is based on faith in Nemesis, whose nature is to show outrage in the face of anything unjust or improper (Hom. Od. 22.39–40).[6] And the indignation of the divine world that Andromeda arouses is connected with the arrogance of this woman who claims to predominate over all. The discourse thus generally runs on the lines of that ethic, which dominated the archaic period but also appears in writers like Herodotus, in which it is the business of the gods to punish mortals for their sins or, more simply, in view of the general equilibrium.[7]

The new sentence that comes after this didactic insertion begins at line 22 with σὺ δ' but remains unfinished. What we have here is the sort of swerve typical of assumed colloquial/intimate discourse, which is a move from first (cf. ἔμοι 20) to third person used by the goddess from line 24 on, as also in the Homeric Hymn to Aphrodite (lines 286–87), and probably at Sapph. F 133.2 (and as e.g. the Dioscuri do when they first appear at lines 1238 ff. of Euripides' Electra).

This transition from first to third person has the obvious function of conferring authority on the discourse of the goddess: Aphrodite tells her protégée that

---

5 Aphrodite is called Κύπρις at F 2.13, 5.18, 15.9, Κυπρογένηα at F 22.16 and 134 and at Alc. F 296b.1.

6 Cf. also Hes. Th. 223–24 and Op. 200, Thgn. 280, Pind. P. 10.43–44, A. fr 266.4–5 R., Soph. Ph. 517–18, Eur. Ph. 182–84 and fr. 1113a K., Hdt. 1.34.1, [Orph.] Hymn. 61.2–9.

7 Cf. Hom. Il. 20.242–43, 15.490–92, Hes. Op. 5–7, Thgn. 661 ff., Sol. fr. 13.67–70 W.², Eur. fr. 420.1–3 K., Hdt. 7.10 ε, Xen. An. 3.2.10, Hor. Carm. 1.34.12 ff.

she has flown in her winged chariot to her father Zeus to request for her the "great gift" of universal fame and a privileged state after death. And Aphrodite's father Zeus has granted her request.

Aphrodite's flight and her preparation of the chariot recall of course the great ode to Aphrodite of Sappho Book 1. Here too the goddess goes to Sappho on leaving her father's house, but the difference is that this time the gods' mountain represents only an intermediate stage during a journey that starts from the Cyprian temple at Paphos.

Furthermore, if Aphrodite flies from Cyprus to Lesbos passing by Mt. Olympus, it is difficult not to see as the hypotext of lines 25–26 Thetis' intervention in favor of her son Achilles in *Iliad* I, a passage that Alcaeus also recalls.[8] There the sea goddess supplicates Zeus at lines 514–15 with νημερτὲς μὲν δή μοι ὑπόσχεο καὶ κατάνευσον | ἢ ἀπόειπ᾽ and the supreme god responds to her at line 524 with εἰ δ᾽ ἄγε τοι κεφαλῆι κατανεύσομαι (cf. line 528 νεῦσε Κρονίων).

§3   The Great Gift

Even if we often find, in Sappho and elsewhere, the concept of "gift" or "gifts" of the Muses or Graces,[9] the "great gift" that Zeus grants on Aphrodite's intercession is something else and has a double valence. It is at the same time *kleos* destined to reach all men who look upon the rays of the sun, and a particular personal fate once one has reached the banks of Acheron.

The motif of *kleos* spreading over space appears in Homer (*Il.* 7.451 τοῦ δ᾽ ἤτοι κλέος ἔσται ὅσον τ᾽ ἐπικίδναται ἠώς) with reference both to the wall the Achaeans construct for their camp and to the quarrel between Achilles and Odysseus at *Od.* 8.74–75 (οἴμης, τῆς τότ᾽ ἄρα κλέος οὐρανὸν εὐρὺν ἵκανε). Laertes' son utters the same expression when he reveals his own name for the first time to King Alcinoos (9.20): καί μευ κλέος οὐρανὸν ἵκει.

Yet it is in an elegy, possibly authentic, of Theognis addressed to Cyrnus that, at least as far as our evidence goes, we find for the first time the motif of fame, intimately linked to a privileged destiny guaranteed by the power of poetry (lines 235–41):

---

8   F 44.7–8 ἁ δὲ γόνων [ἀψαμένα Δίος] | ἱκέτευ[.

9   Cf. F 32, F44 A b.5, F 58.11, Hes. *Th.* 103, Alcm. fr. 59(b).1–2 *PMGF*, Archil. fr. 1.2 W.², Anacr. eleg. fr. 2.3–4 W.² = 56.3–4 Gent., Thgn. 250, Sol. fr. 13.51 W.², B. 19.3–4, Plat. *Lg.* 796e.

Σοὶ μὲν ἐγὼ πτέρ᾽ ἔδωκα, σὺν οἶσ᾽ ἐπ᾽ ἀπείρονα πόντον   235
   πωτήσηι, κατὰ γῆν πᾶσαν ἀειρόμενος
ῥηϊδίως· θοίνηις δὲ καὶ εἰλαπίνηισι παρέσσηι
   ἐν πάσαις πολλῶν κείμενος ἐν στόμασιν,
καί σε σὺν αὐλίσκοισι λιγυφθόγγοις νέοι ἄνδρες
   εὐκόσμως ἐρατοὶ καλά τε καὶ λιγέα   240
ἄισονται.

I have given you wings to fly over the infinite sea   235
   and easily to raise yourself over all the land,
and you will be present at all the festivals and at all
   the banquets placing yourself on the lips of many,
and at the sound of clear-voiced small flutes lovely young men
   will sing of you with beautiful, melodious songs.   240

Theognis is evidently thinking of symposiastic gatherings in which nonprofes-
sional singers (in this case attractive youths like Cyrnus) entertain themselves
by singing to the sound of an aulos around a krater brimful of wine while the
goblets are carried around in a circle among the guests. Cyrnus will be in their
mouths because they will not limit themselves to improvising new songs but
will again perform Theognidean elegies.

   The text does not, however, refer to a possible diffusion of a written collection
of elegies attributed to Theognis as the instrument that will be able to guarantee
Cyrnus' fame. The reference instead is rather to an oral process of transmission
from mouth to mouth and symposium to symposium.

   On the other hand it is with Theognis, Sappho's contemporary, that we have
the most ancient attestation of a poetry collection entrusted to writing. In the
famous "seal elegy" (lines 19–26) the Megarean poet says that he wants to affix
a σφρηγίς to his own verses so that they will be neither "stolen" nor changed.
These words seem in fact to presuppose a model of communication already
preoccupied with aspects (authorship, textual fidelity, preservation over time)
that are to become exactly those of a written culture. This is such a surprising,
or at the very least bizarre, dimension for the early archaic period[10] that some
scholars have tried to get around it by identifying the "seal" as metaphor rather

---

10 Furthermore in the context of an almost exclusively aural circulation of poetry, the presence of the author's name in an isolated fragment could only with great difficulty guarantee to
the poet that the work would not be altered.

than concrete object, whether as the dedicatee's name (the initial "Cyrnus") or that of the poet (the declaration at lines 22–23: "but so everyone will say: 'They are verses of Theognis of Megara' ") or the art itself (σοφίη) of the poet.

Yet, as G. Cerri has observed,[11] even for the archaic period we are not lacking indications that testify to a practice of depositing a certain text near a sanctuary as a form of homage to a god and at the same time as a way of preserving the original form of the text itself. The *Certamen* tells us that, when Homer had recited the *Hymn to Apollo* at the Delian festival, the island's inhabitants transcribed the hymn on a tablet (λεύκωμα) and deposited it in the temple of Artemis (§18, p. 350 West). Heraclitus, according to D.L. 9.6, dedicated his own book in the temple of Artemis at Ephesus; the Boeotians who lived around Mt. Helicon preserved in the area sacred to the Muses a lead tablet on which the *Erga* of Hesiod had been transcribed (Paus. 9.31.4–5). According to the local historian Gorgon (*FGrHist* 515 fr. 18), a copy of Pindar's poem for the local boxer Diagoras (*O.* 7) in gold letters was deposited in the temple of Lindian Athena at Rhodes. Finally, even if chronologically later, we have the precise attestation of a dedication in a temple with the application of a seal by Crantor in D.L. 4.25: the academician had put a collection of poetry in writing and had placed it under seal in the temple of Athena at Soli.

But what might have been the form of the "book" Theognis deposited in a temple? Surely not an instrument for communication between author and public, but rather, as the "seal elegy" expresses, a document destined in the poet's intentions for the future memory of his name and occasional comparison to verify the ownership and genuine character of his elegies. The state in which the *Sylloge Theognidea* has come down to us shows that this objective has succeeded with regard to his name but that it has largely failed with regard to the authenticity of the passages preserved.

As a matter of fact the elegiac texts, old and new, will have continued to be created or recreated within the context of the symposium, working as *aides-mémoire* for the oral communication among the aristocracy of the archaic and late-archaic periods, while the venerated copy placed in the Megarean temple would have been gradually forgotten no less than that which Heraclitus placed in the temple of Artemis at Ephesus.

---

11 See Cerri 1991.

And Sappho? What kind of universal spreading of her fame could she have had in mind? The text does not give us an answer, whether due to the lacuna that begins a little later or because the poet was silent on this. Theoretically speaking, there are two possibilities: fame as teacher in an institution open to girls coming, as we have seen, even from distant regions, or fame, as in Theognis, bound to the quality and charm of her songs. But this is no true alternative: Sappho composed songs to be performed in the context of festivals in which her group participated, and so the fame of her "school" and the fame of her songs would have been two sides of the same coin.

Rather we might ask why Sappho showed herself interested, like an epic hero, in the diffusion of her own name and why Aphrodite besought Zeus for this fame on Sappho's behalf.

The answer must be related to the general process of "panhellenization" with which epic and lyric seem invested in the archaic age.[12] Just to limit ourselves to Lesbos, a nonprejudicial reading of the *Wedding of Hector and Andromache* shows that the Ionic epic of Homer (and likely also of other Ionian singers) had penetrated to the island refashioning its traditional poetic forms. On the other hand a good example of the exportation of the island's traditions is Terpander of Lesbos, who in the twenty-sixth Olympiad won the first citharodic contest at the Spartan Carneia (676–73 BC) and then four times consecutively at Delphi,[13] and who promoted the first Laconian poetic "school."

And the other aspect of the "great gift"? Unfortunately the extant text breaks off at the beginning of a discourse that, given the reference to the infernal river Acheron (image of the afterlife also at F 95.12–13), should have turned to the posthumous existence of the poet. What was in store for her after her death? Not, it would seem, fame, since fame has already been mentioned in the previous line in connection with its diffusion over space. The second element of the "great gift," in keeping with the custom of Zeus who, as Hesiod says, settled "some men, allotting them life and habits apart from the others . . . at the ends of the earth" (*Op.* 167–68), must rather have been a semi-divine existence[14] to be passed not on the Islands of the Blest or the Elysian Fields but in the king-

---

12   Ch. 3 of Nagy 1990, namely entitled "The Panhellenization of Song," is dedicated to this phenomenon.

13   Cf. [Plut.] *De mus.* 4.1132d–e.

14   Cf. Rösler 1980: 73 in relation to F 55.2–4: "eine gewissermassen eschatologische Konsequenz" through which "die Teilnahme an den Geschenken der Musen bedeutet auch ein anderes, besseres Los nach dem Tode."

dom of Hades itself. Here the tenth Muse could have continued to delight and take delight in poetry and music. This same perspective emerges already in the Homeric *Hymn to Demeter* (lines 481–82) and reappears in Pindar (*O.* 2.60 ff. and fr. 129 M.), Sophocles (fr. 278 R.), Aristophanes (*Ra.* 345 ff.), in some Orphic plates (I A 1–4 Pugliese Carratelli) and in Posidippus of Pella (43.1–4, 60.1–2 and 118.24–5 A.–B.), always however in the context of belief in mysteries of various origins and connotations.[15]

§4   Sappho and Alcaeus in the Afterlife of Horace

But there is a more specific witness. At *Odes* 2.13 Horace takes the occasion of an accident—the unexpected fall of a tree that almost killed him—to reflect on the precariousness of the human condition. After saying that he had almost seen Proserpina's dark realm, Horace describes a tableau at whose center appear the two Lesbian poets (lines 21–32):

> *Quam paene furvae regna Proserpinae*　　　　　　　　　21
> *et iudicantem vidimus Aeacum*
> *sedesque discretas piorum et*
> *Aeoliis fidibus querentem*
>
> *Sappho puellis de popularibus*　　　　　　　　　　　25
> *et te sonantem plenius aureo,*
> *Alcaee, plectro dura navis,*
> *durae fugae mala, dura belli.*
>
> *Utrumque sacro digna silentio*
> *mirantur umbrae dicere, sed magis*　　　　　　　　　30
> *pugnas et exactos tyrannos*
> *densum umeris bibit aure volgus.*

Di Benedetto[16] recognized the model, or at any rate a model, of the Horatian picture, and particularly of the ghosts stunned with awe at song worthy of religious silence, in the closure of the poem that in the new "Cologne Sappho" comes immediately before the section on old age (P.Köln VII, 429 fr. 1, col. I.3–8)

15　On eschatological expectations in Sappho see Gentili 1988: 78–80 and Hardie 2005: 29–32.
16　Di Benedetto 2005: 7–12.

]. νῦν θ̣α̣λ̣[ί]α γ.[
_x - ᴗ ᴗ - - - ᴗ ᴗ -]. ν̣έρθε δὲ γᾶς γε̣.[...].. 4
x - ᴗ ᴗ - -].ν̣ ἔχο̣ι̣σαν γέρας ὠ̣ς [ἔ]ο̣ικε̣ν̣
_x - ᴗ ᴗ θαυμά]ζ̣οιεν ὡς νῦν ἐπὶ γᾶν ἔοισαν 6
x - ᴗ ᴗ - -] λιγύραν, [α]ἴ̣ κεν ἔλοισα πᾶκτιν
_x - ᴗ ᴗ - - - ᴗ ᴗ].. ἢ̣ κ̣ὰτ̣ κ̣αλάμοις ἀείδω. 8

3 γέ̣[νοιτο vel γε̣[νέσθω Gronewald-Daniel, π̣α̣[ρέστω vel π̣ά̣ρεστι vel π̣ὰ̣[ρ ἄμμι West 4 γ̇έν̣[εσθ]α̣ι̣ Gronewald-Daniel, π̣ερ̣[ίσχ]ο̣ι̣ West, γεν̣[οίμ]α̣ν̣ Di Benedetto 5 κλέος μέγα Μοίσει]ο̣ν West, κῆ μοισοπόλων ἔσλ]ο̣ν Di Benedetto 6 init. πάνται δέ με West, ψῦχαι δέ με Di Benedetto, αὖθις δέ με Hardie; malim σκίαι κέ με θαυμά]ζ̣οιεν West 7 κάλεισι χελίδω] West, φαίνην δὸς ἀοίδαν] Di Benedetto, αἴνεισί μ᾽ ἄοιδον] Hardie; malim κάλεισι μ᾽ ἀήδων] 8 ἢ̣ κ̣ὰτ̣ scripsi κ̣αλάμοις Gronewald-Daniel ἢ τὰν ἰάχοισάν σε χε]λ̣ύ̣ν̣ν̣α̣ν̣ κ̣άλα, Μοῖσ᾽ Gronewald-Daniel, ἢ βάρβιτον ἢ τάνδε χε]λ̣ύ̣ν̣ν̣α̣ν̣ θ̣αλάμοισ᾽ West, ἔμαισι φίλαισι(ν) ....]....α. κ̣άλα, Μοῖσ᾽ Di Benedetto

[...] now [may we have] the festivity
[...] but that I may also be beneath the earth 4
[in future] as long as I have, as it should be, the gift [of the Muses,]
[and the shades[17]] admire [me], just like now that I am on the earth, 6
[they call me harmonious nightingale] whenever I take up the harp
[either ...] or I sing at the sound of the auloi. 8

The width of the lacunae and the problem of deciphering a number of letters impede a reliable reconstruction of the whole sequence. Yet if we rely on what we have and accept West's likely optative θαυμά]ζ̣οιεν at line 6, there emerges a discursive structure that we may synthesize, with Hardie,[18] in the following way:

A: may this festivity bring us cheer,
B: but may the honor of singing be my lot also below the earth,
C: and the souls of the dead may look upon me with admiration,
D: as now the living admire me when I sing taking up the harp or the cithara(?) or making myself accompany the music of the auloi.

---

17 For σκιά in relation to the souls of the dead cf. Hom. *Od.* 10.495, A. *Sep.* 976, Soph. *Aj.* 1257, Eur. *Hel* .1240

18 Hardie 2005: 23.

Horace's ode imagines Sappho (and Alcaeus) while they sing in the presence of an audience consisting of the souls of those who, for their *pietas*, have received a privileged seat in the afterlife (*sedesque discriptas piorum* of line 23). In the closure of Sappho's poem restored from the Cologne papyrus we find in addition the parallelism between the role Sappho plays, as poet, at present in the festival for which the poem has been composed and the role that she will continue to play among the souls of the dead.

It is precisely this symmetry that highlights the double valence of the "great gift" Zeus has allowed Sappho at Aphrodite's intercession: the universalization of her *kleos* in life and a privileged lot *post mortem* correlate and integrate with one another because the merits that will promote the poet to such a posthumous privilege are the same that legitimate her universal fame in the present.

§5   Elegance and Ostentation

We have already mentioned that, in the new poem we have reconstructed, the form of the prayer—with an invocation of the god and the recollection of aid previously rendered to the poet—is fundamentally the same as that of the *Ode to Aphrodite* of Book 1.

The situation is however very different: here Sappho's objective is not the return of a girl with whom she's in love, but rather getting the better of an arrogant and transgressive woman who presumably threatened the cohesion of Sappho's circle by trying to detach one or more pupils through the display of her own wealth and ostentation.

Both the *kleos* the poet will enjoy in life and the privileged lot reserved for her in the afterlife represent the inverse of Andromeda's punishment: the intervention of Nemesis to condemn her rival and the conferring of posthumous honor and glory on Sappho are complementary divine sanctions.

In fact fame among all men under the sun's rays seems to us to be the projection on a universal scale of a success gained in the struggle against Andromeda and Gorgo within the island's perimeter. It is a gift that is guaranteed from the gods and that, in the context of a religious belief system founded on an ideology of exchange, would make little sense unless it represented a response from Aphrodite to the tribute Sappho rendered her with the composition and performance of songs, the direction of choruses, the organization of religious festivities.

The poem's nucleus seems thus to be founded on themes of wealth, power, punishment and *kleos*, transferred from the context of male struggle for power between individuals and groups to female cliques whose associations must have stood on as precarious a basis.

"Aphrodite's works" essentially concern pleasure and desire, but this time the "Cyprian queen" does not disdain becoming entangled in human relations to protect one of her devotees to whom a special bond ties her.

"Since in love for you" (σὲ φίλ[εισ᾽): this is what Aphrodite says of herself to Sappho at line 24 just as Sappho declares that she loves refinement (ἀβροσύνα) at line 3 of a fragment (F 58.23–26 + F 59)[19] that, after the publication of P.Köln VII, 429, must be considered independent of the poem on age (F 58.11–22 V.) that immediately precedes it in P.Oxy. 1787 fr. 1:[20]

x - ◡ - - - ◡ ◡ - - ◡].μέναν νομίσδει
_x - ◡ ◡ - - ◡ ◡ - - Κρονίδ]αις ὀπάσδοι,
ἔγω δὲ φίληµµ᾽ ἀβροσύναν, [ὔµµι δὲ] τοῦτο καί µοι
_τὸ λάµπρον ἔρως ἀελίω καὶ τὸ κάλον λέλογχε.   4
ἐπιν[
_φίλει.[
καιν[

1]ι Hunt,]ι sive]υ Luppe φθ]ιµέναν Hunt, κεκρ]ιµέναν West   2 ἄλλοισι τύχην ὄσσα θέλωσι Κρονίδ]αις Di Benedetto   3 [ὔµµι δὲ] supplevi   4 ἔρως ἀελίω anon. (1806), Voigt: εροσα ελιω Athen. 15, 687b (cod. A); ἔρος τώελίω Sitzler   5 επῑν[pap.: ἐπίν[ετε γὰρ? 6 φίλειτ[ε?

[Whatever each] considers [the thing of highest value]
[... the son of Cronus to him may] allow,
but I love refinement, [and to you] and to me the love
for the sun has allotted [this] splendor and [this] beauty.[21]

19   Given the distance of the upper line, the horizontal trace beneath fr. 2, l. 1 (= F 58.26) must be a paragraphos, not the remains of a coronis (I owe this important observation to John Lundon). This means that there was no break, that is, between one composition and another, between F 58 and F 59, as Lobel-Page and Voigt maintain.

20   See Di Benedetto 2004, Luppe 2004, West 2005: 3–4, Bernsdorff 2005.

21   For a correct interpretation of the phrase in line with the paraphrase of Clearch. fr. 41 Wehrli (from Athen. 687b) ἡ τοῦ ζῆν ἐπιθυµία τὸ λαµπρὸν καὶ τὸ καλὸν εἶχεν αὐτῆι see Perrotta 1935: 36, Di Benedetto 1985 and 2006: 7–8, Kurke 1992: 93, Burzacchini 1995: 94. But already Aristophanes, as Cavallini 1985: 76 observes, must have understood this in the same way if at *Pl.*

[In fact] you have drunk(?)[22] ...
love ...
and ...

From an analogous point of view Pindar will declare, at the very beginning of *Isthmian* 5, that only thanks to Theia, mother of the sun and origin of light, are men able to appreciate the value of all other good:

Μᾶτερ Ἀελίου πολυώνυμε Θεία,
σέο ἕκατι καὶ μεγασθενῆ νόμισαν
χρυσὸν ἄνθρωποι περιώσιον ἄλλων·
καὶ γὰρ ἐριζόμεναι
νᾶες ἐν πόντῳ καὶ <ὑφ᾿> ἅρμασιν ἵπποι   5
διὰ τεάν, ὤνασσα, τιμὰν ὠκυδινά-
    τοις ἐν ἁμίλλαισι θαυμασταὶ πέλονται.

Mother of the Sun, Theia of many names,
thanks to you men value even
gold as more powerful than anything:
so also the ships
that vie in the sea and horses with their chariots,   5
for your honor, queen, are worthy of admiration
    in the whirlwind of their movements.

The two *iuncturae* φίλημμ᾿ ἀβροσύναν and ἔρως ἀελίω show a clear parallelism: they are two manifestations of the same basic trend.

Moreover the adjective ἅβρος / ἁβρός and its related forms (both adverbial and substantival), represent a key feature of Sappho's lexicon.[23] From time to time they appear in the poetry of the archaic and classical period in relation to the most varied referents: the gesture of mixing water and wine (Sapph. F 2.14), a young woman (Andromache) on her wedding-day (Sapph. F 44.7, cf. Hes. fr. 339.3 M.-W.), and a dying young god (Adonis, Sapph. F 140.1), the way a tune

---

144–45 he ironically repeats Sappho's pair without mentioning the sun: καὶ νὴ Δί᾿ εἴ τι γ᾿ ἔστι λαμπρὸν καὶ καλὸν | ἢ χαρίεν ἀνθρώποισι, διὰ σὲ γίγνεται.

22 A reference, one might think, to the nectar of poetry (see XII, § 2).

23 See Kurke 1992, Broger 1996: 59–91, Snyder 1997: 87–91.

has been composed (Stesich. fr. 212.2 *PMGF*), a musical instrument with strings (the pektis in Anacr. fr. 373–74 *PMG*), woolen clothing (F 100), a myrtle branch (Pind. *I.* 8.65–67), the gait (Eur. *Med.* 830 and 1164), the foot itself that walks (Eur. *Tr.* 506), and a young girl's cheek (Eur. *Ph.* 1486). What these referents have in common is the sensation of pleasure and grace associated with them.

As for the substantive ἀβροσύνα, it is significant that the only other attestation in the archaic period is in an elegy of Xenophanes, where the sage of Colophon refers precisely to the process of acculturation promoted by the Lydians among the cities of the Anatolian coast and the islands opposite to it: we already referred to this process when we spoke about the headdress Cleis demanded (I, § 2 and § 5).

Going over the experiences of his own *polis*, Xenophanes in fact affirms that the Colophonians, who once had rather severe customs, suddenly changed in their taste and fashion when they became bound by alliance to the Lydians. This is how he represents them going to the assembly (fr. 3 W.[2]):

> ἀβροσύνας δὲ μαθόντες ἀνωφελέας παρὰ Λυδῶν,
>   ὄφρα τυραννίης ἦσαν ἄνευ στυγερῆς,
> ἤιεσαν ἐς ἀγορὴν παναλουργέα φάρε᾽ ἔχοντες,
>   οὐ μείους ὥσπερ χείλιοι ὡς ἐπίπαν,
> αὐχαλέοι, χαίτηισιν †ἀγάλλομεν εὐπρεπέεσσιν,   5
>   ἀσκητοῖς ὀδμὴν χρίμασι δευόμενοι.

> ... and after having learned useless luxury from the Lydians,
>   until they were free of hateful tyranny[24]
> they went to the assembly with cloaks gaudy with purple,
>   not less than a thousand in all,
> proud [...] with shining combs,   5
>   wet with oils of fine aroma.

S. Mazzarino[25] writes,

> This is the description of the Colophonian aristocracy, proud in its refined luxury of which it makes a show in the agora; Xenophanes at-

---

24 The reference is to the Persian control of the city after the collapse of Lydian power around the middle of the sixth century BC.
25 Mazzarino 1989: 187.

tributes this ἁβροσύνη to Lydian influence, and knows that "hateful tyranny" put an end to this. Apparently then, at least for a long period, the Lydians had fostered the ἁβροσύνη of the Colophonian aristocracy; the Lydians evidently maintain good relations with the Colophonian aristocracy, which imported types of luxury from Lydia itself and with these could make a show of ἁβροσύνη. Only at a certain point the "hateful tyranny" appeared, which put an end to aristocratic luxury.

It is not by chance that Aeschylus in the parodos of the *Persians* will attribute to the Lydians who make up part of the army of the Great King the epithet ἁβροδίαιτοι.[26] Thucydides (1.6.3), in his turn, will say that because of their ἁβροδίαιτον the Athenian aristocrats only recently gave up wearing linen *chitons* and binding the knot of their hair with brooches in the form of golden cicadas.[27]

Xenophanes is explicit in his condemnation of the "useless luxury" of Lydian culture and so sets himself in an ideological direction that perceived a value in ancient simplicity and the origin of corruption in luxury.

In declaring that she loves *habrosyne* Sappho aligns herself on the opposite side, that of the pro-Lydian aristocracy, but with an important distinction: ἁβροσύνα is not luxury nor arrogant ostentation, nor is wealth *per se* even if wealth is an important prerequisite of refinement. In other words, Sappho gives a precise ideological connotation to *habrosyne*: it becomes a choice of lifestyle founded on art and elegance and nevertheless capable of making up, if necessary, the absence of a Lydian headdress with a purple ribbon or garlands of flowers.[28]

Synonymous only for those who do not know how to scratch the surface of things, Sappho's elegance and Andromeda's ostentation oppose one another in the context of a semantic area concerning social forms and aesthetic manifestations.

26 Lines 41–42: ἁβροδιαίτων δ᾽ ἕπεται Λυδῶν | ὄχλος.

27 Herodotus also uses ἁβρός in relation to the Lydians, cf. 1.55.2 Λυδὲ ποδαβρέ (in the context of a Pythian oracle) and 1.71.4 Πέρσηισι γάρ, πρὶν Λυδοὺς καταστρέφεσθαι, ἦν οὔτε ἁβρὸν οὔτε ἀγαθὸν οὐδέν. Allusions to the refined hairstyles of the ancient Athenian aristocracy appear also at Aristoph. *Eq.* 580 and *Nu.* 14–15.

28 With respect to other supplements proposed for the lacuna at line 3 (e.g., [ἴστε δέ] of Di Benedetto), mine [ὔμμι δέ] implies the involvement also of Sappho's group of pupils in the love of the sun. If we join τοῦτο τὸ λάμπρον ... καὶ τὸ κάλον, ὔμμι δέ introduces a deictic reference to the present performance.

The supreme image of *habrosyne*,[29] Aphrodite has the best reasons to comfort Sappho and to rush to her aid in her own air-borne chariot: protecting Sappho means reaffirming the most authentic value of Eros against the pretenses of arrogant wealth (as Sappho herself declares to Cleis at F 148.1: ὁ πλοῦτος ἄνευθ᾽ ἀρέτας οὐκ ἀσίνης πάροικος, "wealth without virtue is a dangerous neighbor"). In so doing Aphrodite will guarantee Sappho a *kleos* destined to reach all men, and a privileged existence in the afterlife is the just reward for an art that represents a perpetual *hommage* to the goddess's world.

---

29   If in Euripides' *Trojan Women* (ll. 989–90 τὰ μῶρα γὰρ πάντ᾽ ἐστὶν Ἀφροδίτη βροτοῖς, | καὶ τοὔνομ᾽ ὀρθῶς ἀφροσύνης ἄρχει θεᾶς) Hecuba underlines the phonic affinity between Ἀφροδίτη and ἀφροσύνη, it is not illegitimate to imagine that Sappho already perceived the echo of ἀβροσύνα in the name of the goddess.

VI Contrasts

§1 A Good Response

We do not know to what occasion F 133.1 refers:[1]

ἔχει μὲν Ἀνδρομέδα κάλαν ἀμοίβαν ...

Andromeda has a good response.

It seems likely that the word ἀμοίβαν means here "reply" or "response"[2] just as ἀμείβομαι, also in Sappho, means "to respond" (cf. F 94.6 τάδ᾽ ἀμειβόμαν).

After the denial of Andromeda's meek nature in F 70.6 + 75a.7 + 68a.7, the "we sing" of F 68b.2 and the reproach in the vocative at Mika, now gone over to the opposite faction with the invitation to hear the sweet sounds of the spring breezes (F 71), the occurrence of this ἀμοίβαν seems to be a further indication of the practice, in the context of some of the festivals on Lesbos, of organiz-

---

1 Hephaistion (14.7, p. 46 C.) wants to give an example of a metrical sequence having an iambic metron followed by an anaclastic Ionic dimeter (the so-called anacreontic: ⌣ ⌣ – ⌣ – ⌣ – –). He then cites our verse, making it immediately followed by another (F 133.2), namely Ψάπφοι, τί τὰν πολύολβον Ἀφροδίταν ... ; Lobel-Page place the two lines in immediate succession, whereas Voigt follows Blomfield's suggestion in interposing a lacuna of unspecified size between them. This is a good choice, since Hephaistion cites the second verse as an example of variation of time units within the iambic metron, six in the first verse, seven in the second (ἰαμβικὴ ἐξάσημος ἢ ἑπτάσημος). The metrician will then have cited F 133.2 by means of selecting the first line from within the poem to which it originally belonged (which was not necessarily the second of this poem), whose iambic metron consisted of seven time units.

2 While Treu 1954: 97 renders κάλαν ἀμοίβαν with "ihre rechte Antwort" (similarly Aloni 1997: 227: "la sua brava risposta"), Page 1955: 134 understands the line in the sense of an actual reaction ("Andromeda is properly paid out") imagining that "she in turn has lost a lover to Sappho, or one of her captives has done her injury."

ing amoebaic contests between single singers or choral groups. This must have been, we presume, the occasion and context of the greater part of Sappho's satiric poetry (or scoptic or "iambic" or whatever you may call it).

§2   The Munich Krater

But there are also two other witnesses that are closely interconnected. The first is the famous red-figure kalathos attributed to the Brygos painter, now at Munich (Krater 2416), which dates to 480/470 BC and shows the two poets of Lesbos one opposite the other, with a barbitos in hand (Fig. 3).

As Lissarrague well observes,[3]

> ...these two figures are not portraits but, like many others, images of musicians. The identification of the individuals who take this scene out of the ordinary is created by the inscriptions that appear next to Alcaeus' head and alongside Sappho's neck. A vertical inscription reads *damakalos*, "Damas is beautiful." Finally a string of five Os in front of Alcaeus' mouth indicates that he is singing. The use of writing here shows a great deal of variety, and even though the four inscriptions are equally melded into the image, they have three different ranks. The vertical inscription is outside the image and, we might say, parasitical on it; the two proper names next to the heads are captions, or rather labels that identify the two poets and are like their attributes. Finally, the string of vowels before the singer's mouth is the graphic equivalent of his song, the visual symbol of his melody.

The scene is generally interpreted as a poetic dialogue between the two Lesbian singers and has been related to the tradition of Alcaeus' presumed courtship of Sappho as it appears in the *Leontion* of Hermesianax. In this poem the Alexandrian poet, addressing the beloved who gives the name to his poetry collection, recalls (fr. 7.47–48 Powell) "how many symposiastic gatherings Alcaeus welcomed / singing his burning passion for Sappho on the lyre."[4]

The courtship does not seem unlike the one that appears a little further down in the same poem of Hermesianax concerning Anacreon and Sappho (F 7.50–

---

3 Lissarrague 1990: 126.
4 See Wilamowitz 1913: 41; Treu 1954: 230–31; Aloni 1997: 232–33.

56) and also in Chamaeleon's small treatise *On Sappho* (fr. 26 Wehrli = Sapph. T 250). Here Chamaeleon interpreted Anacreon's poem on the Lesbian girl of the many-colored sandal (fr. 358 *PMG*) as an address of Anacreon himself to Sappho and considered the anonymous lyric fragment 953 *PMG* as Sappho's reply to the Tean poet.

§3   "I would like to tell you something"

But in our case there is something more to it. Aristotle in the *Rhetoric* (1.9, p. 1367a7 ff.), speaking of those who are ashamed at saying, doing, or thinking shameful things, gives as an example—and this is the second of the *testimonia* quoted below—a fragment that can be laid out as an alcaic strophe in which Alcaeus apparently said (= Sapph. F 137.1–2):

θέλω τί τ' εἴπην, ἀλλά με κωλύει
αἴδως ...

I would like to tell you something, but shame
prevents me ...

And Sappho replied (ll. 3–6):

αἰ δ' ἦχες ἔσλων ἴμερον ἢ κάλων
καὶ μή τί τ' εἴπην γλῶσσ' ἐκύκα κάκον,
αἴδως κέ σ' οὐ κάτηχεν ὄππατ',   5
ἀλλ' ἔλεγες περὶ τὠδικαίως.

5 κέ σ' οὐ κάτηχεν Mehlhorn: κέν σε οὐκ εἶχεν codd.   6 τὠδικαίως Lobel: τὼ δικαίω fere codd.

But if you had desire of something good or beautiful
and your tongue were not stirring up something bad,
shame would not veil your eyes,
but you would speak of what you wanted.[5]

---

5 With some hesitation I accept Lobel's hypothesis that τὼ δικαίω is a corruption of τὠδικαίως (= τὼ ἐδικαίως).

The editorial vicissitudes of this fragment are instructive. Stephanus was the first to include it in an edition of lyric poets (1560), while a few years later F. Orsini proposed a bold *collage*: in a note (p. 313) of his *Carmina novem illustrium feminarum ... et lyricorum* (1568) he suggested making the first two lines of F 137 be immediately preceded by a verse cited in another *testimonium* (Heph. 14.4, p. 45 C.), namely Alc. F 384:[6]

ἰόπλοκ᾽ ἄγνα μελλιχόμειδε Σάπφοι.

Violet-haired Sappho, venerable, sweetly smiling.

In this way Orsini not only accepted the tradition of a relationship between Sappho and Alcaeus, but combined it with a verse whose author Hephaistion does not indicate but which is to be attributed to Alcaeus, since it is cited as an example of alcaic dodecasyllables.

Orsini's *collage* had a long if intermittent fortune and eventually gained the consensus of Paul Maas (1920), who however assigned the sequence represented by lines 3–6 of F 137 to an anonymous "story-teller" of the sixth century BC.

This deletion of lines 3–6 was ignored, without even a mention in the apparatus, by Lobel-Page, but has been taken up again by Voigt. However, Voigt has not accepted the verse added by Orsini and in the wake of Lobel-Page has articulated the whole series of lines according to the metrical pattern of the alcaic strophe. Voigt goes on to note in the apparatus: "res incerta, cum neque de stropha Alcaica apud Sappho constet neque metri ia ^hipp alterum exemplum inveniatur."

§4   Page's Hypotheses

Meanwhile Page had studied the whole question in detail, and in his opinion Aristotle's words could be theoretically interpreted along three possible lines:[7]

- The first part of the citation (lines 1–2: "I would like to tell you something, but shame | prevents me") is taken from an ode of Alcaeus in alcaic strophes, while the rest comes from Sappho's reply. A series of questions

6 In order to make the two verses two alcaic dodecasyllables Orsini, followed later by A. Schneider (1802), had to understand -ει αι- (in κωλύει αἴδως) as a monosyllable by synecphonesis.
7 Page 1955: 106–9.

then arises: were both poems offered, each by its author, to the same audience on different occasions? In that case should we suppose that Sappho composed her reply with the presumption that most of her audience had heard Alcaeus' ode addressed to her? Or was Alcaeus' poem a kind of private letter? In that case Sappho could have shown a copy of Alcaeus' text to her companions or alternatively could have repeated its substance within her own reply.

- The two fragments from Aristotle come from one and the same poem of Sappho. This poem was composed in the form of a dialogue between herself and Alcaeus in a way analogous to what Horace does in *Carm.* 3.9 (a love "quarrel and reconciliation song" between the poet and Lydia).

- Aristotle did not really know what he was talking about or expressed himself inaccurately. His citations could have been taken from a poem by Sappho (perhaps an *epithalamium*) composed in the form of a dialogue between a man and a woman, both unnamed. From the use of the alcaic strophe Aristotle drew the incorrect conclusion that Alcaeus was the man and Sappho the woman cast in the text.[8]

Page himself dismissed the third alternative, or at any rate set it aside as an *extrema ratio*: Aristotle's citation, and the words with which it is introduced,[9] admit a perfectly linear interpretation that exempts us from making any such supposition.

The second line of argument also is declared impracticable by Page whether because there are no other pertinent examples of the kind of dialogue one would have to attribute to Sappho among her extant poetry, or because we do not have definite cases of Sappho using the alcaic strophe.

The first case is the one that Page opted for (Page 1955: 107), without however being willing to be precise about its exact articulation; rather, he refuses to "pursue these shadows further." Yet one must say that the idea of Sappho and Alcaeus exchanging amorous messages (on little pieces of papyrus? wax tablets? ostraka?), or of a Sappho responding to an absent Alcaeus upon show-

---

8   See already Wilamowitz 1913: 41 n. 3 on this line of thought. It should be added that in the discussion of the Aristotle passage found in the so-called *Commentary of Stephanus* (p. 280.30 ff. Rabe), dating to the twelfth century, Sappho is named as the author of the whole dialogue, but doubts are expressed about the presence of Alcaeus as her interlocutor. Besides, the commentator suggests that the female figure may be an unknown girl.

9   His text reads: τὰ γὰρ αἰσχρὰ αἰσχύνονται καὶ λέγοντες καὶ ποιοῦντες καὶ μέλλοντες, ὥσπερ καὶ Σαπφὼ πεποίηκεν εἰπόντος τοῦ Ἀλκαίου.

ing her own pupils the message of the love-torn Alcaeus, unfolds unreal scenes worthy of *Sappho's Leap* (2003), Erica Jong's novel, where the author lingers over, among many other things, the love affair between the two singers of Lesbos.

This is not to say that a dialogue at some distance between poets in archaic Greek poetry is an impossibility, as shown by the case of Solon's well-known "correction" (fr. 20 W.²) of a word of Mimnermus (fr. 16 W.²), who had wished to die at 60. But here we are concerned with something completely different, namely Solon's poetic contribution in the context of a symposium where another guest had offered the lines of Mimnermus (likely in the context of a series of exchanges on the theme of old age). What sounds so improbable in Page's idea is the occurrence of a performance of the two poems "on different occasions." In the context of oral communication a dialogue only makes sense if it occurs in the course of one and the same occasion.

§5   A Compatible Scenario

A nonproblematic feature of the passage Aristotle cites is that it concerns a contrast in which the beginning lines for both figures A and B coincide with the beginning of a strophe.

This technique—by which each figure alternatively sings a strophe—has nothing in common with the dialogic exchange that we see for instance at the start of Sappho F 94. There the dialogic articulation does not follow the division of stanzas, and in any case the direct discourse is introduced, in the manner of Homeric dialogue, by expressions of the type "I replied to her thus," "I said" (cf. also F 95). The very same technique of F 137 can instead be found in an exchange between a girl on the eve of marriage and Virginity in F 114 or in the threnodic dialogue on the death of Adonis in F 140.

Furthermore, the way in which the lines of the two interlocutors—man and woman—alternate in F 137 recalls those agonistic pairs that we know so well from the *Sylloge Theognidea* and the *Carmina Convivalia* in the symposiastic collection transmitted in Athenaeus 15.694c (*Carm. Conv.* 900/901 *PMG*). Here the two distichs both begin with εἴθε ... γενοίμην: they form a pair in which one part hooks onto the other, following a particular kind of symposiastic practice based on a contrast or a different response to the same theme or point.[10]

A particular case within this pattern is represented by those exchanges in which two symposiasts each assume a mimetic mask, as in the contrasting duet/altercation of an elegiac couplet each between wife and husband in Thgn. 579–82:

- Ἐχθαίρω κακὸν ἄνδρα, καλυψαμένη δὲ πάρειμι,
    σμικρῆς ὄρνιθος κοῦφον ἔχουσα νόον.   580
- Ἐχθαίρω δὲ γυναῖκα περίδρομον ἄνδρα τε μάργον,
    ὃς τὴν ἀλλοτρίαν βούλετ᾽ ἄρουραν ἀροῦν.

- I hate a bad man (here I am covered with a veil),
    with a head as empty as a sparrow's.   580
- I hate a roving woman and a lecherous man,
    who wants to plow a furrow that is not his.

That Alcaeus and Sappho, taking on the roles of the young suitor and the marriageable girl respectively, could have done something similar within a symposiastic context is incompatible with everything we know about Sappho's poetry and the archaic symposium. The latter was accessible only to aristocratic males and, as far as women are concerned, only hetairai were allowed to be present as players of the harp or aulos. On the other hand, such a scenario is not incompatible with festive gatherings featuring musical performances of the most varied kind.

This also explains well why Sappho on this occasion has for once composed in alcaic strophes. This was not a meter habitual to her repertory, but rather was used because the "contrast" required the repetition not only of the theme but also of the metrical frame and the melody of the one (in this case Alcaeus) who sang first.

The Munich kalathos seems an apt confirmation of this hypothesis. Suffice it here to note that the one figure (Alcaeus) sings while accompanying himself on the barbitos while the other (Sappho) listens intently but already has the plectrum raised at mid-height in her right hand, like one who is in turn about to play the lyre that she holds with her left arm. Nor is it by chance that the two

10   On this see Reitzenstein 1893: 91–97; Vetta 1980: xxx; Ferrari 1989: 33–38.

figures appear dressed with a certain deliberate finery that adds to the festive occasion: both are wearing a closely embroidered chiton and a cloak with elegant folds. The Munich krater and Aristotle's citation (with lines 1–2 assigned to Alcaeus and 3–6 to Sappho) seem reciprocally to supplement and confirm one another.

However, no space remains in this picture for Alcaeus' assumed greeting to Sappho (Alc. F 384), which would represent an act of homage to the poet in her sacral role as priestess of Aphrodite.[11] The linguistic problems here of hypothesizing for metrical reasons the metaplastic form μελλιχόμειδε instead of μελλιχόμειδες and of giving the poet, contrary to her own usage (F 1.20, 65.5, 94.5, 133.2), the name Σάπφω and not Ψάπφω seem to me insurmountable.[12]

---

11 See Gentili 1988: 222.

12 Liberman 1999: II.169 n. 339 has revived a hypothesis by Pfeiffer, communicated orally to Maas (see Maas 1973: 4). Pfeiffer's suggestion was to correct Σάπφοι transmitted by Hephaistion into Ἄφροι, diminutive of Aphrodite. The sequence ΜΕΛΛΙΧΟΜΕΙΔΕΣΑΦΡΟΙ would thus have been wrongly divided as μελλιχόμειδε(ς) Σάπφοι, and Σάπφοι would have resulted from fixing Σάφροι. The epithets used seem to agree with an invocation of a divinity: ἰόπλοκος is referred by Bacchylides to Aphrodite (9.72), the Nereids (17.37), and the Muses (3.71); in Pindar it also refers to the Muses (*I.* 7.23). Sappho uses ἄγνος for a sanctuary (F 2.3), a wedding-song (F 44.26), and the Graces (F 53 and 103.5). Alcaeus too refers it to the Graces (F 386) and also to Athena (F 298.17). In μελλιχόμειδες the second element recalls Aphrodite φιλομμειδής of Hom. *Il.* 3.424, *Od.* 8.362, Hes. *Th.* 989, and fr. 176.1 M.-W. However, we cannot exclude a more economical solution from a palaeographical point of view if, with Lobel, we read μελλιχόμειδες ἄπφα ("dear"), or, with Voigt, μελλιχόμειδες ἄπφοι. In both cases we would then have an erotic apostrophe.

VII Gorgo

§1 Leather Phalloi?

Few details remain about Gorgo, whose name also recurs in two wretched little papyrus fragments.[1] Some individuals (male) are "quite sated with her" (F 144 μάλα δὴ κεκορημένοις | Γόργως), presumably with allusion to her sexual incontinence.[2]

At the head, like Andromeda, of a rival group (Maximus of Tyre attests this: Sapph. T 219), Gorgo was paid off by Sappho with the ironic line (F 155):

πόλλα μοι τὰν Πωλυανακτίδα παῖδα χαίρην

Many greetings to the daughter of the Polyanactid![3]

On the basis of a detailed cross-examination of the available evidence we have suggested the hypothesis that the daughter of the Polyanactid must be Gorgo (and not Andromeda). It remains now for us to identify who is this Polyanactid.

1 F 29c.9]ντε Γόργοι and 103Aa col. II 9 Γόργ[(beginning of poem).

2 For κορέννυμι in a sexual sense cf. Thgn. 1269, Anacr. fr. 366 *PMG*. The theme also appears in Semon. Amorg. fr. 7.54 W.[2] τὸν δ᾽ ἄνδρα τὸν παρεόντα ναυσίηι διδοῖ.

3 The fact that the manuscripts of Maximus of Tyre have -νάκτιδα is obviously not binding for the original text. Both Lobel-Page and Voigt, following Bergk, accept -νάκτιδα, but "the Polyanactid daughter" as a way of saying "the daughter of Polyanax" would be a very anomalous expression, and in fact G. Hermann conjectured -τίδαο, Maas -τιδαίαν. On the other hand, as in itself the form -τίδα of the genitive is completely correct (cf. Κρονίδα), at issue here is the daughter not of Polyanax, but of the Polyanactid. As for the metrical structure of the sequence πόλλα ... -τίδα, one might consider a scansion cr^gl|| (so also Voigt (p. 17) who assumes a period end after -τιδα). The alternative scansion cr ^hipp^da|| suggested by Voigt (p. 19) on the basis of -νάκτιδα does not have attested parallels.

Another papyrus (P.Oxy. 2291), unfortunately very difficult to read, may, with due caution, come to our assistance. P.Oxy. 2291 preserves the remains of three poems that Lobel attributed to Sappho in the *editio princeps* (1951) and then consequently edited with Page as Sapph. F 99.[4] Other scholars have attributed these fragments to Alcaeus (in Voigt's edition they appear as Alc. F 303A a-c).

The reference in line 5 of the first fragment (F 303Aa) to ὄλισβοι ("leather phalloi") has surprised many. *Olisboi* are occasionally mentioned in Old Comedy as means of solitary sexual pleasure (e.g., in Cratin. fr. 354 K.-A. and in Aristoph. *Lys.* 109–10);[5] they feature substantially also in Herondas' sixth mimiambus (but the word used here is βαυβών, cf. line 19).

According to Page "the beginning of col. i. 5 appears to prove that Sappho used in her poetry a word of quite unique coarseness, referring to practices about which silence is almost universally maintained."[6] More recently Aloni, charging Voigt's decision to assign the fragment to Alcaeus as "philological hypocrisy," has suggested that Sappho is accusing the "ladies of the rival clan of being given, not so much to homosexual practices, as to masturbation." In other words, "the attack would seem directed, even more than against the women, against the Polyanactid men, evidently unable to satisfy the needs of their women."[7]

But let us take a look at the incriminating passage in its context (that is, the first poem preserved by P.Oxy. 2291: Alc. F 303Aa = Sapph. F 99 col. I, 1–9 LP):

_.].γας πεδὰ βαῖο[v - x - ⌣].α
δ[.]οῖ Πωλυανακτ[ίδ]αις
_...αις Σαμία<ι>σιν ε.[.]...[.]
<ἐν> χόρδαισι διακρέκην
_ὀλισβοδόκοισ<ι> περκαθ....ενος   5
τεούτ[οι]σι φιλοφ[ρό]νως,
_π]ᾶκτις δ᾽ ἐλελίσδ[ε]ται προσανέως,
...]ωνος δὲ δι᾽ ὀ[στί]ων
.....] μυάλω δ᾽ ἐ[π]εί κ᾽ ἔνη τρ[έχε]ι.   9

---

4 Aloni 1997: lxvii, 166–69 and Liberman 1999: I.xcii-xciv also favor attribution to Sappho.
5 See Henderson 1975: 221–22.
6 Page 1955: 144 n. 1.
7 Aloni 1997: lxvii.

1 init. fort. ὄ]ργας   3 Σαμία<ι>σιν Voigt   4 <ἐν> supplevi   -σι διακρέκην vel -σ' ἴδια κρέκην
Lobel   5 fin. fort. περκαθ[θ]ώμενος   7 π]ᾱκτις legi et supplevi   8 init. εὔφ]ωνος West   δι'
ὀ[στί]ων Gallavotti   9 init. e.g. ἔρπει]   μυάλω Voigt   ἐ[π]εί κ' ἔνη τρ[έχε]ι legi et supplevi   marg. dext. χ

... a little later [...]

[...] the Polyanactid
... Samian... takes pleasure

striking on the chords
that receive *olisboi*, dining[8]   5

in a friendly manner with similar people,
and the harp vibrates gently,

and [the sound penetrates] through
the bones and, when it's within the marrow,[9] runs.[10]   9

There has been some discussion whether at line 2 Πωλυανακτίδαις stands
for a male or female accusative plural, and means then "Polyanactids" (m.)
or "Polyanactids" (f.), or a nominative masculine singular ("the Polyanactid").
Yet since the name is followed at the end of line 5 by what is almost certainly
a middle masculine singular participle in the nominative (hence the possible
sequence: "dining in a friendly manner with similar people"), the second solution seems unavoidable. The subject of the last part of this poem (we know line
9 to be the end) was a sympotic reunion where "the Polyanactid" was having

---

8   For περκαθ[θ]ώμενος (= περικαταθώμενος) cf. A. fr. 47a.818 R., Epichar. fr. 198 K.-A.
9   For δι' ὀ[στί]ων (Gallavotti) cf. Archil. fr. 193.3 W.[2] δι' ὀστέων. For ἐ[π]εί κ' ἔνη cf.
Sapph. F 88.15 ἄς κεν ἔνη μ[(for the retaining of ἔνη in the papyrus, corrected by Lobel to ἔνηι,
see Hamm 1958 § 249a) and Alc. F 249.8 ἐπεὶ δέ κ' ἐν πόντωι γένηται. For τρ[έχε]ι cf. Sapph. F
31.10 χρῶι πῦρ ὑπαδεδρόμηκεν.
10   For the end of line 9 Lobel-Page, followed by Voigt, transcribe]..ενητε[..].χ.. . Yet the χ
(after which only tiny ink spots can be glimpsed, not necessarily ascribable to traces of letters)
seems written in a rather smaller size and with a *ductus* similar but not identical to that of the
text. In my opinion this is a marginal χ (used to indicate something remarkable, see Turner 1968:
116–17), that we find, e.g., also in Sapph. F 85(*a*) (3) 6 LP (this papyrus scrap is omitted in Voigt's
edition) and F 62.11.

a good time with despicable people[11] and beginning to strike the chords of an instrument (the πᾶκτις of line 7). The effects of such a performance are defined sarcastically in the last three words with the hyperbolic sonority of the instrument, whose echo penetrates the bones and runs across the marrow.

In this context, uncertain in some details but sufficiently clear in its general outline (in particular there is no doubt that someone is playing on a lyre), it's not obvious what role the leather *phalloi* could have had.

West proposed the correct solution:[12] ολισβο- here has the meaning of "plectrum," since, given the form of the plectrum itself, it is possible to imagine a semantic development from "plectrum" to "artificial phallus."

§2   The Hetaireia of Pittacus

But who is the fragment's author? Lobel's main reason for attributing the fragment to Sappho is that three-line stanzas are attested for our poet (as for instance the second ode transmitted by P.Oxy. 2291) but not for Alcaeus. However, as Voigt recognized, Alc. F 130 is indeed a poem of five three-line stanzas: in Lobel-Page it is erroneously joined to the following poem (F 130b Voigt), but should rather be kept separate from it, as the latter poem is articulated in four-line stanzas.

The meter itself favors attribution to Alcaeus. While the Alexandrian edition of Sappho was characterized by a strict observation of metrical homogeneity, this was only true of the first books. In particular we have variations in the fifth book (see F 94, 96, 98, and 101), but these variations occur only in the context of three-line strophes. The immediate juxtaposition of a poem in distich stanzas with one of three-line stanzas is not documented for Sappho.[13]

A further argument that favors Alcaeus as composer of this fragment is that satirical iconography of a masculine figure is frequent in Alcaeus, but, as far as we know, altogether lacking in Sappho.

---

11   The use of τεούτ[οι]σι at the beginning of line 6 has a clearly censorious tone. Since, as Lobel already noted, the reading τεουτ[is decidedly preferable to τουτ[, the first verse of this distich is a glyconic rather than a telesillean, see West 1990: 1: "I assume the loss of a syllable before χόρδαισι, since the responding lines 6 and 8 seem to have been glyconics, and 2 δ[.]οῖ Πωλυανακτ[ιδ]α..[, though difficult to restore, is perhaps easier if δ[.]οῖ represents two syllables. The metrical scheme of the stanza is then gl|tl ia |||." For my integration ἐν at the beginning of line 4 cf. Pind. *P.* 2.69 τὸ Καστόρειον δ᾽ ἐν Αἰολίδεσσιν χορδαῖς θέλων | ἄθρησον and Adesp. *A.P.* 9.584.3 αἰόλον ἐν κιθάραι νόμον ἔκρεκον.

12   West 1990: 1–2.

13   Against a possible exception for book IV see II, § 3.

If we change the attribution of the fragments of P.Oxy. 2291 to Alcaeus, the strict correlation between the scene described in F 303Aa and the situation represented in Alc. F 70.3–5 cannot escape our notice:

ἀθύρει πεδέχων συμποσίω.[
βάρμος· φιλώνων πεδ᾽ ἀλεμ[άτων
εὐωχήμενος αὔτοισιν ἐπα[5

3 ἐπα[νδάνει Liberman, ἐπά[δεται Diehl

... taking part in the symposium the harp [...]
resounds: dining together with foolish
companions [...] to these [it pleases]   5

The subject of the phrase that sets off at line 4 is the lyre (βάρμος) personified as a symposiast,[14] while immediately after, Pittacus is sarcastically invited to devour the city (cf. F 129.23–24), now that he has married a Penthilid, as he used to do once with Myrsilus. There is a strong "parallelism" between the imagery of the banquet and the metaphor of "devouring the city."[15]

§3   Drinking in the Thracian Manner

Similarly in Alc. F 72.3–6 some people are represented in the act of filling cups with neat wine while they amuse themselves at the kottabos game.[16] We are then told that this wine boils day and night (contrary to the Greek custom of drinking only from sunset):[17]

---

14 See Liberman 1999: II.209–10, who refers to Hom. *Od.* 8.99 and *H.Merc.* 31 and 478–79. At the beginning of line 6 κῆνος δέ, referring to Pittacus (cf. F 72.7), marks out a new start in the discourse that makes it impossible also to trace the subject of the verb that stood at the end of line 5 back to Pittacus again, as Rösler 1980: 165 seeks to do.

15 Lentini 2002: 5.

16 Cf. F 322 and Athen. 665e–668f and see Friis Johansen 1986 and Lentini 2002: 12–13. The game consisted of flinging drops of wine so as to hit either the center of a saucer (πλάστιγξ) set on top of a pole (kottabos κατακτός) or goblets floating on water in a basin (kottabos ἐν λεκάνηι). The references to the wine "boiling" (at contact with the water) and to the notion of "over-turning" show that Alcaeus had the second form in mind.

17 At Alc. F 346 (echoed by Asclep. *A.P.* 12.50.5) beginning to drink a little before dark is already considered an exceptional event.

```
....].[
_ἐν[..].λα[.].....[
λάβρως δὲ συν στεί[.]..[..]ειαπ..
πίμπλεισιν ἀκράτω [....]π᾽ ἀμέραι [
καὶ νύκτι παφλάσδει λάταχθεν,
_ἔνθα νόμος θάμ᾽ ἐν.[.].[.].νην.                              6
κῆνος δὲ τούτων οὐκ ἐπελάθετο
ὤνηρ ἐπεὶ δὴ πρῶτον ὀνέτροπε,
παίσαις γὰρ ὀννώρινε νύκτας,
_τῷ δὲ πίθω πατάγεσκ᾽ ὁ πύθμην.                               10
σὺ δὴ τεαύτας ἐκγεγόνων ἔχης
τὰν δόξαν οἴαν ἄνδρες ἐλεύθεροι
ἔσλων ἔοντες ἐκ τοκήων....
```

4 [τὸ δ᾽ ἐ]π᾽ Page   5 λάταχθεν Lobel   6 fort. ἔνε[σ]τ᾽ Diehl [ὀρ]ίννην Wilamowitz

...

...

... and furiously with [...]
they fill [the cups] with neat wine [and both] day
and night [it] boils with resonant drops[18]
where it is often the custom to make [merry].   6

And that man did not forget these habits
from when he first changed his status (?):
since for whole nights he made merry,
and the bottom of the jar resounded.   10

And look, you the son of such a mother[19] enjoy
the fame that free men have, those
born of noble parents.

If, as it appears, σύ at the beginning of line 11 has Pittacus as its target, the κῆνος ... ὤνηρ of lines 8–9 who has not forgotten the ways of his country of

---

18   In favor of λάταχθεν of Lobel cf. Alc. F 322 λάταγες ποτέονται | κυλίχναν ἀπὺ Τήιαν.

19   We know nothing of Pittacus' mother except that according to *Suda* (Π 1659) she was from Lesbos. Her fault, according to Page 1955: 173, consisted in the fact that "by marriage with a foreign drunkard she had forfeited her claim to rank and respect."

origin must be Hyrras,[20] Pittacus' father. We know that this was his name from Alcaeus himself (F 129.14 and F 298.47) and other sources (Call. *Ep.* 1.2 Pf., Duris, *FGrHist* 76 fr. 75, Schol. Dion. Thrac. p. 368.15 Hilgard). He was of Thracian origin (which had not however prevented him, according to the same scholion to Dionysius Thrax, from becoming a member of the Mytilenean aristocracy[21]). All this is perfectly consistent with the fact that drinking neat wine was considered a Thracian custom (and Scythian too), as Plato mentions in a passage of the *Laws* (637d–e):

> Let us then go on speaking a bit more about drunkenness in general, for this practice is no small thing nor one for a lawgiver of little worth to discern. I don't refer to drinking or not drinking wine at all, but to drunkenness itself, whether to practice it as the Scythians practice it and the Persians, and further the Carthaginians and the Celts and Iberians and Thracians, all these being bellicose peoples, or as you do. For you, as you mention, totally abstain from it, while the Scythians and the Thracians drink unmixed wine, all, women and men, even pouring it over their clothes and believe they practice a good and fortunate habit.

We would then be dealing here with a stigmatization of the irregular symposiastic style and of a "barbaric" manner of drinking[22] by Pittacus' entourage. A confirmation in this direction is provided by a passage of Plutarch (*Quaest. Conv.* 8.6, p. 726b) that mentions how Alcaeus characterized Pittacus as ζοφοδορπίδαις because he enjoyed the company of low and despicable companions (ἀδόξοις τὰ πολλὰ καὶ φαύλοις ἡδόμενον συμπόταις).

§4   Hyrras

If then F 303 Aa represents another tessera of this mosaic, "the Polyanactid" must be precisely this Hyrras, Pittacus' Thracian father, and the more so as

---

20   See Wilamowitz 1914: 235–36, Page 1955: 173 n. 2, Liberman 1999: I.50.

21   P. 368.15 Hilgard: Ὕρρας δὲ Μυτιληναίων ἐγένετο βασιλεύς (VN: τύραννος Σ). For βασιλεύς in the sense of aristocrat or magistrate see Mazzarino 1943: 43 n. 2 and Page 1955: 170 n. 8.

22   A fragment of Anacreon (fr. 356 *PMG*), where drinking "in the Scythian manner" (σκυθικὴν πόσιν 9) is associated with uproar, disorderly shouting, and *hybris*, is emblematic of this opposition (see Pretagostini 1982). According to Hdt. 6.84.3 the Spartans thought that Cleomenes went mad after learning from the Scythians to drink pure wine.

the only attestation of the name Polyanax known to us is an inscription from Apollonia Pontica, on the western coast of the Black Sea (*IGBulg* I² 458.1 and 5, from IV/III BC).[23]

On the other hand Alc. F 112.24 would seem to delineate a connection between Pittacus and the Archeanactids. Here, in the right margin of a line almost entirely lost in the lacuna except for the end] ἤ (Ἀ)ρχεανακτίδαν (or the "Archeanactid" or "of the Archeanactids"), appears an explicative gloss τ(ὸν) Φιττακ(όν) (analogous to the gloss τ(ὸν) Μυρσίλ(ον) in the preceding line to the end of the verse Κλεανακτίδαν, i.e., "the Cleanactid" or "of the Cleanactids" (see I, § 4).

Two explanations have been proposed:

- "Pittacus" is "the Archeanactid" (or "of the Archeanactids") of the text, but then the first member of the disjunctive formulation (swallowed by the lacuna of the first part of the verse) would remain without explanation.[24] Furthermore Pittacus, whom we know to have been the son of Hyrras (and therefore Hyrradios), would end up being associated with a different family group.
- "Pittacus" explains the first member (now in the lacuna) of the disjunctive formulation: we could supplement, e.g., Ὑρραδίων with Diels (1920) or Καικίδαν (Kaikos is given as an alternative name of Hyrras in *Suda*, Π 1659), with Mazzarino (1943). With this explanation we no longer have a contradiction with the *genos* of Pittacus, but, as in the first hypothesis, the gloss does not explain one of the two parts of the alternative, that is, Ἀρχεανακτίδαν.

It is possible to escape this impasse if we hypothesize that the scholiast is explaining only one of the two parts of the disjunctive formulation because only one of the two was a true patronymic, and needed to or could be explained in such a way. This is a real possibility, if we consider that the form "Archeanactid" appears as a proper name, and not as a patronymic, in Alcaeus (F 444) according to a scholion to Nicander. The poet had related that Apollo, holding a branch of tamarisk in his hand, appeared to a certain Archeanactides and his family in a dream at the time of the war between Lesbos and Erythra.[25]

23 The homonymy, noticed by Mazzarino 1943: 47, between Pittacus and an Edonian prince whom Thucydides mentions at 4.107.3, is also worth noting.

24 See Page 1955: 175.

25 Schol. Nic. *Ther.* 613 καὶ Ἀλκαῖος φησιν ἐν <ᾱ> (suppl. Bergk) τοῖς περὶ Ἀρχεανακτίδην

Three figures, Myrsilus, Pittacus, and the (for us) not better known Archeanactides,[26] would then have been implicated in a curse that, on the basis of the
remaining line ends of the verses immediately preceding (lines 21–22),

x x - ᴗ ᴗ τό]σσουτον ἐπεύ[χο]μαι
x x - ᴗ ᴗ]ησθ᾽ ἀελίω φ[ά]ος

[...] so much do I pray,
[... that they no longer see] the light of the sun

we can imagine as being very similar to that flung at Pittacus in F 129.13–14:

τὸν Υ̓́ρραον δὲ πα[ῖδ]α πεδελθέτω
κήνων Ἐ[ρίννυ]ς

And the son of Hyrras
let their Avenger pursue him

From this we can deduce that the Archeanactids, as far as we know, had nothing to do with Pittacus. He, on the other hand, as the son of a noble of Thracian
origin named Hyrras, was part of the clan of the Polyanactids.

From this perspective the "Polyanactid" of F 303Aa.2 and b.14 is Hyrras, Pittacus' father, whereas the daughter of the Polyanactid of Sapph. F 155 is Gorgo,
Pittacus' sister.[27]

κατὰ τὸν πρὸς Ἐρυθραίους πόλεμον φανῆναι τὸν Ἀπόλλωνα καθ᾽ ὕπνον ἔχοντα μυρίκης κλῶνα.
The same scholion adds that Apollo was worshiped at Lesbos as Myrikaios. Perhaps the context
is the war between Erythra and Chios (supported by Miletus), to which Hdt. 1.18.3 refers (see
Liberman 1999: II.261).

26   Other *testimonia* on the Archeanactids are (1) Strab. 13.1.38: Archenax of Mytilene forti-
fied the promontory of Sigeum with rocks taken from the ruins of Troy (the date is unknown,
but should however precede the duel between Pittacus and the Athenian Phrinon in 607/6 BC).
(2) A citharode Archeanax of Mytilene is mentioned in a Delphic inscription from the end of the
sixth or beginning of the fifth century BC (see Liberman 1999: II.261 and 220–21). (3) In Sapph.
F 213 a female figure whose proper name was Pleistodike is called "Archeanassa" on the basis of
her *genos* (see VII, § 5).

27   F 213Ab.9]παι πολυα[could be another reference to her. In that case Gorgo would have
been involved with the events concerning Charaxos (mentioned at line 7).

§5   Devouring the City

Several times Alcaeus uses the epithet κακοπατρίδαις in relation to Pittacus and his group: F 348.1–2 (the Mytileneans have unanimously elected κακοπατρίδαις Pittacus "tyrant" of the city), F 67.4 (genitive plural), F 75.12 (nominative plural), F 106.3 (κακο]πατρίδα̣[). The once-current opinion was that Alcaeus had attacked the "plebeian" Pittacus for his humble birth.[28] Mazzarino has been the first to argue against it:[29] in particular he observes that a "plebeian" could not have been a member of Alcaeus' *hetaireia*, as Alc. F 129 attests. Rather Pittacus must have been descended from a family of Thracian nobles who long entertained close connections of ξενία with one or more Mytilenean aristocratic groups (Mazzarino speaks à propos of archaic "metoikia").

Nonetheless Mazzarino himself, and others with him,[30] have continued to argue for the existence of a strong connection between Alcaeus' use of κακοπατρίδαις and the Thracian origin of Pittacus' father.

Rösler,[31] by contrast, wants to understand the use of the epithet as a denunciation of the character of Pittacus' politics: likewise in the *Sylloge Theognidea* (cf. e.g. lines 305–8) the charge of being κακοί is used also of those who, while of noble origin, have distanced themselves from the code of aristocratic behavior by entertaining contacts with those who are not nobles.

Yet the Theognidean κακοί is a much vaguer term than the one Alcaeus uses,[32] and our perplexity on this point can probably be explained away with an ideological tension underlying the world of the Mytilenean elites. If, in the eyes of those who were Pittacus' sympathizers (and among them we must count also Alcaeus before the "betrayal"), a noble of Thracian origin could be received on terms of equality in the circle of aristocratic citizens, his foreign origin could always be resurrected and dusted off as a political weapon against him.

Besides characterizing Pittacus as κακοπατρίδαις, Alcaeus branded him with a whole series of insults, some of which are recorded by D.L. 1.81 (Alc. T 429):

28   See, e.g., Wilamowitz 1914: 235–36.
29   Mazzarino 1943: 38–52.
30   See especially Page 1955: 170–73.
31   Rösler 1980: 186–91.
32   See Lapini 2007.

Alcaeus called this man σαράποδα and σάραπον because he had large feet and shuffled with them; χειροπόδην because of the chilblains that they call "chapping"; γαύρηκα because he boasted for no reason; φύσκωνα and γάστρωνα because he was fat; but also ζοφοδορπίδαν because he didn't use lamps[33] and ἀγάσυρτον because he was slovenly and dirty.

What emerges from this picture is a contrast between arrogant pride (the boasting) and physical deformity associated particularly with the feet[34] and the stomach. This mixture of arrogance, deformity, and inadequacy for aristocratic company has its undisputed archetype in Homer's Thersites, whose name is formed from the noun θέρσος (Aeolic form of θάρσος). Thersites insults the heads of the army and has a series of deformities or disharmonious features: he shuffles, is lame in one leg, his shoulders curve down to his chest, his head comes to a point, and sparse hair covers his whole body (Il. 2.216–19).

Compared with these traits the epithet "potbelly" (φύσκων and γάστρων) seems on the other hand to refer to a greediness similar to that Alcaeus attributes to him, as we have mentioned, in two fragments in which the link between δάπτειν and πόλις recurs to indicate his greed in his relations with his fellow citizens, namely F 70.7 δαπτέτω πόλιν ὡς καὶ πεδὰ Μυρσί[λ]ῳ and F 129.23-24 ἔ]μβαις ἐπ᾽ ὀρκίοισι δάπτει | τὰν πόλιν.

The voracious greed of Alcaeus' portrait of Pittacus has its model no longer in Thersites but rather in Agamemnon, whom Thersites, in the wake of Achilles, harshly attacks.

In fact it is very likely, as Lentini has well observed,[35] that the Alcaic phrase δάπτειν (τὰν) πόλιν is modeled on the epithet δημοβόρος, with which Achilles brands Agamemnon in the first book of the Iliad.[36]

---

33 Plutarch, as noted at VII, § 3, gives a different interpretation of the epithet. For other explanations offered by ancient sources see Liberman 1999: II.188 n. 384.

34 On the vulnerability of the lower limbs of various μόναρχοι see Catenacci 1996: 246–48.

35 Lentini 2000: 9–12.

36 Hom. Il. 1.231 δημοβόρος βασιλεύς. Similar are the connotations of δωροφάγοι at Hes. Op. 39, 221, and 264, and of δημοφάγος at Thgn. 1181 (see Catenacci 1996: 212–14).

As Lentini himself summarizes,[37]

> the sharing of a characteristic like city- (or people-) eating is not co-
> incidental, given that the tyrant Pittacus claimed relationship with the
> Atreid line, that of Agamemnon: he received κῦδος[38] from a divinity
> (as Agamemnon from Zeus) and aroused the wrath of Alcaeus (as Aga-
> memnon does that of Achilles).

§6   A Denunciation to Apollo

This very same temperamental trait, greed, qualified by an adjective (μάργον)
that takes on itself notions of madness, ravenousness, and lust, is assigned to
the "Polyanactid" in the second of the two fragments preserved by P.Oxy. 2291,
namely Alc. F 303 Ab + Ac.1–3 (= Sapph. F 99, col. I ll. 10–24 + col. II, ll. 1–3
LP):[39]

Λάτως] τε καὶ Δί[ος] πάϊ[.]
   ].. ε...[.] ἔπι[θ'] ὀργίαν
_Γρύνηαν] ὑλώδη<ν> λίπων
   ].εν χρη[σ]τήριον
      ].[ ].ευμεσ[..].[.]ων   5
  _   ]....[ ]
      ]...... ἀ[μ]έραις
      ]ρσανον[.]..ργιαν
  _   ]υσομεν [ ]
      ]ν ὑμνε[10
κα[   ]ενα[.] φο.[...].. ἀδελφέαν
_ὤσπαι[ ] .ιο.[...].[
οὔτις δε[...]κει.θέλη[
δειχνυσ[...]ε, δηῦτε Πωλυανακτίδαν

---

37 Lentini 2002: 6.

38 Cf. Alc. F 13 Φιττάκωι δὲ δίδοις κῦδος ἐπήρ[ατ]ον with Hom. *Il.* 1.279 σκηπτοῦχος
βασιλεύς, ὦι τε Ζεὺς κῦδος ἔδωκεν.

39 I include in the poem also the remains of the first three verses of Alc. F 303 Ac, which
ought to belong to it. As Voigt notes in her apparatus, "ad v. 2 marg. sin. coronis et schol. οὐκ ἦν
κορωνίς, quam ad v. 3 ponere deb. ut docent paragr."

_τὸν μάργον ὄνδειξαι θέλω   15
..στοσ.[
ϝ..πα[
ὤνηρ[

2 ἔπι[θ'] ὀργίαν Snell: επι[ ]βοργιαν[pap.   4 καὶ σὸν κλύ]τον Snell   7 ἀ[μ]έραις Voigt
8 πό]ρσανον Treu   9 fort. χορε]ύσομεν   16 fort. ὤστ' ὄσσ[(α)·   17 ϝῶν Voigt

Son of Leto and Zeus
[...] come to your rite
leaving wooded Grynea

[and your famous] oracle
...   5
...

[...] in days
[...] do accomplish ...
[...] we shall dance? [...]

[...] sing- [...]   10
the sister [...]
...

and no-one [...]
denounces [...], again the greedy Polyanactid
I mean to indicate,   15

so that all the things that [...
of his[...]
that man [...]

The text of the poem is even more damaged than that of Alc. F 303Aa, and we
cannot even succeed in getting a handle on the metrical scheme of the second

verse[40] of these three-line strophes (it is clear though that the first and third lines are iambic dimeters), but two aspects are still easy to grasp.

First of all, this is a violent attack against "the greedy Polyanactid." The poet, or rather the speaking voice, means to point him out, to denounce him (a form of the verb (ὀν)δείχνυμι = (ἀνα)δείκνυμι occurs twice, at lines 14 and 15) to the gods (Apollo and his sister Artemis), apparently to ask their help against this transgressor and his group.

Aloni understands Πωλυανακτίδαν as a genitive feminine plural ("of the female Polyanactids"), and supposes that the substantive governing this genitive occurred in the following verse (that is, at the beginning of col. III = F 303 Ac).[41] Yet Aloni's hypothesis is refuted by the fact that the initial letters of this following verse (..στοσ.[) do not seem compatible with a substantive but rather, it would seem, with the beginning of a consecutive clause (ὥστ᾽ ὄσσ[(α)).

Therefore the accuser means to denounce the Polyanactid "again." The pattern in which the adverb δηὖτε signals, especially in Sappho,[42] the recurrent character of a certain experience (for instance *eros*) is well known. In this particular case we are not concerned with a phenomenon that recurs in relation with the rhythm of nature or human existence, but rather with an event tied to the speaker's experience within a specific context (a festival of Apollo). The "again" refers then to something that the subject does now as he has done in the past on the same occasion or to something that he does for a second time in the context of the same occasion: in an analogous way in a dithyramb (fr. 75.8 M.) Pindar says through the mouth of his chorus that he comes "for the second time" (δεύτερον) to Athens near the Altar of the Twelve Gods.[43]

This indication provided by δηὖτε is connected to the second aspect that emerges from the fragment, namely a ritual setting that separates this and other poems from the customary symposiastic setting of Alcaic lyric.

According to Snell's fortunate reconstruction,[44] the ritual setting must have been a festival in honor of Apollo, who was worshiped at the oracular sanctuary

40   As Voigt notes *ad* 14, "cum fieri nequeat ut tres cons. in lac. perierint (ia ^gl), nullum in metrum versus quadrat." For the sequence ia ^gl cf. Sapph. F 138.2 and (with ia ^gl ia) *Inc. Auct.* 21.1 and 2.

41   Aloni 1997: 169.

42   Cf. Sapph. F 1.15 and 18, 22.11, 83.4, 127, and 130.

43   Pind. fr. 75.7–9 M. Διόθεν ... σὺν ἀγλαΐαι | ... πορευθέντ᾽ ἀοιδᾶν δεύτερον | ἐπὶ τὸν κισσοδαῆ θεόν. On δεύτερον see Lavecchia 2000: 263, who rightly postulates "un precedente ditirambo pindarico eseguito ad Atene."

44   Snell 1953.

of Grynea, on the Anatolian coast between Elea and Cuma. And it is precisely from Grynea that the speaking voice summons the god to come, presumably to Mytilene, to attend a celebration that, similar to what we have seen in Sappho, must have included amoebic contests with the exchange of satiric poems among different poets or choral groups.

Particularly cogent in this regard is the parallel between the attitude of lines 14–15 "again I mean to indicate the greedy Polyanactid" and the "but [now] I will go attack the one guilty [for these] torments / [and these] anxieties" of the lines 4–5 of the Sapphic poem we have reconstructed at II § 3 (where, immediately after, the speaker expressed her trust in the punitive intervention of Artemis against Andromeda).

§7   The Yoke

At a certain point Pleistodike and Gongyla passed to Gorgo. We have this from a commentary transmitted by P.Oxy. 2292 (= Sapph. T 213):[45]

```
]..[.].τα, Γο[γγύλα δὲ αἶ-
ψ᾽ ἰαχ[ηθ]ήσε<τ᾽> ἔμα κ Ἀρχεάνα[σ-
σα Γόργω(ι) σύνδυγο(ς)· ἀντὶ τοῦ
σ[ύν]ζυξ· ἡ Πλειστοδίκη
    τ]ῆι Γ[ο]ργοῖ σύνζυξ με-          5
τὰ τ[ῆς] Γογγύλης ὀν[ο]μασθή-
σετ[αι· κ]οινὸν γὰρ τὸ ὄνο-
μ[α δ]έδοται ἢ κατὰ τῆς [ο]ἰκί-
α[ς, διὸ] Πλ[ε]ιστοδίκη [μὲ]ν
αὔτη ὀνομ]ασθήσετ[αι] κυ-          10
[ρίως        ]ηι ].ατετουτ
             ].νο αν
```

1–2 legi et supplevi   3 Γόργω(ι) sive Γόργω(ς) Lobel   8–9 [ο]ἰκί-|α[ς, διὸ] et [μὲ]ν supplevi cetera suppl. Lobel   10 αὔτη supplevi ὀνομ]ασθήσετ[αι] Lobel   10–11 κυ-|ρι( ) Lobel

---

45 For the reconstruction of the text see Ferrari 2007: 22–28.

[...] "and suddenly my [Gongyla]
and Archeanassa will be called
companions of Gorgo": σύνδυγος
    for σύνζυξ. Pleistodike
    will be named together with Gongyla a follower of Gorgo: 5
    in fact the name (Archeanassa) is given
    as a common name or in relation to the kinship
    [hence she] will be called
    Pleistodike on the basis of her proper name,
    [but ...]   10

The assertion that Pleistodike will be called, together with Gongyla, "yoke-mate" (σύνζυξ) of Gorgo has been linked to a passage of Himerius (*Or.* 9.4 p. 75–76 Colonna = Sapph. T 194) on "the rites of Aphrodite" to support the existence of initiatory marriages within Sappho's circle, analogous to what apparently happened at Sparta within the local ἀγέλαι, and that would be mirrored in the role played by Agido and by Hagesichora in Alcman's *Louvre Parthenion*.[46] "Within the women's communities of archaic Lesbos"—writes Gentili[47]—"there were liaisons of an 'official' character, which could involve a genuinely matrimonial type of relationship, as is shown by Sappho's (F 213.3 V.) use of the term σύνζυξ."

Di Benedetto has objected that "even in ancient Greece marriage was a union of two, not three" and that "Sappho speaks not of an actual event but of something that will be said."[48] Stehle, with reference to a passage of Euripides on the cooperation of the Muses and the Graces,[49] has observed that "since 'wife' is an extension of the metaphorical meaning 'fellow-worker' or 'companion' and takes on its specificity from its context, it should not be substituted for 'companion' where the context does not warrant it."[50]

But the understanding of the passage must first of all take into account the fact that, while the commentator's paraphrase speaks of Pleistodike as the one who will be called σύνζυξ of Gorgo together with Gongyla, in the lemma (lines

---

46 By contrast, on the "communal perspective" of Alcm. fr. 1 *PMGF*, confirmed by the *Parthenion for Astymeloisa* (Alcm. fr. 3 *PMGF*), see Stehle 1997: 73–88.
47 Gentili 1984: 106–7.
48 Di Benedetto 1987: 16 n. 17.
49 Eur. *HF* 673 ff. ἀδίσταν συζυγίαν.
50 Stehle 1997: 276.

2–3) apart from the absence of Gongyla presumably swallowed in the lacuna of line 1, the reference is not to Pleistodike but rather to Archeanassa.[51]

Treu suggested a promising solution, the more so since the commentary speaks of "appellation" and "proper name":[52] "Pleistodike ist identisch mit Archeanassa, letzeres dann als Bezeichnung der Sippe gebraucht,"[53] and in fact our reconstruction of the text is founded on this hypothesis.[54]

If this is the case, in our poem the emphasis was not on an initiatory union between Pleistodike/Archeanassa and Gongyla, but rather on the strong sense of reciprocal belonging to each other that united the pupils in that all were under the same "teacher."[55]

In the case of Mika in F 71 (see above IV, § 7) it was the suspicion of the young woman's mockery of her former companions that aroused a reaction of pride. This time it is the anticipation of two new adherents of Gorgo's "party" that provokes a sorrowful reaction.

The lemma allows us to recover little more than a single verse and we can say nothing certain about the performative occasion of the poem. Yet the use of the third person ("she will be called") seems to prefigure a discursive strategy

51 We again encounter the name Archeanassa in a rather lacunose context in F 103CA.4 Ἀρ]χεάνασσα[.

52 Treu 1954: 165–66.

53 Di Benedetto 1987: 16 n. 17 understands κ]οινόν of line 7 as a remark that σύνδυγος is a "common" name in the sense of being able to be used without variation in form either in the masculine or in the feminine. But this interpretation is problematic for several reasons. First, it does not allow an understanding in this particular context of either the slippage from the Archeanassa of the lemma to Pleistodike in the commentary nor the fact that δέδοται κοινόν shows a certain possibility as regards an alternative introduced with ἢ κατὰ τῆς [of line 8. Secondly, it does not explain the emphasis (ὀνομασθήσεται twice as well as ὄνομα δέδοται) on the way in which Pleistodike will be called, nor finally the very probable presence, as Lobel saw, of a form of κυρι- (κυρίως?) between line 8 and line 9: all things that Treu's explanation clarifies. Therefore, considering that in the grammatic tradition the κύρια (or ἴδια) ὀνόματα are our "proper names" and that the adjective κοινός is sometimes used of *appellativa nomina* (see Uhlig's index to the *Opuscula* of Apollonius Dyscolus in GG II 2.218–19), it follows that κοινόν must indicate here "common" or *appellativum* name (προσηγορικόν) in contrast to a "proper" name. This antithesis is cleary expressed in Ap. Dysc. *Pron.* 105.4 'σὸς' κοινόν, ἐπὶ πάντων, τὸ δὲ 'Ἐκτόρειος' ἴδιον and 112.17 ὁ μὲν γὰρ δυικὸς ὡς κύριον ὄνομα κατὰ τοῦ δύο ἐτάχθη, ὁ δὲ πληθυντικὸς κοινὸς παντὸς πλήθους καθέστηκε.

54 Metrically, if we consider the sequence αἴ-]ψ' to Γόργω(ι) as one verse, we have a series |3cho ba| (Γο[γγύλα δὲ] | αἴψ' ἰαχ[ηθ]ήσε[τ'] ἔμα κ Ἀρχεάνα[σ]σα Γόργωι | σύνδυγος [) attested for Sappho at F 114.1 and F 128. This may be a case of distichs organized by cho ba (= aristoph) ||3 cho ba |||, as at Hor. *Carm.* 1.8 *Lydia, dic, per omnis / te deos oro, Sybarin cur properes amando.*

55 We find an example of the use of a form of συζυγ- not to a pair but to a larger group, in the συζύγιαι Χάριτες of Eur. *Hipp.* 1148.

very different from that suggested in relation to Mika by the use of the second person ("you have chosen"). The poem mentioned in the commentary of P.Oxy. 2292 was not addressed to Gongyla, or Pleistodike, or Gorgo, but rather to those pupils who remained faithful.

VIII Iconography

§1 The Bochum Krater

We have already mentioned (IV, § 1) that one mark of Andromeda's rustic boorishness—her inability to let her gown elegantly fall above her ankles—is paralleled in two vase representations, one from the first and one from the second half of the fifth century BC.

Let us now consider how Attic vase painters visualized Sappho and her group in greater detail.[1] Obviously these representations are not faithful snapshots of a world that, on the other side of the Aegean Sea and at a century of distance, must have already been perceived as remote and obscure. Yet it is nonetheless possible that an examination of this evidence can tell us something interesting about the earliest phase of reception of Aeolic poetry and the culture to which it gave expression.

We have already referred to the Bochum krater of 480/70 BC for the girl who is holding up the hem of her skirt with both hands. Regarding this krater, D. Yatromanolakis garners credit for having recognized the symposiastic features that characterize Sappho's portrait. In particular he has given full value to the B face of the vase, where he has identified the inscription Η ΠΑΙΣ above the girl's head. On the basis of these data Yatromanolakis has suggested the presence of a further erotic nuance.[2]

Sappho's figure on face A holds the barbitos and suggests a dance step, whereas the girl represented on face B moves in the same direction as Sappho, turning

---

1 On the arguments see the important review offered by Yatromanolakis 2001. See now Yatromanolakis 2007: ch. 2.
2 Yatromanolakis 2001 and 2005; Yatromanolakis 2007: 88–89, 103–10, 161–64.

her face back[3] in the same way. Both figures thus advance neither to meet nor to look at one another. Rather, as the observer turns the vase in an attempt to understand exactly what is going on, the two scenes together could represent the eternal cycle of a fruitless pursuit,[4] similar to the one dramatized in Sapph. F 1.19–24.

But on the vase there are no indications that Sappho is pursuing a beloved yet unruly girl. Actually, the scene seems to be of unproblematic interpretation: Sappho marks a dance step from left to right (from the point of view of the observer), and precisely for this reason turns her head back to balance her movement and to show off the lovely chiton that falls from her outstretched right arm.

With her left hand the poet holds a barbitos, a type of lyre generally used at symposia, from which hangs a συβήνη (a case for an aulos), to show that she will perform either plucking a lyre or singing to the sound of the aulos. This alternative, as we have seen (V, § 4), emerges at the end of the fragment of the new Sappho on the Cologne papyrus that precedes the poem on old age.

Sappho's outstretched right arm aligns with the backturned movement of her head and ends with the plectrum she holds between her fingers. Her mouth is closed, just as the plectrum is far from the lyre-strings, signaling that both instrumental and singing performance will happen in the immediate future, but have not yet commenced.

As we have already seen, the general pattern is of young men moving from one symposium to another and is consistent with the reverse side of the vase, where the παῖς repeats exactly Sappho's posture and movement. On the other hand this girl has with her neither musical instrument nor any case for such. Rather, as we observed, her gesture is one of holding up the two hanging folds of her dress with both hands.

Moreover, while Sappho wears a himation with many vertical folds and an elegant chiton that leaves the right part of her breast revealed, the girl seems enveloped in a heavy cloak that winds up to her neck. This is a clear sign that the scene is taking place outdoors.

When put together, the two images represent a komos, a festive procession in an unspecified setting, but certainly one that is outside of the domestic space.

---

3 But one cannot say that she moves "in the opposite direction from Sappho" (Yatromanolakis 2005: 18): at least it is as legitimate to say that she follows in Sappho's steps.

4 Yatromanolakis 2005: 18–19.

§2   The Warsaw Kalpis

The oldest of the extant images of the poet (Fig. 4) was depicted c. 500/490 BC by the Sappho Painter on an Attic kalpis preserved in Warsaw. Here we have a Sappho (her name is incised below the stringed instrument) who, as on the Bochum krater, holds a barbitos in her hand and raises her heel (rather, here both her heels), but is already undertaking to pluck at the instrument with the plectrum (and, consistent with this, she does not turn her head and right hand backward).

As already observed, neither in the extant fragments of Sappho nor in the indirect testimonia on the poet do we find any signs or indications of symposiastic reunions of the type customary in the poetry of Alcaeus and Anacreon. It would thus be arbitrary to imagine that Sappho (the historical Sappho, not the one represented on the vase) is leading a komos towards a symposiastic gathering.

It is possible that the Attic vase painters, ignorant of the original context, reinterpreted the occasion as that of a female komos on the model of the contemporary "Anacreontic" vases. But it is also equally possible that they were led to adapt Sappho's role to the pattern of a symposiastic komos from the fact that the original festive contexts, of which some memory remained either through oral tradition and earlier iconography or through clues embedded in her texts, exhibited a real affinity to komastic celebration. The komos is a procession not only tied to symposiastic situations but also to other festivities, particularly Dionysiac ones.

What is certain is that the Bochum krater and the Warsaw kalpis both work out a model of Sappho as musician who plays (or will play) at the head of a komos.

§3   The Vari Hydria

A further iconographical model is offered by the red-figure hydria of the Polygnotus group (440/30 BC), found at Vari (Fig. 5) and now in the National Archaeological Museum of Athens (Inv. 1260). Here the poet, who wears a chiton and himation, appears seated on a chair with curved legs and surrounded by two young female figures. One of these holds, or rather offers, the lyre, and both (Nikopolis, who holds a garland over Sappho's head, and Kallis, the figure with the lyre) are indicated by name, as is the poet. Another young woman, anonymous, appears farther to the right.

The iconographic scheme whereby a famous poet is on the point of playing and is surrounded by young female figures clearly does not recall a performance in action but a moment in preparation for the same. Hence the iconography shows Sappho holding a papyrus roll in her hands, in keeping with a well-attested tradition of joint scenes of music and reading that we find, e.g., in the red-figured kylix of Onesimos, dated c. 485 BC, from Naucratis, preserved at Oxford's Ashmolean Museum (G 138.3). It is worth noting that the two recognizable sequences of letters on the roll, ἔπεα πτερόεντα, refer to a frequent epic formula and hence do not allude to a text that the poet has composed or is in the act of composing. Instead, they refer to an epic episode that has come to her memory and whose exact diction she has decided to verify.

In such a way the Vari hydria, while it appears to confirm for us that Sappho "was certainly understood by later generations to have been a music-teacher and chorus-leader to whom people sent their daughters for some sort of education,"[5] does not seek to reconstruct a performative context so much as to recreate an image of the private sphere, where Sappho elaborated her own songs and instructed choruses made up of her pupils.

---

5 West 1992: 36. For a survey on the origins of music instruction see West 1992: 36–38. On the iconographic evidence on the matter see Pöhlmann 1988: 15–20 and Prauscello-Pernigotti 2002: 30, 34 n. 5.

Fig. 1 Red-figure krater, side A. 480/70 BC. Attributed to the Tithonos Painter. Inv. S 508. Reproduced courtesy of the Ruhr-Universität Kunstsammlungen, Bochum.

Fig. 2 Red-figure krater, side B. 480/70 BC. Attributed to the Tithonos Painter. Inv. S 508. Reproduced courtesy of the Ruhr-Universität Kunstsammlungen, Bochum.

Fig. 3 Red-figure kalathos. 480/70 BC. Attributed to the Brygos Painter. Inv. 2416. *RV*² 385 and 1649; *Paralipomena* 167. Reproduced courtesy of the Staatliche Antikensammlungen und Glyptothek, Munich.

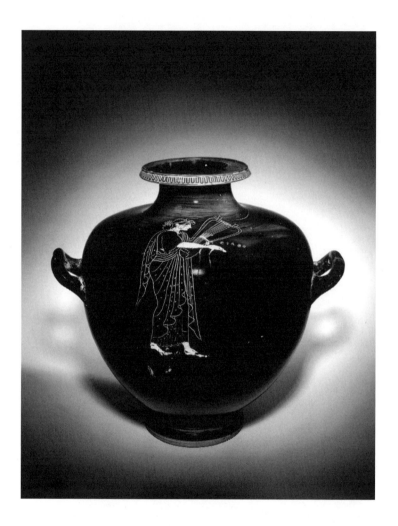

Fig. 4 White-figure Attic kalpis. 500/490 BC. Attributed to the Sappho Painter. Inv. 142333. *ARV*² 300. Reproduced courtesy of the National Museum, Warsaw. Photo by Piotr Ligier.

Fig. 5 Red-figure hydria of Vari. 440/30 BC. Polygnotus group. Inv. 1260. Reproduced courtesy of the National Archaeological Museum, Athens.

IX Nocturnal Celebrations

§1 Lovely Like Helen

The confusion between the role Sappho plays as teacher of music and poetry in a domestic and informal sphere and the designation of her poems for a wider audience at public festive contexts, or, to put in another way, the confusion between interiors and externals, is at the root of an intimist perception of Sappho's production. This perception has long dominated the field and continues to appear even among scholars who have argued against false premises and a priori readings.

With one apparent exception to which we will return (F 150), Sappho's poetry is externally oriented, destined to be sung by an individual or a chorus before a variously articulated audience but one nonetheless participating in a festive celebration. This is a reality that is obviously not traceable in every fragment but one that emerges from a nexus of references.

A kind of festival that appears the most like the symposiastic komoi, revelling through the Athenian streets and Attic countryside, is the so-called παννυχίς. This is a nocturnal vigil[1] connected, like the Roman *pervigilia*, either to wedding ceremonies or festivals in honor of Aphrodite or another divinity.[2]

F 23 exemplifies a song performed at such a nocturnal celebration:

---

1 On the παννυχίδες see Bravo 1997: 53–84. In Posid. 53 A.-B. a girl named Calliope falls from the roof during a nocturnal vigil (cf. l. 2 λυγρὴν τὴν τότε παννυχίδα).

2 Just as Night in [Orph.] *Hymn.* 3.5, so also Aphrodite is invoked as φιλοπάννυχε in [Orph.] *Hymn.* 55.2. On the possible ritual premises underlying the *Pervigilium Veneris,* see Cucchiarelli 2003: 38–44.

] ἔρωτος ἠλπ[

—   ]   2

αν]τιον εἰσίδω σ[ε

]Ἑρμιόνα τεαύ[τα

] ξάνθαι δ᾽ Ἑλέναι σ᾽ ἐίσ[κ]ην

—   ]κες   6

].ις θνάταις, τόδε δ᾽ ἴσ[θι] τὰι σᾶι

] παίσαν κέ με τὰν μερίμναν

]λαισ᾽ ἀντιδ[..]᾽[.]αθοις δὲ

—   ]   10

]τας ὄχθοις

]ταιν

παν]νυχίσ[δ]ην

3 -- ὡς γὰρ ἄν]τιον Hunt, καὶ γὰρ ὡς ἐν]άντιον Castiglioni   σ[ε Hunt   4–5 φαίνεταί μ᾽ οὐδ᾽] ... | ἔμμεναι] Page   6 οὐδὲν ἄει]κες Wilamowitz   7 αἰ θέ]μις Wilamowitz   8 καρδίαι] Diehl   11 δροσόεν]τας Lobel

... of love ...

...   2

[... as soon as] I see you face to face,

[not even] Hermione [seems to me to be]

your equal, and to liken you to blond Helen

[is not at all] improper,   6

[if it is permitted] for mortal women, but know in our

[heart] that me from all these anxieties

...

...   10

the [dewy] banks

...

... to keep watch through the night...

A female figure is compared not only to Hermione but even to Helen, Hermione's mother. It is indeed possible that the designee of this message was, in the context of a marriage rite, the bride-to-be,[3] as also seems to be confirmed by the frequency with which, in epithalamic poetry, bridegroom and bride are assimilated to divinities, heroes, or natural elements.

However, notwithstanding the lacunose nature of the text, it is undeniable that references to Eros and to the gaze (ll.1–3), and to "all these anxieties" (l. 8) after a confidential gesture such as the phrase "but know in your [heart]" of lines 7–8, introduce a markedly subjective mood that recalls on the one hand F 31.7 ("indeed as soon as I look on you"), and on the other the "oppressive anxieties" of the *Ode to Aphrodite* (F 1.25–26).

If then the speaker confided his/her thought regarding all his/her present anxieties to one particular female figure, the distance that separates a composition like this one from ritual songs, such as those that in the Alexandrian edition composed a specific book of *Epithalamia* (on which see X, § 1), is very clear.

The allusions to an open space (the "banks" of line 11, cf. F 95.12–13 and Alc. F 325.4) and to a nocturnal rite (παν]νυχίσ[δ]ην of line 13)[4] seem to belong to a ritual frame that coincides with the *pervigilium*. Yet, notwithstanding the frequently attested connection between nocturnal rites and performances of female choruses in particular,[5] we can see that, within the space of the festivity, here Sappho offers a poem decidedly monodic at least in the sense that it features a personal, subjective voice, capable of opening a close dialogue with a woman as lovely as Helen.

§2   Waiting for Dawn

References to a nocturnal rite also appear in F 30 (ll. 1 and 3), but linked to stage directions of the kind that we observed in F 27 (see III, § 1):

---

3   See Treu 1954: 190; Rissman 1983: 93; and Aloni 1997: 45. For the use of the comparison in epithalamic context cf. Himer. *Or.* 9.16 = T 218 and Contiades Tsitsoni 1990: 94–97. Cf. also F 115.1 σ᾽ ... ἐικάσδω.

4   If παννυχίσδην was part of an exhortation, we would have something similar to *Perv. Ven.* 46 *detinenda tota nox est, pervigilanda canticis.*

5   Cf. Soph. *Ant.* 1151 ff., Eur. *Ba.* 862, Aristoph. *Ra.* 370 ff., Men. *Sam.* 46, *Phasm.* 95, Crit. fr. 88 B 1.8 D.-K. For the performance of a female chorus during a nocturnal vigil at Orchomenos (Pind. fr. 333 M.), see D'Alessio 2000: 260 ff.

_   νύκτ[...].[
πάρθενοι δ[
παννυχίσδοι[σ]αι[
σὰν ἀείδοισ[ι]ν φ[ιλότατα καὶ νύμ-
_   φας ἰοκόλπω·   5
ἀλλ᾿ ἐγέρθεις ἤϊθ[
στεῖχε σοὶς ὐμάλικ[ας
ἤπερ ὄσσον ἀ λιγύφω[νος
ὔπνον [ἴ]δωμεν.   9

6 ἤϊθ[έοις Lobel-Page fin. καλέσσαις Page   7 fin. ὡς ἐλάσσω Lobel   8 fin. ὄρνις Lobel; malim
ἄμμες

night...

and the girls [...] ˙
keeping festive watch through the night [...]
sing[6] of your love and of the bride
    of violet bosom.   5

But come, upon rising, [having called] the young men,
your age-mates, come, [so that we] may look upon a sleep
[more brief] than that of
    the clear voiced-one.   9

In the closure of the ode (line 9 is the last line of the poem, as signaled by the
corresponding coronis set in the left margin), the "I" addresses the groom
and first tells him that a group of young girls is celebrating, in a nocturnal
ritual, the love[7] that binds him to his violet-bosomed bride, then urges him to
rise and summon a group of his age-mates so that—as the poem concludes

---

6 Lobel preferred ἀείδοιεν to ἀείδοι[σ]ιν on the grounds that in Sappho the ν ephelcystic does
not make position, but this is not correct: cf. F 44Ab 9 θνάτοισιν· πεδέχ[, F 58.17 κεν ποείην and F
103.9]σε φόβαισι<ν> θεμένα λύρα.[(where φόβαισι of P.Oxy. 2294 would involve a sequence of
three short syllables, which is incompatible with Aeolian versification: see Treu 1954: 162 and 170).

7 For φιλότας referring to the first wedding night cf. Alc. F 42.9–11 (where the supplement
φιλό[τας at l. 13 is virtually certain) and Theocr. 18.54 ff.

—"[we] may look upon a sleep more brief than that of the clear voiced-one" (the nightingale).[8]

To the hypothesis, frequently proposed,[9] that this poem must be considered an example of the so-called epithalamium on waking it has been objected that "the verb ἐγέρθεις has nothing to do with the morning arousal of the spouses, but is to be understood as an invitation to the groom to rise from the symposium at which, in a period of the ceremony that follows on the *agogé*, he participates alone, while his wife has already retired to the nuptial chamber. On rising, he is to gather his age-mates, who will join with the girls mentioned at line 2 in their dancing and singing; together they will sing for a large part of the night."[10]

Actually the summons for the groom to gather his coevals so that they may form a male chorus complementary to that of the young girls[11] hardly suits the perquisites of a *Morgenlied*. But we should also bear in mind that the wedding banquet took place in the house of the bride's father *before* the beginning of the wedding procession, and that at such a banquet both the spouses and their relatives and friends took part in two separate groups of men and women.[12]

Also in Catullus 62 the initial summons of a young man, who has taken on the role of chorus leader, to his companions to rise and leave the banquet precedes the hymeneal songs and the *deductio* of the bride (lines 1–4):

> *Vesper adest: iuvenes, consurgite. Vesper Olympo*
> *expectata diu vix tandem lumina tollit.*
> *Surgere iam tempus, iam pinguis linquere mensas.*
> *Iam veniet virgo, iam dicetur hymenaeus.*

---

8   ἀ λιγύφωνος is most likely a *griphos* of Hesiodic fashion (cf. Hes. *Op.* 524 ἀνόστεος, 571 φερέοικος, 778 ἴδρις, see West 1978: 289–90). This seems to be suggested also by the necessity of a first-person plural pronoun at the end of l. 8 (ἄμμες) that contrasts the friends of the groom. Such a pronoun would not leave room for a possible supplement like ὄρνις or the like. Also in Theocritus (18.56) the chorus of Spartan maidens uses an allusive expression to denote the cock (πρᾶτος ἀοιδός) when it promises to come back to sing the "epithalamium on waking." The nightingale's indifference to sleep was proverbial (cf. Hes. fr. 312 M.-W.), and according to Plin. *HN* 10.29.43 (81) when the buds are budding its song lasts fifteen days and nights without any interruption.

9   See Treu 1954: 193, Contiades Tsitsoni 1990: 100 ff., Stehle 1997: 279 ff.

10   Aloni 1997: 61.

11   Cf. F 27 where a female chorus is summoned to take part in the nuptial festivity.

12   Illuminating instances of the articulation of the wedding feast, at least in an Attic context, and of the role played by the symposium therein are provided by Menander's *Samia* (ll. 71 ff., 120 ff., 189 ff., 210 ff., 219 ff, 673 ff., 729 ff.) and *Dyskolos* (esp. ll. 941 ff.).

Evening is come: rise up, young men. Evening long awaited
has only just borne the lights from Olympus.
It is time to rise, to leave the rich tables.
Now the bride will come, and now the wedding hymn will be uttered.

If this is the imagined context of Sappho's ode, the "I" means to alert the
groom that the girls have already begun to sing the hymeneans[13] and therefore urges him to rise from the banquet (cf. *surgere* and *linquere mensas* in
Catullus 62) and to begin the final phase of the festivity by calling his friends
together.[14]

It is possible that the "I" is that of a choral group, and that this choral group
refers to itself first in the third person ("they sing") and then in the first person
plural ("we see"). However, we should not exclude the possibility of a monodic
voice that maintains an equal distance from the chorus of young men and that
of young women except for merging finally with the plurality of the female
group that is put under its direction.

A comparable situation emerges at the end of another poem, this one con-
taining instruction relevant however to the conclusion of the festivity (F 43):

>]αι·
>]
>]λεται
>]αλος
>]. ἄκαλα κλόνει   5
>] κάματος φρένα
>]ε κατισδάνε[ι]
>] ἀλλ᾽ ἄγιτ᾽, ὦ φίλαι,
>] ἄγχι γὰρ ἀμέρα.

7 ὄσσ]ε Mehrwaldt

---

13   We are most probably dealing with those kinds of evening songs interspersed with jokes
to which Pindar refers when he narrates that Coronis (*P.* 3.16–19) οὐκ ἔμειν᾽ ἐλθεῖν τράπεζαν
νυμφιδίαν | οὐδὲ παμφώνων ἰαχὰν ὑμεναίων ἅλικες | οἷα παρθένοι φιλέοισιν ἑταῖραι | ἑσπερίαις
ὑποκουρίζεσθ᾽ ἀοιδαῖς. On the playful nuance conveyed by the verb ὑποκουρίζεσθαι see Gentili
1995: 410–11.
14   For the link between στεῖχε and ὡς ἴδωμεν of F 27.7 and 9 cf. F 6.7–8; for the integration
of Page καλέσσαις see Alc. F 368.1 Μένωνα κάλεσσαι.

... [the wind] stirs sweetly...   5
... toil [has invaded] the heart
... [sleep] settles [on the eyes]
... but now you, friends,
... day is near.

The silent rustle of the leaves at the soft breath of the wind, the toil that seizes the spirit, the sleep that settles on the eyes, [15] all explain the exhortation to a group of "friends" (l. 8) to complete an action, now lost in the lacuna, that should have taken place near the end of the night: more likely the dismissal at the festival's end[16] than the continuation of "refrains de l'hyménée jusqu'au point du jour." [17]

§3   Persian Mantles

Similarly, the varied colors of crocuses, purple peploi, Persian mantles,[18] and garlands depicted in F 92 all refer to an outdoor scene of a festival (whether noctural or not we do not know):

...
πε[
κρ[.........]περ[
πέπλον[...]πυσχ[5
καὶ κλε[..]σαω[
κροκόεντα[
πέπλον πορφυ[ρ........]δεξω[.]
χλαιναι περσ[
στέφανοι περ[10
καλ[.]οσσαμ[
φρυ[
πορφ[υρ

<hr/>

15   Cf. F 149 ὅτα πάννυχος ἄσφι κατάγρει (perhaps, as Voigt observes, with ὕπνος as the subject).
16   Treu 1954: 197: "zum Aufbruch mahnt Sappho, denn der Tag ist nahe, die Pannychis am Ende."
17   Lasserre 1989: 40.
18   Also the "royal scent" of F 94.18–20 μύρωι ... βασ]ιληίωι should be of Persian or Median origin; cf. Hor. *Carm.* 3.1.44 *Achaemeniumque costum* and Plin. *HN* 13.18.

τα̣π̣α̣[

...

9 Πέρσ[ικαι Schubart   12 Φρυ[γ- Schubart

...

a peplos ...   5

...

of crocus ...
a purple peplos [...]
Per[sian...]mantles
garlands around [...]   10
beau- [...]
Phry[g-...]
purple...

...

In another poem[19] there is a reference to a diaphanous mantle of oriental origin (βεῦδος), which corresponds to Aristoph. *Lys.* 52 Κιμβερικόν. The poem to which F 39, already mentioned (see I, § 2), belonged includes a reference to a scarlet slipper and perhaps also to a "cloak worthy of Adonis" ([φᾶ]ρο̣ς̣ ... Ἀ[δω]νίδηον: suppl. Vogliano) in F 96.23.

---

19 Cf. Poll. 7.49 = Sapph. F 177: βεῦδος, ὡς Σαπφώ, κιμβερικόν. ἔστι δὲ τὸ κιμβερικὸν διαφανής τις χιτωνίσκος.

X Nuptial Songs

§1 The Book of the *Epithalamians*

The poems with nuptial overtones that we have analyzed so far, i.e., poems in which a monodic or choral voice imparts stage directions to a group or a single individual, and in which that voice is capable of dialoguing with the groom on confidential terms, belonged either to the first (F 24, 27, and 30) or to the second (F 43) book of Sappho's Alexandrian edition, in Sapphic stanzas and Aeolic pentameters (gl^{2da}) respectively. We must thus try to explain the presence of poems with nuptial content outside the so-called *Book of the Epithalamians*.[1]

It is commonly held that the Alexandrian philologists did not include in this book (whether the eighth or the ninth we do not know) the entirety of Sappho's nuptial songs but only those composed in a meter different from that of the "epithalamians" scattered in the other books. Yet as Carlo Pernigotti has observed, as far as the nuptial content is concerned, only the small corpus represented by F 104–17, reconstructed as it is by modern editors through putting together poems explicitly mentioned by ancient sources as epithalamic (F 113 and 116) and poems with certain nuptial themes,[2] provides us with songs whose

---

1 See Page 1955: 119–26 and Contiades Tsitsoni 1990: 69–71.

2 The sequence of ten lines (all beginnings of poems) preserved by P.Oxy. 2294 (= F 103) constitutes a different issue. These *incipits* are followed by a *subscriptio* that allows us to infer that the relevant poems must have included in their entirety about 130–39 verses (cf. l. 14 στίχ(οι) ρ̄λ̄ [)) and belonged to the *Book of the Epithalamians* (l. 16 f.). On the problems raised by this piece of evidence, see Treu 1954: 167–71 (a selection for the celebration of a given wedding feast), Page 1955: 116–19, Lasserre 1989: 17–80 (who arbitrarily reconstructs a very long choral hymenean), Contiades Tsitsoni 1990: 71–91, Aloni 1997: 176 ff., Yatromanolakis 1999a (who posits a sylloge not exclusively epithalamic in content).

"ritual purpose seems always obvious, concrete, and often achieved by means of direct, folk-like tones and forms of address such as, for instance, apostrophe, dialogue, or straightforward mockery."[3]

[Demetrius] had already observed this tendency when in *De eloc.* 166–67 he stated:

> This is why Sappho sings of beauty in words which are themselves beautiful and attractive, or on love or spring or the halcyon. Every beautiful word is woven into the texture of her poetry, and some she invented herself. But it is in a very different tone that she mocks the clumsy bridegroom and doorkeeper at the wedding. Her language is then very ordinary, in the diction of prose rather than poetry.[4]

Furthermore, the hypothesis traditionally shared would require that the songs included in the *Epithalamians* were composed in meters different at any rate from those used in the nuptial poems of the other books. But we can see that some meters used in F 104–17 occur also in poems which were not likely to be of an epithalamic nature. We find dactylic hexameters[5] not only in F 105a and F 105b, but also in a line of a mythical-narrative turn as F 142 (Λάτω καὶ

A good explanation is provided by Puglia 2008: within a process of excerpting and selecting, a grammarian (or anyway a passionate reader of poetry) would have compiled some kind of bibliographical notes on Sappho's books according to the current Alexandrian edition, recording the number of poems contained in each single book and then quoting the beginnings of the most beautiful ones and their line number (thus, from l. 18 onwards, the reference would no longer be to the book entitled *Epithalamians* but to a new one). Furthermore, as already posited by Page 1955: 118–19, at l. 15, the erudite writer most probably wanted to signal that the ten poems selected from the book of the *Epithalamians* were composed, the first excepted, in the same meter (cf. Page's supplement ὁμοιόμετροι δὲ] at the beginning of the same line 15). In fact this hypothesis seems compatible with an analysis of the incipit. The line endings Πιέριδέ[ς τε] Μοῖσαι at l. 8, λιγύραν [ἀοί]δαν at l. 10 and χρυσοπέδιλ[ος] Αὔως at l. 13 are best interpreted as acephalic hipponacteans with double choriambic expansions, that is, ^hipp²ᶜʰ (as the lengths of the lines suggest itself). The other line beginnings, even if not of unambiguous interpretation, are all consistent with such metrical scheme (the first line excepted). Alternatively one could posit that the anonymous compiler did observe that all the line beginnings (with the exception of the first line that exhibits a dactylic rhythm) were metrical sequences with internal choriambic expansion.

3 Pernigotti 2001: 15.

4 A rustic tone is emphasized also by Longus (4.40.1 ff.) when he remarks that all the members who took part in the nuptial procession "when close to the door, started singing with a hard and rasping voice" (ᾖδον σκληρᾶι καὶ ἀπηνεῖ τῇ φωνῆι).

5 Hephaist. p. 293.15 ff. C. (= Sapph. T 240) calls "specifically Sapphic" hexameters with initial spondee, but instances of a dactylic incipit are not absent (F 105b.2 and 106).

Νιόβα μάλα μὲν φίλαι ἦσαν ἔταιραι) and in another one equally narrative in tone (F 143 χρύσειοι δ᾽ ἐρέβινθοι ἐπ᾽ ἀιόνων ἐφύοντο).

The structure of three ionics *a minore* that we find in F 113 occurs also in F 135 in an apostrophe by the speaking voice to its beloved girl[6] (Eirene, reproached in F 91): τί με Πανδίονις, ὦ Εἴρανα, χελίδων.

The use of a sequence of pherecrateans with dactylic expansion in F 110 occurs also in a proverb ironically recalled (F 146) with regard to someone (not necessarily Sappho herself) who claimed to be ready to renounce a good so far as its negative consequences may be avoided:[7] μήτε μοι μέλι μήτε μέλισσα.[8]

The formation of a book of epithalamians did then not happen mechanically, by way of merely inserting in one and the same recipient nuptial songs not yet ascribed to other books. It involved instead a generic awareness rooted in stylistic and performative features that could be found in the text itself.[9]

§2   The Start of the Procession

The Alexandrian editors had also then to identify and isolate, apart from the songs belonging to the first books, those poems that exhibited, with respect to the marriage rite, a precise pragmatic function by articulating its phases and highlighting its main features.[10]

This operation was feasible inasmuch as the ancient Greeks' wedding rite, as

6   A comparison with Meleager's epigram *A.P.* 5.172 ("Dawn hostile to the lovers, why have you quickly arrived to this bed …?") suggests here the presence of the erotic motif of the dawn descending too early (cf. Di Benedetto 1987: 14–15).

7   See the list of *testimonia* in Voigt's edition.

8   It is instead likely that the opening invocation of the Charites and Muses of F 128 δεῦτέ νυν ἄβραι Χάριτες καλλίκομοί τε Μοῖσαι, which exhibits the same metrical sequence of 3 cho ba as F 114.1 παρθενία, παρθενία, ποῖ με λίποισ᾽ ἀποίχηι, might well represent the beginning of the poem: cf. F 103.5].. ἄγναι Χάριτες Πιερίδε[ς τε] Μοῖ[σαι (the very beginning of an epithalamian). Also F 136, with a nightingale announcing the spring (ἦρος ἄγγελος ἰμερόφωνος ἀήδων), might have belonged to a nuptial song: a pherecratean with double dactylic expansion can be found also in F 115 τίωι σ᾽, ὦ φίλε γάμβρε, κάλως ἐικάσδω; | ὄρπακι βραδίνωι σε μάλιστ᾽ ἐικάσδω.

9   If we accept Puglia's hypothesis mentioned above, the fact that all the *incipits* of F 103 (with the exclusion of the first) must have been in ^hipp[2ch], that is, in the meter characteristic of Book 4, is particularly telling.

10   For a pragmatic approach see the study by Lyghounis 1991 (cf. in particular the scheme at 175–79, where the extant Greek hymeneans preserved to us are correlated with the various stages of the marriage rite).

is well known, presented itself, just like the funeral rite, as a rite of passage: the bride had to accomplish a journey from one house to another, moving from one family context to a new one.

The scanty remnants of the group F 104–17[11] are cited for the most varied reasons (generic: F 105, F 108, F 110, F 113; stylistic: F 104, F 105b, F 111, F 114; morphological and semantic: F 107, F 109, F 116, F 117A; metrical: F 110, F 111, F 112, F 115, F 117, F 117B).[12] Yet, in keeping with their pragmatic function, simplicity of diction and choral performance[13] executed by homogeneous groups (the age-mates of the bride and those of the groom), they may largely be read against the background of the different stages of the wedding rite, according to a synchronization of song and ritual in which the former is almost a function or mode of the latter.

This dimension is especially emphasized and easily recognizable even now, in those passages that belong to songs performed respectively either at the actual start of the wedding procession which accompanied, on foot or on a wagon, the newlyweds from one house to the other, or before the nuptial chamber.

The procession took place after the banquet at the bride's house (on which we have commented in relation to F 27: see IX, § 2), thus starting at the very beginning of the evening with the lighting of torches. F 104a refers to this very moment of incipient twilight, marked by the appearance of Hesperus:

> Ἔσπερε πάντα φέρων ὄσα φαίνολις ἐσκέδασ᾽ Αὔως,
> φέρηις ὄιν, φέρηις αἶγα, φέρηις ἄπυ μάτερι παῖδα.

_____Hesperus, you bring back everything that Dawn has scattered away:

11 But with the exclusion, in all likelihood, of F 106. A praise of someone excelling as the "Lesbian aoidos" (perhaps Terpander, cf. Aristot. fr. 545 Rose) over those coming from foreign lands (πέρροχος, ὡς ὄτ᾽ ἄοιδος ὁ Λέσβιος ἀλλοδάποισιν), F 106 does not contain anything epithalamic in itself and has been included among the wedding songs only because of its dactylic rhythm.

12 F 110 and F 111 appear in two different categories because Hephaistion quotes them for metrical reasons, whereas [Demetrius] quotes them in relation respectively to generic conventions and the phenomenon of hyperbole.

13 Lasserre 1989: 36 ff. has expressed doubts on the choral nature of epithalamians and already [Demetrius] (*De eloc.* 167) claimed that wedding songs "are more appropriate to recital than song, and would not suit either a chorus or a lyre; unless something like a dialogic chorus may exist (χορὸς διαλεκτικός)." Yet a choral execution is typical of the whole epithalamic tradition (Lyghounis 1991: 180 points out Hom. *Od.* 4.15 ff. as the only sure exception). Furthermore it is evident that [Demetrius] is discussing the question on a merely stylistic basis without being able to exploit a specific record of evidence (and he himself however posits the possibility of lyric "contrasts").

you bring back sheep and goats and take away the daughter from her mother.[14]

Catullus 62.20–23, performed by the semichorus of the maidens singing against the male, refers to the same moment:

> *Hespere, qui caelo fertur crudelior ignis?*   20
> *Qui natam possis complexu avellere matris,*
> *complexu matris retinentem avellere natam*
> *et iuveni ardenti castam donare puellam.*

> Evening star, what fire more cruel does the sky bear?   20
> You who can tear a daughter from the embrace of her mother,
> tear away a daughter who clings to her mother's embrace,
> and give the chaste girl to a young man on fire.

And the young replied (62.26–29) in a way which may look back at Sapph. F 104b (ἀστέρων πάντων ὁ κάλλιστος):[15]

> *Hespere, qui caelo lucet iocundior ignis?*   26
> *Qui desponsa tua firmes conubia flamma,*
> *quae pepigere viri, pepigerunt ante parentes*
> *nec iunxere prius quam se tuus extulit ardor.*

> Evening star, what more pleasing fire shines in heaven?   26
> You who with your flame affirm matrimonial vows,
> vows men have sworn, sworn before their parents,
> not to join before your splendor has gone out.

---

14 Lobel-Page inserted *cruces* (but perhaps the second *crux* should be written after the second φέρηις, limiting thus, even if only a little, the extension of the corruption), whereas Voigt has posited for line 2 a sequence ia + pher[2da] (for pher[2da] cf. F 136). Yet, as shown by the Catullan imitation, a change of meter within a stanza sung by the one and same group of singers is highly unlikely and does not find parallels in Sappho's other dactylic hexameters. As many have recognized, l. 2 must also have been originally a hexameter.

15 The witness of Himerius (in two different passages: *Or.* 46.8 and 47.17) guarantees that this portion of the text echoing Hom. *Il.* 22.318 ἕσπερος, ὃς κάλλιστος ἐν οὐρανῶι ἵσταται ἀστήρ refers to Hesperus.

From Sappho Catullus picks up not only the motif of Hesperus bringing anxiety to the maidens and joy to the young men but also a stylistic fabric based on iteration. To these features Catullus adds the epanalexis *complexu ... matris / complexu ... matris,* in keeping with a process of oral mimesis that wants to communicate the impression of extemporaneity and immediacy.

What is certain is that both poets aim at representing with the greatest formal polish a traditional theme that leaves very little room for originality or innovation.

Likewise, two passages (F 107 and F 114) that touch upon the end of the status of maidenhood well suit a group of maidens, but this time we have a contrast between a single voice and the chorus of female companions who, as a collective entity, embody the condition of virginity itself. First F 107:

ἦρ᾽ ἔτι παρθενίας ἐπιβάλλομαι;

shall I still keep hold of virginity?

And then F 114:

ΝΥΜΦΗ—Παρθενία, Παρθενία, ποῖ με λίποισ᾽ ἀ<π>οίχηι;
ΠΑΡΘΕΝΙΑ—†οὐκέτι ἤξω πρὸς σέ, οὐκέτι ἤξω.†

BRIDE—Virginity, virginity, why are you leaving me? Where are you going?
VIRGINITY—I shall never come back to you, never.

Furthermore, in the anadiplosis of line 1 (Παρθενία, Παρθενία) and presumably also of l. 2 of the latter fragment we find again the same taste for iteration that we have observed in the previous fragments.[16]

[Demetrius] is an obscure Hellenistic author of a treatise (*On Style*) entirely focused on defining and exemplifying the canon of the different stylistic registers (grand, elegant, plain, and passionate), a work probably addressed to advanced students of rhetoric. At *De eloc.* 140 he remarks about the anadiplosis:

---

16 On the tropes of sound in hymenaic context see Neri 2003: 424 on Erinn. fr. 4.51 (= fr. 401 *SH*).

The attractive charms which derive from the use of tropes are evident and most numerous in Sappho. For instance the bride who addresses her own virginity by means of anadiplosis saying: [quotation of line 1 of F 114] and Virginity replies to her using the same trope [quotation of line 2 of F 114]. In this way more charm is achieved than if the words have not been repeated and we did not have the trope. Although the anadiplosis seems to have been invented more to engender emotion, yet in Sappho even stylistic devices that aim at emotion are used charmingly.

What [Demetrius] wants to single out is the process of mingling different styles so that a trope proper to a given style (in this case the anadiplosis, that in itself would belong to the passionate style) may occur within a style that is altogether different (in this case the elegant style, proper of Sappho).

If deprived of the rhetorical frame imposed upon it, the remark is in itself correct inasmuch as Sappho was able to express, in ways that combined immediacy and elegance, features typical of a poetic tradition that must have had its strength in popular verbal jest and easy memorization of its contents.

§3   In Front of the Bedchamber

Another essential moment of the wedding ritual, upon which our scarce fragments allow us to shed some light, is that of the choral song performed in front of the door of the nuptial chamber once the spouses had entered and the door had been locked. F 111, also echoed by Catullus (61.76 *claustra pandite ianuae*) refers to the entrance of the newlyweds in the thalamos: the refrain ὐμήναον is repeated after each single verse following a rhythmical movement that seems to alternate[17] pherecrateans and enoplians:

ἴψοι δὴ τὸ μέλαθρον·
ὐμήναον,
ἀέρρετε τέκτονες ἄνδρες·
ὐμήναον,
γάμβρος (εἰσ)έρχεται ἶσος Ἄρευι,   5

---

17 The reconstruction of l. 5 is uncertain: see Voigt's apparatus.

<ὑμήναον>
ἄνδρος μεγάλω πόλυ μέζων.
<ὑμήναον>,

5 εἶσ᾽ ἴσ᾽ Lobel

High up, the chamber lintel
Hymenaon!
Raise up, carpenters!
Hymenaon!
Is arriving a groom who resembles Ares,   5
Hymenaon!
Much bigger than a big man.
Hymenaon!

These lines are a concentration of performative and illocutory utterances that articulate the ritual action with perfect synchronism.

What is highlighted is what is traditional: suffice it to mention the refrain ὑμήναον, the comparison with Ares (analogous to the comparison with Achilles in another epithalamian alluded to by Himerius[18]) and the emphasis on the physical superiority of the groom (ἄνδρος μεγάλω πόλυ μέζων), assimilated thus to the Homeric Ajax, ἠΰς τε μέγας τε | ἔξοχος Ἀργείων κεφαλήν τε καὶ εὐρέας ὤμους (*Il.* 3.226–27) by means of that kind of hyperbole so common in folk songs and particularly dear to Sappho elsewhere as well (cf. F 31.14–15 χλωροτέρα δὲ ποίας | ἔμμι; 98a.6–7 ξανθοτέρα<ι>ς ... τα<ὶ>ς κόμα<ι>ς δάιδος; 156.1–2 πόλυ πάκτιδος ἀδυμελεστέρα ... | χρύσω χρυσοτέρα; 167 ὠίω πόλυ λευκότερον) which has been called "supra-superlative."[19]

F 110 refers instead to a different phase of the wedding ritual, that succeeding the locking of the bed-chamber. This is the moment when, according to the established ritual custom, the female friends of the bride, in the jocular tone discussed above by [Demetrius], pretended to want to re-

---

18   *Or.* 9.16 = Sapph. T 218.

19   See Zellner 2006: 293: "an extreme is surpassed in a way that is impossibile, or which at least is conceptually or imaginatively difficult." As Zellner himself observes, the recognition of this stylistic device preempts any other explanation for F 111.7, especially that by Kirk 1963, who saw in the sentence a phallic allusion.

claim their companion and take her back. So they commenced mocking the groom's friend who was in charge of locking the thalamos[20] and forbidding access to it:

θυρώρωι πόδες ἐπτορόγυιοι,
τὰ δὲ σάμβαλα πεμπεβόηα,
πίσσυγγοι δὲ δέκ᾽ ἐξεπόνησαν.

Seven arms' length long are the porter's feet,
his sandals are made of five ox-hides,
ten shoemakers worked on them.

Here too, as in the case of the assimilation of the groom to Ares or Achilles, the rhetorical figure of the hyperbole is what triggers the jocular mood. Even in the cases for which we do not have positive precedents, it is thus legitimate to posit that Sappho presented these touches of rustic humor as drawing on conventional motifs. In this case Sappho's artistry is visible entirely in its refined, polished form; this is especially evident here in the parallelism between the first two sentences, both of them having at the end of the line a five-syllable compound whose first element is a numeral, and the inversion in the third sentence, with the numeral in the middle of the line.

The jocular mood that seems to be prevalent in these songs performed in front of the bed-chamber ("epithalamians" in the literal sense of the word)[21] recalls by contrast the pathetic mood at the beginning of the ritual, which was tinged, from the point of view of the bride and her companions, with the realization of the impending loss of maidenhood.

§4 Farewells

Though not entirely unambiguous in their interpretation, the two forms of address that we find in F 116 and F 117 are most likely understood as a farewell to the couple at the end of the wedding ritual.

---

20 Cf. Poll. 3.42 and Hesych. Θ 957.
21 On the relationship between "hymenaon" and "epithalamian," see Muth 1954.

While in F 116:

χαῖρε, νύμφα, χαῖρε, τίμιε γάμβρε, πόλλα ...

Farewell, bride, and farewell you too, honored bridegroom!

we find the use of imperative addressed to both the bride and the bridegroom, in F 117:

†χαίροις ἀ νύμφα, χαιρέτω δ' ὀ γάμβρος

1 fort. χαίροις σύ, νύμφα

Farewell to you, bride, and farewell to you, bridegroom!

the use of the second person (but expressed with a desiderative optative)[22] for the bride is paralleled by the third-person singular imperative addressed to the groom. The two formulations differ anyway only in tonal nuances.

The farewell nature of the markers χαῖρε and χαίροις is made most evident by the comparison both with Theocr. 18.49 χαίροις, ὦ νύμφα· χαίροις, εὐπένθερε γαμβρέ, a line which introduces the conclusive section of the *Epithalamian for Helen*,[23] and with ὦ χαίρετε χαίρετ᾽, ἄνδρες in the final of Aristophanes' *Pax* (l. 1357), immediately after the last refrain "Hymen, Hymenaeus!" (a farewell addressed not to the spouses but to the participants of the feast).[24]

§5   Praise and Felicitations

Pinning down the praise of the bride or bridegroom exactly within the temporal frame of the wedding rite is problematic, no doubt also because such praise was most likely to be repeated at different stages. Yet the motif of the

22 This is true only if the corruption of the textual tradition of Heph. 4.2, p. 13 C., and of the other witnesses does not also involve the verbal form χαίροις. Since from the same Hephaistion we find out that the line must consist of a catalectic iambic trimeter, what really does not fit in is the long syllable ἀ after the initial iambic foot with spondaic form χαίροις: hence my conjecture χαίροις σύ, νύμφα (other emendations are recorded in Voigt's apparatus).

23 Cf. also Luc. *Symp.* 41 νυμφίε, καὶ σὺ δὲ χαῖρε and P.Ryl. 17.3 νύμφα φίλη μέγα χαῖρε.

24 Likewise, also χαῖρε, φίλος addressed to the winner in Pind. *N.* 3.76 is a farewell form of address, even if outside an epithalamic context.

felicitations (μακαρισμός) addressed to the spouses must have been related to the final phase of the ritual in front of the nuptial chamber, that is, immediately before the final farewell.

We have only one certain extant instance of this motif in Sappho, that is F 112, a fragment otherwise inopportunely reproduced in the editions of both Lobel-Page and Voigt as a continuous piece. F 112 instead consists most clearly of the remnants of a poem in which the chorus addresses the bridegroom first and the bride second (or, alternatively, a semichorus of maidens addresses the groom first and a semichorus of young boys the bride second), with a change of direction in address between ll. 2 and 3 :

- ὄλβιε γάμβρε, σοὶ μὲν δὴ γάμος ὡς ἄραο
ἐκτετέλεστ᾽, ἔχηις δὲ πάρθενον ἂν ἄραο.

- σοὶ χάριεν μὲν εἶδος, ὄππατα <δ᾽ ....>
μέλλιχ᾽, ἔρος δ᾽ ἐπ᾽ ἰμέρτωι κέχυται προσώπωι
<.............> τετίμακ᾽ ἔξοχον Ἀφροδίτα.   5

5 init. <καί σε κόραν> Di Benedetto (καί σε iam Lobel)   ἔξοχον Lobel: ἐξόχως ἡ codd.; ἔξοχά σ᾽ Weil

To the Bridegroom—Happy bridegroom, behold, for you the wedding rites
you desired are complete, and you possess the virgin you desired.

To the Bride—Enchanting is your countenance, and your eyes [...]
sweet as honey, and love is poured over your lovely face,
[and among virgins you] Aphrodite has honored to the highest degree.   5

Theocritus will pick up the very same apostrophe ὄλβιε γάμβρε at line 16 of his *Epithalamian for Helen*, which is imagined as performed in front of the nuptial chamber freshly decorated (πρόσθε νεογράπτω θαλάμω 3). Likewise, the words ἐκτετέλεστ᾽ and ἔχηις at l. 2 seem also to refer to something that has just been concluded or is about to be over.

On the level of signifiers, we find here a new feature of popular orality, the use of the "rhyme" ἄραο / ἄραο between lines 1 and 2. This is an element that finds in Sappho a precise parallel, and not by chance, in another epithalamic passage (F 115):

τίωι σ᾽, ὦ φίλε γάμβρε, κάλως ἐικάσδω;
ὄρπακι βραδίνωι σε μάλιστ᾽ ἐικάσδω.

To what, dear bridegroom, would I well liken you?
Best to a slender bough would I liken you.

Summing up, Sappho composed nuptial songs intended to become an integral element of the different moments of the wedding ritual, and we cannot detect any hint suggesting that one and the same poem may relate to different moments of the rite itself. Sophisticated as Sappho's art may have been, our poet refashioned traditional motifs according to the specific performative needs of the various phases of the festival. Catullus also reproduces very ancient topoi and patterns and it is indeed possible that his poem 61 had been actually performed during the wedding ceremony for the marriage of Lucius Manilius Torquatus and Junia (or Vinia) Aurunculeia. But in 61, unlike the contrasting songs in 62, Catullus has certainly revolutionized the stage direction and pragmatics of the traditional epithalamian. Suffice it here to recall that his long poem—a sort of *summa* of the different potentialities of the epithalamic genre—is structured in various sections, each one referring to a different ritual phase of the ceremony and marked by its typical orders and instructions. In 61 we have thus the hymn to Hymenaeus prompting him to take part in the feast, the invitation to the bride to appear on the stage, the procession, the bride entering the thalamos and the songs sung in front of it.[25]

§6   Hector and Andromache

How should one consider the epicizing re-evocation[26] of the wedding of Hector and Andromache in the last poem of the second book (F 44), if compared to the epithalamians of the sequence F 104–117, so immediately linked to the occasion and essential in their expressive register?

25   See Tomsen 1992: 26 ff.

26   On the redeployment of epic formulae (τάχυς ἄγγελος 3, κλέος ἄφθιτον 4, ἄχω θεσπεσία 27) and the relationship of F 44 with the diction of the Ionian epic, see Marzullo 1958: 115–94 and Ferrari 1986.

We possess a fairly large part of F 44 thanks to the contributions of two papyri published respectively in 1914 (P.Oxy. 1232) and 1927 (P.Oxy. 2076):

Κυπρο.[   ]ας·
κᾶρυξ ἦλθε θε[   ]ελε[...].θεις
Ἴδαος ταδεκα...φ[..].ις τάχυς ἄγγελος
<"   >   3a
τάς τ᾽ ἄλλας Ἀσίας .[.]δε.αν κλέος ἄφθιτον·
Ἕκτωρ καὶ συνέταιρ[ο]ι ἄγοισ᾽ ἐλικώπιδα   5
Θήβας ἐξ ἰέρας Πλακίας τ᾽ ἀπ᾽ [ἀϊ]ν<ν>άω
ἄβραν Ἀνδρομάχαν ἐνὶ ναῦσιν ἐπ᾽ ἄλμυρον
πόντον· πόλλα δ᾽ [ἐλί]γματα χρύσια κάμματα
πορφύρ[α] κὰτ αὔτμενα, ποίκιλ᾽ ἀθύρματα,
ἀργύρα τ᾽ ἀνάριθμα ποτήρια κἀλέφαις."   10
ὣς εἶπ᾽, ὀτραλέως δ᾽ ἀνόρουσε πάτη[ρ] φίλος,
φάμα δ᾽ ἦλθε κατὰ πτόλιν εὐρύχορον φίλοις.
αὔτικ᾽ Ἰλιάδαι σατίναι[ς] ὑπ᾽ ἐυτρόχοις
ἄγον αἰμιόνοις, ἐπ[έ]βαινε δὲ παῖς ὄχλος
γυναίκων τ᾽ ἄμα παρθενίκα[ν] τ..[..].σφύρων   15
χῶρις δ᾽ αὖ Περάμοιο θύγ[α]τρες [
ἴππ[οις] δ᾽ ἄνδρες ὔπαγον ὐπ᾽ ἄρ[ματα
π[άντ]ες ἠίθεοι, μεγάλω[σ]τι δ[
δ[   ]. ἀνίοχοι φ[.....].[
π[   ]ξα.ο[20
<   desunt aliquot versus   >
                       ἴ]κελοι θέοι[ς
                    ] ἄγνον ἀολ[λε-
ὄρμαται [   ]νον ἐς Ἴλιο[ν
αὖλος δ᾽ ἀδυ[μ]έλης [   ]τ᾽ ὀνεμίγνυ[το
καὶ ψ[ό]φο[ς κ]ροτάλ[ων   ]ως δ᾽ ἄρα πάρ[θενοι   25
ἄειδον μέλος ἄγν[ον, ἴκα]νε δ᾽ ἐς αἴθ[ερα
ἄχω θεσπεσία γελ[
πάνται δ᾽ ἦς κὰτ ὄδο[ις
κράτηρες φίαλαί τ᾽ ὀ[...]υεδε[..]..εακ[.].[
μύρρα καὶ κασία λίβανός τ᾽ ὀνεμείχνυτο,   30
γύναικες δ᾽ ἐλέλυσδον ὄσαι προγενέστερα[ι,

πάντες δ' ἄνδρες ἐπήρατον ἴαχον ὄρθιον
Πάον' ὀνκαλέοντες Ἑκάβολον εὐλύραν
ὕμνην δ' Ἕκτορα κ Ἀνδρομάχαν θεο<ε>ικέλο[ις.

2 θέ[ων Jurenka 3 τάδ' ἔκαστα Diehl 9 κὰτ ἀύτμενα Lobel (cf. F 101.2) 15 τ' ἀπ[αλ]οσφύρων
Pfeiffer 20 ἔ]ξαγο[ν Hunt 25 λιγέ]ως Lobel

Cyprus [...]
the herald came r[unning ...]
Idaos, swift messenger, [...] each of these things:
["   ]   3a
and of the rest of Asia [...] glory everlasting:
Hector and his companions conduct the bride of glancing eyes   5
from holy Thebe and from Placia [ever]-flowing,
gentle Andromache on ships across the salt sea;
and behold many bracelets of gold and gowns
of purple go with the wind's breezes, playthings of many kinds
and countless goblets of silver and ivory."   10
So he said, and swiftly (Hector's) beloved father rose to his feet
and along the broad streets of the city the rumor came to his friends.
Straightaway the ladies of Ilion upon well-wheeled chariots
drove their mules, and up mounted the whole crowd
of ladies and of virgins of [slender] ankles,   15
and apart the daughters of Priam [...]
and below the chariots all the youths
yoked the horses, and splendidly [...]
[...] the charioteers [...]
...bore out...   20
...
[...] like the gods
[...] sacred [...]all
rushes to Ilion [...]
and the sweet sounding flute [...]mingled with
the noise of castanets, and [with clear voice] the virgins   25
intoned the holy song and [came] up to the sky

the infinite echo […]
and everywhere there was in the streets […]
wine bowls and goblets […]
myrrh and cassia and incense mingled together   30
and the elder women cried "eleleu"
and all the men raised the lovely clear cry
calling upon Paean, the far-shooter, of the beautiful lyre,
and hymned Hector and Andromache like the gods.

Two extreme interpretative approaches to F 44 are exemplified on the one hand by those critics who recognize in it a kind of "ballad" detached from any specific occasion,[27] and on the other hand by Rösler's view,[28] according to which there would be a specific correspondence between the temporal phases of the feasts and the stage directions embedded in the text about the arrival of the bride, the movements of the relative groups, the singing of the paean.

At first sight the former interpretative approach seems unassailable but it is not without some objections, either: place and time of performance are left suspended in an unlikely vacuum and the resulting narrative structure is most peculiar. We are presented with a record of events that seems to be cut out from between the arrival of the ship of the spouses and the paean sung by all the men in honor of the "godlike" couple. In between, once the herald Idaos had enumerated the gifts brought by Andromache and Priam has stirred from his throne, we have a kind of "script" where the poet/regisseur establishes the different movements of a whole city:

- the women of Ilios yoke the mules to the wagons on which mature women and maidens alike step;
- a closer framing on Priam's daughters;
- the men yoke the horses to the chariots;
- lacuna (arrival of the ship carrying the spouses and the bridal gifts?);
- a tuned concert of auloi and crotala;
- song of the maidens;
- myrrh, cassia, and incense are spread around;
- ritual cry of the mature women at the slaughter of the sacrificial victims;
- paean sung by the men.

27 See Lesky 1962: 194 and Kakridis 1966.
28 Rösler 1975.

What is the core or the sense of such a chain of motifs? Within Greek choral lyric Stesichorus and Bacchylides do indeed compose lyric narratives with a strong acoustic and visual impact but free from an immediate link to a specific concrete occasion; however, these are in any event stories that have the breadth and development of a narrative tale. In Sappho we find instead a series of framed images that are as essential and persuasive as they are inadequate to build up a self-contained story.

An opposite approach is no less debatable and Pernigotti[29] has effectively dismantled it, observing that "a coincidence between the time of song and sung time" is ruled out by the sheer "quantity of actions and movements described in the text, once we relate them to the duration of the poem itself."

The re-evocation of Hector's arrival at Troy from Thebe below Placia and of the enlivening that animates Ilios like a wave may instead assume an exemplary value if we consider it as a "typical epic scene" (as for instance a scene of visit or sacrifice): that is, as a series of actions that preserves the memory of a social practice by describing its distinct features and by performing through a narrative mode a function that is also prescriptive.

In other words, the so-called *Epithalamian for Hector and Andromache* does not reveal, unlike the epithalamians of F 104–17, an immediate pragmatic value, but it is not necessarily a song entirely deprived of an occasion or context, either.

As usual, we do not possess the documentary evidence necessary to reconstruct the specific occasion, but we would like to know whether the setting of the wedding in the Troad and the arrival of the bride by ship bear some reference to the real situation.[30] Yet, the general function of mythical narratives linked to the nuptial theme could but perform a "proemial" function. They were narratives that worked as proems to the actual rite and its songs, just as the rhapsodic hymns (called "proems" already in Pindar and Thucydides as is well known)[31] introduced the recital of episodes relative to the great epic saga.

Pausanias (10.8.10) speaks of a proem with reference to a hymn (in alcaic stanzas) to Apollo by Alcaeus (F 307), of which we have only the mere beginning (ὦναξ Ἄπολλον, παῖ μεγάλω Δίος). Of similar nature must have been also

---

29 Pernigotti 2001: 15.
30 See Pernigotti 2001: 16.
31 Pind. *N.* 2.3, Thuc. 3.104.

a hymn in Aeolic pentameter ascribed to Sappho by Voigt (F 44 A a), and to Alcaeus by Lobel-Page (F 304 col. I), about the privileges that Artemis has obtained from her father Zeus in a colloquium sanctioned by a solemn oath.

From such "proems" derive also some fragments, minimal as they are, of Terpander, fellow country-man of Sappho but fifty years earlier than our poet. These are fr. 697 *PMG* (= fr. 2 Gostoli) and 698 *PMG* (= fr. 3 Gostoli): the former introduced a νόμος in honor of Apollo, the latter a hymn to Zeus.[32] Some of Alcman's poems too performed a proemial function, as fr. 10 (b), fr. 14, and fr. 26 *PMGF* (the last one in dactylic hexameters).[33]

Sappho's F 44, with its tale of the ship-journey of Hector and Andromache from Thebe below Placia to Ilion, of the movements within the city that led up to the welcoming cry of the women at the slaughtering of the sacrificial victims, and the paean calling for good wishes sung by the men at the first sight of the spouses who have just arrived, might have worked very well as a "proem" performed immediately before the banquet on separate tables hosting the members of the two familial groups.

From this perspective the time of the song and the sung time are not in "synchrony," except inasmuch as there is a "zero point," namely the concluding moment of the poem. Here begins the sacrifice that leads to the wedding banquet, and the newly arrived spouses are welcomed to the cry of the paean. It is at this moment that the two temporal sequences of ceremony and song might collapse the one into the other and the mythical narrative open into the actuality of the wedding feast.

---

32 On the problematic nature of Terpander's proems and especially on the two quoted here, see Gostoli 1990: xxix–xxxiii and 128–36. In particular, there is debate about whether our ancient sources quoting these passages used "proem" simply to refer to the initial part of a poem or to a whole introductory poem in its entirety. However, of fundamental importance for our discourse is the evidence provided by [Plut.] *De mus.* 6.1133c, according to which Terpander's "citharodic proems" introduced, like the Homeric Hymns, the performance of passages from Homer and other poets.

33 On F 26 see especially Calame 1983: 472 ff.

XI Contexts

§1 The Song of Farewell

The ten more or less complete strophes of F 94 (one of the fragments recovered from the Berlin parchment, P.Berol. 9722) have often been at the
center of the debate on the nature of Sappho's circle and on the relationships
that developed within it.[1] There have been rather fewer attempts to specify the
destination and the occasions of this poetic performance,[2] even though in the
two last remaining strophes the lyric discourse focuses precisely on these aspects:

τεθνάκην δ᾽ ἀδόλως θέλω·
_ἄ με ψισδομένα κατελίμπανεν   2
πόλλα καὶ τόδ᾽ ἔειπέ [μοι·
ὤιμ᾽ ὡς δεῖνα πεπ[όνθ]αμεν,
_Ψάπφ᾽, ἦ μάν σ᾽ ἀέκοισ᾽ ἀπυλιμπάνω.   5
τὰν δ᾽ ἔγω τάδ᾽ ἀμειβόμαν·
χαίροισ᾽ ἔρχεο κἄμεθεν
_μέμναισ᾽, οἶσθα γὰρ ὡς <σε> πεδήπομεν·   8
αἰ δὲ μή, ἀλλά σ᾽ ἔγω θέλω
ὄμναισαι [...(.)].[..(.)].εαι

---

1 See Wilamowitz 1913: 48–52, Di Benedetto 1987: 55–59, Greene 1996c, Stehle 1997: 306–
11, Tsomis 2001: 223–26.
2 Aloni 1998: 230 opportunely notes that the succession of actions accomplished in the past
by "Sappho's" interlocutrix seem to describe a linear progression "in the direction of choral activity, that is perhaps first described at lines 25–28" even though he sees in this ode a typical
example of a poem directed to a restricted audience.

_ὀσ[..........] καὶ κάλ᾽ ἐπάσχομεν·   11
πό[λλοις γὰρ στεφάν]οις ἴων
καὶ βρ[όδων κρο]κίων τ᾽ ὔμοι
_κα..[.......] πὰρ ἔμοι π<ε>ρεθήκα<ο>   14
καὶ πόλλαις ὑπαθύμιδας
πλέκταις ἀμφ᾽ ἀπάλαι δέραι
_ἀνθέων ε[.......] πεποημέναις   17
καὶ π.....[   ]. μύρωι
βρενθείωι.[   ]ρυ[..]ν
_ἐξαλ<ε>ίψαο κα[ὶ βασ]ιληίωι   20
καὶ στρώμν[αν ἐ]πὶ μολθάκαν
ἀπάλαν παρ[...]..ων
_ἐξίης πόθο[ν   ].νίδων,   23
κωὔτε τις [οὔ]τε τι
ἶρον οὐδ᾽ ὐ[   ]
_ἔπλετ᾽ ὄππ[οθεν ἄμ]μες ἀπέσκομεν,   26
οὐκ ἄλσος .[   ].ρος
                ] ψόφος
                ]...οιδιαι   29

11 ὄσ[σα Schubart, dein τέρπνα τε Jurenka 13 κρο]κίων Sitzler 14 κάρα[ι σῶι] Perrotta 17 ἐ[ράτων Schubart 18 καὶ πόλλωι λ[legit Schubart 19 ῥύ[δο]ν Zuntz 22]ονων Schubart,].διων Zuntz; παρ[ὰ Μαι]όνων Theander, παρ[ὰ Σα]ρδίων West 23 νεα]νίδων olim Lobel, νε]ανίδων Zuntz (negant Lobel-Page), ὐμε]υνίδων Page 24 [γάμος Bowra 27 χ]όρος Lobel-Page 28 κροτάλων] Theander 29]ενιοιδιαι vel]ενεοιδιαι Zuntz (δ᾽ ἴαι?)

... and truly I wish I were dead.
She left me weeping   2

copiously and said this [to me] :
"Alas, how terribly we suffer,
Sappho: truly unwillingly I leave you."   5

And I responded to her thus:
"Farewell, and remember
me, since you know that we cared for you: 8

and if not—but I want
to recall to your memory [...]
how many [pleasant] and good things we enjoyed: 11

[for] many [garlands] of violets
and of roses and also of [crocuses]
you placed [about your head] next to me   14

and many plaited necklaces
made of [enchanting] flowers³
around the delicate neck,   17

and with much [...] perfume
floral [...]
and royal did you anoint yourself in profusion   20

and on soft coverlets
[...] you placated the desire [...]
of tender [...],   23

and there was neither [wedding festival] nor
sanctuary nor [...]
from which we were far   26

nor wood [nor] dancing ground
[nor] sound [of castanets]
...   29

§2   Interiors

Sappho, whose name appears in the vocative at line 5, recalls her parting from
a young woman who shortly before left her in tears, perhaps for a marriage in
a faraway place.

---

3 I believe that the lacuna of line 17 can be filled, rather than with a verb parallel to περεθήκαο
14 (e.g., ἔ[βαλες of Theander), with an adjective that determines ἀνθέων, as ἐ[ράτων of Schubart
(for the construction with the simple genitive in place of ἐκ + genitive cf. e.g. Thuc. 4.31.2 ἔρυμα
... λίθων ... πεποιημένον). In such a case also ὑπαθύμιδας 15 is governed by περεθήκαο.

That the parting is a very recent event is suggested by "truly I wish I were dead" of line 1. This phrase, notwithstanding some opposing voices who attribute it to the girl at the moment of departure,[4] should be assigned to Sappho above all on stylistic grounds. We know of no case, whether in Sappho or Homer, of lines spoken by one person that are interrupted *ex abrupto* and then taken up again with a "he/she said."

Furthermore, if we are able to attribute the phrase to the girl at the moment of her departure, we would be faced with an "incongruent emotional climax. It is not possible to say 'this separation makes me desire death,' as sorrowful as that is, and then 'truly unwillingly I leave you.'"[5]

Finally, the asyndeton of line 2 can be interpreted as a symptom of the anguish expressed in the first line,[6] but it would be ill understood at the juncture between direct discourse and narrative.

Now, Sappho would like to be dead but—she recalls—at the actual moment of parting she was able to pronounce words of comfort to soothe the girl's lamentation.

After the first words of farewell, the recall of the past is prompted by a colloquial mode that in turn promotes an exercise in memory.[7] The memory of the shared past seems to consist of three images, each of which occupies a strophe. First (lines 12–14) garlands (cf. F 81) of violets, roses, and crocuses, with which the young woman frequently plaited her own hair next to Sappho. Then follow (lines 15–17) the floral necklaces that she often placed about her delicate neck. Finally (lines 18–20) there is the precious ointment with which she perfumed her skin.

The scene places Sappho and the young woman in the former's home, if it is true that already in the Homeric poems[8] a combination like πὰρ ἔμοι (line 14) usually denotes, analogous to *chez moi*, finding oneself not only near but in the house of someone.

---

4 See especially Burnett 1983: 293–300.

5 Vetta 1999: 140.

6 Robbins 1990: 114.

7 The turn of line 9 ff. αἰ δὲ μή, ἀλλά σ' ἔγω θέλω | ὄμναισαι finds an interesting parallel (but with the transition from "and if you don't remember" to "and if you wish to recall") in a line of Socrates in the *Symposium* of Plato (201a): ἐπὶ δὲ τούτοις ἀναμνήσθητι τίνων ἔφησθα ἐν τῶι λόγωι εἶναι τὸν Ἔρωτα· εἰ δὲ βούλει, ἐγώ σ' ἀναμνήσω. For the juxtaposition "farewell" / "remember" cf., with Page 1955: 77, Hom. *Od.* 8.461 ff. χαῖρε, ξεῖν', ἵνα καί ποτ' ἐὼν ἐν πατρίδι γαίηι | μνήσηι ἐμεῖ'.

8 Cf. Hom. *Il.* 13.627, *Od.* 9.427 and 11.490, and see *LSJ* s.v. παρά, B II 2: "at one's house or place" and, in reference to the passage of Sappho, Hutchinson 2001: 145: "at my house."

A strophe follows (lines 21–23) in which on "soft covers" the girl, now far away, satisfied the desire (her own or that of her young friends). This strophe, whatever its exact sense, with καί at the beginning and its syntactic articulation, shows itself to be parallel to the three that precede it. The whole sequence of lines 12–23 is configured as one homogenous distillation of memories.

And further we should note that these στρῶμναι should be covers used not for a picnic or seat on which to repose, but for a bed on which they are spread for the entire night.[9]

§3   Sleeping Together

But let us look more closely at lines 21–23. For this strophe Wilamowitz was only able to read the area of text to the left of the lacunae, as he was basing his judgments on the second edition of the parchment made by W. Schubart (1907). He was thus not able to use the readings relative to the verse ends (the fruit of the discovery of another parchment fragment) that were to be published by Lobel in 1925.[10] Accordingly, he thought that the girl was satisfying her own need for rest.[11]

Rather, on the basis of comparison with several Homeric passages (*Il.* 1.469 ἐξ ἔρον ἔντο, 13.636 ἐξ ἔρον εἶναι, 24.227 γόου ἐξ ἔρον εἴην), it is generally thought that the girl satisfied her own or her companions' sexual impulses on soft covers.

Both lines of interpretation are partly true and partly forced.

If that of Wilamowitz inevitably did not take into account a word in the genitive plural, i.e.,].νίδων,[12] dependent on πόθον, and he supplemented the sense of desire as desire of sleep, the other interpretation has often exaggerated πόθον with a concrete sexual sense that is not appropriate.

---

9   Cf. Pind. *P.* 1.28, *N.* 1.50, A. *Ch.* 671, Eur. *Ph.* 421, Plat. *Prot.* 321a and see Page 1955: 79.

10   Lobel 1925: 123.

11   Wilamowitz 1913: 49–50: "auf weichem Polster ... hast du das Bedürfnis (der Ruhe) gestillt"; Lardinois 1996: 164 n. 70 has recently understood "the girl is taking a nap."

12   The supplement νεα]νίδων of Lobel (1925) was confirmed by Zuntz (1938) with the reading]ανιδων, but subsequently Lobel-Page (1955) printed].νίδων, denying the possibility that the traces of the first letter after the lacuna could be restored as an α (rather one could make out "circuli arcus sup. dext.").

So Page, upon concluding that there are insufficient factual data to define the general sense of the stanza, added with embarrassed convolution that "there are obvious indications that it contained matter incompatible with the modern theory of Sappho's character."[13] By this he means, as he summarizes elsewhere,[14] the theory (reconstructed by Page himself through a cento of citations from W. Schmid, Wilamowitz, and Bowra) that Sappho had pupils to whom she imparted lessons in moral, social, and literary subjects, and that consequently she was "a highly respected member of society, a lady of unblemished character occupying with distinction a more or less official position in Mytilene." More recently Di Benedetto, after having observed that "there would be in effect a falling off, if, after having evoked in the first three strophes episodes of communal life (garlands, necklaces, unguent), in the final strophe Sappho recalled her naps to the girl," concluded that "it is very probable that in lines 21–23 of F 94 Sappho refers to erotic experiences of the girl in which she was herself in some way involved."[15]

Even if it is impossible to reconstruct every word and every syllable of the strophe, if we compare the text with other fragments of Sappho the answer is simple. To say that the girl satisfied the πόθος of delicate νεάνιδες or ὑμεύνιδες or similar is the same as saying that she occasionally satisfied the desire of this or that companion to sleep (i.e., to pass the night) on soft covers with her (that we are concerned here with another's desire and not her own seems guaranteed by the πάρ of line 22).

Whether it expresses a wish or a fact (the difference depends on an elision), the motif of sleeping together with a "companion" appears in F 126:

δαύοισ(') ἀπάλας ἑταίρας ἐν στήθεσιν

that you sleep/in sleeping on the breast of a gentle companion.[16]

We can compare a distich from the *Sylloge Theognidea*, where the act of sleeping together is effectively specified in a sense that incorporates gestures and acts of a homoerotic character (Thgn. 1063–64):

13 Page 1955: 80.
14 Page 1955: 111 (where, at n. 1, there are references to representatives of such a "theory").
15 Di Benedetto 1987: 14.
16 Against a reading of the passage in the sense of an epithalamium proposed by Welcker, see Burzacchini 1977: 180.

ἐν δ' ἥβηι πάρα μὲν ξὺν ὁμήλικι πάννυχον εὔδειν,
ἱμερτῶν ἔργων ἐξ ἔρον ἱέμενον.

In youth it is permitted to sleep the whole night with an age-mate,
satisfying the desire of [the] act of love.[17]

But in Sappho there is not this degree of specification (and it is unlikely to lie
hidden in the lacuna), nor should we look for it. Attentive to the as-yet unde-
fined and aimless sexuality of adolescence, the poet does not speak explicitly
or allusively, but recalls to the mind of her interlocutor the sensual pleasure of
sleeping together among age-mates and the affectionate ties that follow.

Moreover we also find in Sappho the negative inverse of this desire—passing
the night in solitude (the μονοκοιτεῖν of Aristoph. *Lys.* 592 and of *Lyr. adesp.* F
1.35 Powell)—in the very well-known F 168B, which Lobel-Page denied was by
Sappho but which was restored to her by Voigt. In this fragment it is probable
that the "I" is to be identified generically with a woman in love:[18]

Δέδυκε μὰν ἀ σελάννα
καὶ Πληΐαδες· μέσαι δὲ
νύκτες, παρὰ δ' ἔρχετ' ὤρα,
ἔγω δὲ μόνα κατεύδω.

The moon has set
and the Pleiades; it is the middle
of the night, time
goes by; I sleep alone.

---

17   Cf. also Thgn. 1335 ff.: ὄλβιος, ὅστις ἐρῶν γυμνάζεται οἴκαδε ἐλθών, | εὔδων σὺν καλῶι
παιδὶ πανημέριος and see Vetta 1980: 110.

18   Marzullo 1958: 1–60 adduces various important arguments in favor of the authenticity
of the quatrain, which is presumably complete. Rather less convincing is his rejection of the
hypothesis that Sappho here remodels a *Volkslied* (the affinity between lyric fragments of Sappho and Anacreon and the so-called Locrian songs was observed by Clearchos, fr. 33 Wehrli).
The more appropriate parallel is the little song which the young woman sings at Aristoph. *Ec.*
911–13 αἰαῖ, τί ποτε πείσομαι; | οὐχ ἥκει μοὐταῖρος· | μόνη δ' αὐτοῦ λείπομ'· ἡ | γάρ μοι μήτηρ
ἄλληι βέβηκεν (see Vetta 1989: 240). On the interpretation of ὤρα of l. 3 see Ferrari 1983; for a
reexamination of the notion of "popular poetry" in ancient Greece see Palmisciano 2003; for the
tradition of the lament of the abandoned woman see Esposito 2004: 59–70.

§4   Externals

Beginning with the opening of the strophe of lines 24–26, the poem's rhythm undergoes a quick acceleration as if through a dissemination of negative particles (οὔτε, οὐδέ, οὐ) a series of spaces or situations is enumerated, from which the lyric subject and the girl who dominates the scene were never absent.

Some references are certain: mentions of a sanctuary (ἴρον at l. 25),[19] woods (l. 27), the sound of musical instruments (l. 28, perhaps castanets),[20] conjectural, but very likely, a dancing space (l. 27).

Posidippus of Pella will summarize the sense of Protis' youth in the participation of "festivals of virgins" and in the modulation of the musical tune called "Boeotian" (58.1–3 A.-B.):

Ὡς ἐπ]ὶ νυμφίον ἦλθε λέχος Πρῶτις [˘˘--
    μητ]ρόθε, παρθενίους οὐκέτ᾽ ἔβη θα[λίας
ἠχήσ]ασα νόμον Βοιώτιον.

[When] Protis, [daughter of ...] on her mother's part, came
    to the marriage bed, no more did she come to festivals of virgins
[letting sound] the Boeotian tune ...

In a succession of communal occasions only with difficulty could wedding ceremonies have been lacking, ceremonies that not only would have represented for Sappho an occasion for which she was asked to compose songs but which, as we have seen especially in the case of F 27 (see III, § 1), also engaged the group in the formation of correctly instructed choruses. And so it is with a certain confidence that we can keep Bowra's supplement γάμος in the central lacuna of line 24.

Moreover, at l. 27, either the contiguity with vocabulary denoting fixed spaces or the comparison with l. A 11 (= F 70.11) of the poem discussed in II, § 3, leads us to understand χόρος not as "choral group" or "dance," but as "dancing space."

---

19 Cf. Hom. *Il.* 10.571, Alc. F 401Ba.2 ἐς Γλαυκώπιον ἴρον.

20 On κροτάλων] ψόφος (Theander) cf. F 44.25 ψ[ό]φο[ς κ]ροτάλ[ων, and more generally, on ψόφος in relation to sound given out by musical instruments cf. Eur. *Ba.* 687 λωτοῦ ψόφωι and *Cyc.* 443 ff. ψόφον | κιθάρας.

We have then, putting in parentheses the cases that are not sure, the series:

- (wedding festival)
- temple
- ?
- wood
- (dancing space)
- noise (of castanets)

The expressive dichotomy that characterizes the unraveling of the poem was accompanied therefore by a contrast between spaces internal and external to Sappho's[21] house. This is at one time an opposition between private activity related to elegance, beauty, and the pleasure of sleeping together, and activity tied to festive occasions and musical performances.

§5   Mourning Becomes Not Sappho

An apparent exception that actually confirms the tendencies that have appeared thus far in relation to the contextualization of Sappho's poetry appears in F 150, which Maximus of Tyre (18.9 = T 219) cites, saying that Sappho, like Socrates with Xanthippe, had reproached her daughter Cleis for excessive lamentation connected with bereavement:[22]

οὐ γὰρ θέμις ἐν μοισοπόλων <δόμωι>
θρῆνον ἔμμεν’ <.......> οὔ κ’ ἄμμι πρέποι τάδε.

---

21   See Greene 1996c: 11: "the interior space ... expands outward to the seemingly endless spaces of groves, shrines, and dances."

22   It is not immediately obvious in what meter the poem to which this fragment belonged was composed. Yet, on the one hand we can recognize a double choriamb γὰρ ... μοισοπόλων at line 1 and the choriamb ἄμμῐ πρέποι at line 2 (for the correption of the second syllable of ἄμμι—Lobel suggested the transposition of τάδε πρέποι—cf. F 16.19; 44.8 and 14; 105a.2, Alc. F 249.9 and 332.1 and see Marzullo 1958: 87–98, Gentili 1984, Martinelli 1997: 54). On the other hand we can also see at line 2 an incipit (- ⌣) and an ending (... - ⌣ -) both of the glyconic type. Voigt has hypothesized, with the implicit revival of a suggestion of Wilamowitz 1913: 20 n. 1, that the poem was in glyconics with choriambic expansion (greater asclepiads) used in a series (and so belonged to Book III of the Alexandrian edition), with the consequent necessity of postulating a lacuna of five syllables (⌣ - - ⌣ ⌣) between ἔμμεν’ (Blomfield: εἶναι codd.) and οὔ κ’ (Lobel: οὐκ codd.). Hence my suggestion <ἄπαυστον, Κλέϊς,>.

2 ἔμμεν' Lobel-Page (ἔμμεν iam Wilamowitz): εἶναι codd.   lac. statuit Wilamowitz, <ἄπαυστον, Κλέϊς,> suppleverim

... for it is not permitted in the house of the Muse's servants
that there be [incessantly, Cleis,] the song of mourning: this could not
suit us.

The textual tradition of Maximus of Tyre does not clarify for us whether Sappho intended programmatically to ban the threnos (understood as a disorderly manifestation of grief) from the houses of those who were the Muse's servants or, rather, limited herself to declaring that ritual lament should not at length suppress the practice of other types of song even after a sorrowful event. Yet it is also certain that the threnos from Homer on was part of the Muses' archive, in that it was a song type meant to be sung by specialized singers (*Il.* 24.720–21) if not, in a mythical sense, by the daughters of Mnemosyne (*Od.* 24.60). And it is precisely in a threnos (fr. 128c M.) that Pindar mentions the genres of paean and of dithyramb, and then focuses on particular forms of funeral lament (Linus, amoeban, Ialemus).[23]

Sappho herself composed a threnos on the death of Adonis (cf. F 140 and see below § 7), and an epigram of Posidippus directed to girls of Caria (51 A.-B.)[24] seems to allude to epikedia composed by Sappho, with its final exhortation to couple songs of Sappho to tears:

> Δακρυόεσσα[ι ἔπεσθε, θε]οῖς ἀνατείνατε πήχεις·
> τοῦτ' ἐπὶ πα[ιδὸς δρᾶτ' αὐ]τόμαται, Καρύαι,
> Τειλεσίης ἧς [νεῖσθε πρὸ]ς ἡρίον· ἀλλὰ φέρουσαι
> εἴαρι πορφυρέ[ου φύλλ' ἐς ἀ]γῶνα νέμους   4
> θῆλυ ποδήν[εμον ἔρνος] ἀείδετε, δάκρυσι δ' ὑμέων
> κολλάσθω Σα[πφῶι' ἄισμ]ατα, θεῖα μέλη.

1 ἔπεσθε, θε]οῖς Austin   2 πα[ιδὸς δρᾶτ' supplevi   3 [νεῖσθε Gronewald   4 φύλλ' Battezzato

---

23   For a comprehensive interpretation of the Pindar fragment, and especially the inclusion of the wedding hymn among funeral songs, see Cannatà Fera 1990: 136–44 and Neri 2003: 426–27.

24   On this epigram also in relation to Sappho's "threnodic" production see Battezzato 2003; for the text of lines 1–3 cf. Ferrari 2005: 203.

[Come] in tears, hold out your arms [to the gods: do]
    this of your own accord, Carian virgins, [for Telesia's]
daughter to whose tomb [you go]. Come, bringing
    in spring to the contest [flowers] of the [purple] wood   4
Sing of the gentle [bough] fleet as the wind, and to your tears
    let [songs of Sappho] be joined, divine melodies.

According to Aristoxenus of Tarentum (fr. 81 Wehrli) it was indeed Sappho who invented the Mixolydian harmony defined as "pathetic" and "adapted to tragedy" by [Plutarch] (*De mus.*16), which Plato (*R.* 3.398e) places in first position among the threnodic ἁρμονίαι and which, according to Aristotle (*Pol.* 8.1340b), makes us mournful and restrained in spirit.

Unless we give threnos a diverse and more generic value compared to the term's use continuously from Homer almost to Aeschylus and Pindar—that is, of a ritual funeral song quite distinct from spontaneous lamentation[25]—it is inconceivable that Sappho is saying that funereal song is unsuitable to a house animated by the cult of the Muses.

There would, however, be an explanation for the γάρ of l. 1, from the perspective of an exhortation to end a song of lament that risks becoming endless. This implies that suddenly Sappho said something like "enough already with the lament!" This is equivalent to saying that, as the conclusion, our distich should itself have been a part of a threnos composed by Sappho for a funeral that involved her familiar group.[26]

Now it is entirely natural that the poem be sung on such an occasion in the house of the poet at the moment that the house became something that it habitually was not, i.e., the theater of a ritual event: the focus of a ceremony in which a family of the Mytilenean aristocracy made the community a participant in the grief that had smitten it.

In this setting the reference to "servants of the Muses," tied to the practice of

---

25 Cf. Hom. *Il.* 24.720 ff., *Od.* 24.60–61, Hes. fr. 305.2–3 M.-W., Pind. *P.* 12.7–8 and *I.* 8.57–58, A. *Pers.* 686 and 937 ff., A. 990 ff., 1075, and 1541, *Ch.* 334–35 and 926, and see Palmisciano 1998, who claims this significance also for Sapph. F 150. For θρῆνος as spontaneous lament see Burzacchini 1977: 186.

26 Taking the parallelism of Socrates and Xanthippe a little too *à la lettre*, it has been thought that Sappho turns to Cleis at the moment of her own death, but see Treu 1954: 220.

a full range of songs, would have simultaneously signaled the close of the threnos and the dismissal from mourning—that is, not a break with the tradition of funeral lament, but an allusion to the knowledge that other festive occasions are imminent and that it is fruitless to continue to mourn.

Aloni[27] has opportunely recalled F 11,

> οὐδέ τι γὰρ κλαίων ἰήσομαι, οὔτε κάκιον
> θήσω τερπωλὰς καὶ θαλίας ἐφέπων

> neither will I find a cure in lamenting nor will I make worse
> these things through busying myself with pleasure and festival

and fr. 13 W.[2] of Archilochus, this last culminating in an exhortation to banish lament by passing through the phase of grief and returning to everyday life with its festive pleasures (ll. 9–10):

> ἀλλὰ τάχιστα
> τλῆτε, γυναικεῖον πένθος ἀπωσάμενοι.

> ... come, as soon as possible
> be strong and drive away feminine lamentation![28]

While F 11 and 13 (the so-called *Elegy to Pericles*) appear to be consolatory rather than threnodic fragments, the Sapphic distich seems to fit with the final movement of an effectively threnodic development that appears in another Archilochean elegy (to which the fragment cited by Plutarch, *Aud. poet.* 6.23b, belonged), to illustrate the poet's self-possessed reaction on hearing of the shipwreck of his brother-in-law. The fragment centers on the recollection, in the context of a commemorative threnos, of a rite (cremation) that was frustrated by the impossibility of burning the body of a man, wound in his funeral garments, because he had been lost at sea (fr. 9.10–11 W.[2]):[29]

---

27   Aloni 1997: 247–48.

28   On the motif of "satiety" and of the fruitlessness of lament cf. already Hom. *Il.* 23.157 γόοιο μὲν ἔστι καὶ ἆσαι, 24.524 οὐ γάρ τις πρῆξις πέλεται κρυεροῖο γόοιο, and 550 οὐ γάρ τι πρήξεις ἀκαχήμενος υἷος ἑῆος (Achilles speaks in all three cases).

29   On the orientation of this elegy see Palmisciano 1998: 195–201; more generally on threnodic elegy see Aloni 1998: 195–200.

εἰ κείνου κεφαλὴν καὶ χαρίεντα μέλεα
Ἥφαιστος καθαροῖσιν ἐν εἵμασιν ἀμφεπονήθη.

Oh if Hephaestus had attended to
his head and fair limbs in pure garments.

§6   A Cult Association?

Giuliana Lanata has maintained that with the term μοισόπολοι Sappho does
not intend to denote generically those who cultivate poetic activity, as do Euripides (*Alc.* 444–47, *Ph.* 1499–1501) and Nonnus (*Dion.* 45.185), but rather
declares her membership in a cultic association whose members were bound
to the cult of the Muses.[30] In support of her hypothesis Lanata has adduced an
epigraphic document from second century BC Thebes (*IG* 7.2484) in which,
in the context of a dedication to Dionysus, a guild of actors is designated as
ἐ[σ]θλὴ τεχνιτῶν μουσοπόλων σύνοδος. Gentili has restated that "the close-
ness of the Muses can only be explained by the hypothesis of an actual cult in
their honor within the community. Its existence is proven by the presence of
moisopolos, a word with precise religious meaning."[31]

But the use of μοισόπολοι is easily comparable, as Aloni observes,[32] to ex-
pressions such as ἀοιδός | Μουσάων θεράπων of Hes. *Th.* 99–100 and Μουσῶν
θεράποντα καὶ ἄγγελον of Theogn. 769, in which the poet affirms that he is the
Muses' servant without thereby presupposing any institutional link. One might
also adduce the case of ἱεραπόλος, which appears as a cult title in a variety of
epigraphic documents[33] but which Pindar uses in a metaphorical sense, with
allusion to the actual role of the poet, as an epithet of μάντις in *Parth.* 1.5–6 (=
fr. 94a M.) μάντις ὡς τελέσσω | ἱεραπόλος.[34]

---

30   Lanata 1969: 67.
31   Gentili 1988: 84 (and see also Calame 1977: I.162–72 and Grandolini 2000).
32   Aloni 1997: 248. Against the notion of a cult association see also Lasserre 1989: 116–18
and Hardie 2005: 15–17.
33   Cf. *IG* 14.256 (Gela) and 5(1).29 (Sparta) and *TAM* 2(1).174.*E* 9 (Sidyma).
34   For μάντις as a metaphor of the poet's activity cf. also Pind. fr. 75.13, *Pae.* 6.6 (= fr. 52f
M.) and fr. 150 M.

§7   Rites of Aphrodite

Another testimonium on Sappho's community as a cult association might be
provided by a sequence of an epithalamium in Himerius (*Or.* 9.4, p. 75–76 Colonna = Sapph. T 194), who means to illustrate "Aphrodite's rites" as directed by
Sappho (we mentioned this earlier in VII, § 7).

The passage is textually problematic in many respects and has been occasionally interpreted as a paraphrase of a lost epithalamium,[35] a description of
a ritual belonging to Sappho's community,[36] or a rhetorical embellishment on
some Sapphic expressions:[37]

... τὰ δὲ Ἀφροδίτης ὄργια <μόνηι> παρῆκαν τῆι Λεσβίαι Σαπφοῖ {καὶ}
ἄιδειν πρὸς λύραν καὶ ποιεῖν τὸν θάλαμον· ἦ καὶ εἰσῆλθε μετὰ τοὺς
ἀγῶνας εἰς θάλαμον, πλέκει παστάδα, τὸ λέχος {Ὁμήρου} στρώννυσι,
ἀγείρει παρθένους <εἰς> νυμφεῖον, ἄγει καὶ Ἀφροδίτην ἐφ᾽ ἄρμα<τι
μετὰ> Χαρίτων καὶ χορὸν Ἐρώτων συμπαίστορα, καὶ τῆς μὲν ὑακίνθωι
τὰς κόμας σφίγξασα, πλὴν ὅσαι μετώπωι μερίζονται, τὰς λοιπὰς ταῖς
αὔραις ἀφῆκεν ὑποκυμαίνειν, εἰ πλήττοιεν. τῶν δὲ τὰ πτερὰ καὶ τοὺς
βοστρύχους χρυσῶι κοσμήσασα πρὸ τοῦ δίφρου σπεύδει πομπεύοντας
καὶ δᾶιδα κινοῦντας μετάρσιον.

μόνηι ex apogr.   καὶ del. Wernsdorf   Ὁμήρου del. Neue   ἀγείρει παρθένους <εἰς>
νυμφεῖον Dübner: γράφει παρθένους νυμφίον cod.; ἄγει παρθένους, νυμφίον ἄγει καὶ
Ἀφροδίτην Stenzel   ἐφ᾽ ἄρμα<τι μετὰ> suppl. Köchly   πομπεύοντας Dübner: πολιτεύοντας
cod.

... and to Sappho of Lesbos alone do they accord the right to sing, with
the accompaniment of the lyre, the rites of Aphrodite, and to set up
the bedchamber. And she enters the chamber after the contests, con-

---

35   Lasserre 1989: 46–61.
36   Gentili 1988: 76. Also Grandolini (2000: 357–60) sees in the passage proof of "a strong
religious connotation" of Sappho's circle, but interprets the ritual as "a solemn procession during which Aphrodite occupies a post of central importance [as her statue is] conducted into the
nympheum," without specifying whether this concerns an event within the Sapphic group.
37   Treu 1954: 235. See also Stehle 1997: 267: "he attributes to her the motions described
in her poetry."

structs the canopy, prepares the bed, assembles the virgins near the nuptial chamber and leads also Aphrodite to her chariot together with the Graces, and leads the chorus of Erotes that accompanies the festival. And upon having bound the hair of one with hyacinths she lets the others flutter with the wind's breaths as these strike them, except those that part the hair on the forehead. And after having decorated with gold the wings and the curls of the Erotes she hangs them before the chariot while they go forth in procession and brandish torches on high.

Some points remain obscure or problematic, but the scene appears too detailed to be nothing but a patchwork of Sapphic phrases cooked up on a whim by a late-antique rhetorician. We are witness, with an abundance of detail, to a nuptial procession in which the bride (Aphrodite) is conducted in a chariot escorted by two choruses, one male, of Erotes, and one female, of young girls.

Even the reference to "contests" that precede the poet's entrance into the bedchamber to arrange it for the arrival of the newlyweds is easily explained in the sense of "repartees" of boys and girls that preceded the moment of the procession and in the wake of which Catullus constructed his poem 62.[38]

As to the assertion that only Sappho was entrusted with the office of celebrating the rites of Aphrodite, this seems to allude to a public commission and seems in line with the biographical papyrus from Cologne (see III, § 2), when the latter mentions that at Mytilene Sappho received the privilege of a front seat at festivals in honor of Aphrodite.

What we have here is not the description of a rite belonging to a group, but a public ceremony Sappho organized. Whether it was in regard to the verbal web of songs and choral instruction or the overall direction of a festival that had Aphrodite as bride in the ritual, the rite found its culminating moment in the entrance to the bedchamber of the goddess and of her companion, human or divine.

On this last figure Himerius is strangely silent, but we happen to possess a precious fragment that relates to a funeral lament on the death of Adonis, the Semitic god of vegetation whom Aphrodite loved. This lament was articulated as a ritual dialogue between a single voice that gave instructions (and that impersonated the goddess) and a chorus that responded (F 140):

---

38 On this point see Lasserre 1989: 48.

-κατθνα<ί>σκει, Κυθέρη᾽, ἄβρος Ἄδωνις· τί κε θεῖμεν;
-καττύπτεσθε, κόραι, καὶ κατερείκεσθε κίθωνας.

-He's dying, Cytherean, your gentle Adonis. What can we do?
-Strike your breast, girls, rend your chitons!

This proto-dramatic ritual must have taken place in the context of the *Adonia* (as is well known, at Athens on the occasion of this festival women constructed a wooden image of Adonis and displayed it upon the roofs, lamenting and beating their chests),[39] just as in the context of the *Adonia* organized at Alexandria in the royal palace by Arsinoe II, a γυνὴ ἀοιδός recalls the wanderings of Adonis and Aphrodite (whose figures are laid down with care upon beds surmounted by canopies of plants) in Theocr. 15.100–44.

---

39 Cf. Aristoph. *Lys.* 389–98 and see Alexiou 1974: 55–56.

XII The Grove and the Temple

§1   Cretan Aphrodite

A confirmation of one of the scenarios—the sacred grove—that we find in the last two partially preserved stanzas of F 94 comes to us from the so-called ode of the Florentine ostrakon (F 2= *PSI* 1300), first published in 1937. Consideration of this poem has in the past been confused by a line before those printed below, which can now be shown, by virtue of its Ionic dialect, not to represent a part of the Sapphic ode.[1] We can therefore consider what follows as a complete poem:[2]

---

1   As Pintaudi 2000 has shown, at the beginning of the text copied on the ostrakon one must read ΟΥΡΑΝΟΘΕΝ (a reading suggested to Norsa by U. Wilcken in a letter of 20 November 1947 published by the same Pintaudi) and not ΟΡΡΑΝΟΘΕΝ. The dactylic rhythm and Ionic dialect of ΟΥΡΑΝΟΘΕΝ ΚΑΤΙΟΥ[of l. 1 (=l. 1ᵃ in Voigt's numeration) indicate that this represents a verse of a lost hexametric hymn (already Pfeiffer derived the origin of the collocation οὐρανόθεν κατιοῦ[σα from the conflation of Hom. *Il.* 17.545 οὐρανόθεν καταβᾶσα and *Il.* 4.475 Ἴδηθεν κατιοῦσα). The ostrakon, probably dating to the second half of the third century BC, might represent the record of a "class lesson" (either within a school or, as suggested by Vetta 1999: 128, within a female community akin to the Sapphic one) on the epiphanies of Aphrodite: the (for us) lost hexametric hymn has been referred to only by quoting its initial verse evoking the epiphany of the goddess, whereas Sappho's ode has been written down in full.

2   Unlike Lobel-Page, Voigt has used Lanata's 1960 transcription as the basis for her text, a transcription that does not represent a substantial improvement from Norsa's (to whom Lobel wrote on 16 July 1937: "you have done wonders in making out so much"). With the precious help of Rosario Pintaudi I had the opportunity to study the ostrakon at the Biblioteca Laurenziana (see Ferrari 2000) and I can confirm the following: at l. 1 π̣ρ̣[rather than π[.]ρ must be read; at l. 13 Malnati's reading δ̣ο̣σμ[(Malnati 1993) is compelling; and at l. 16 one must read οἰνοχόαισα[.

Once we accept Malnati's reading δ̣ο̣σμ[(that is, δός μ')—a reading that, I should mention, has the authority of experts like Pintaudi and Bastianini (whom I have personally consulted

Δεῦρύ μ' ἐ<κ> Κρήτας πρ[οσίκαν'] ἔναυλον
ἄγνον ὄππ[αι τοι] χάριεν μὲν ἄλσος
μαλί[αν], βῶμοι δ' ἔ<ν>ι θυμιάμε-
_   νοι [λι]βανώτωι,   4
ἐν δ' ὕδωρ ψῦχρον κελάδει δι' ὕσδων
μαλίνων, βρόδοισι δὲ παῖς ὁ χῶρος
ἐσκίαστ', αἰθυσσομένων δὲ φύλλων
_   κῶμα κὰτ ἴρον·   8
ἐν δὲ λείμων ἰππόβοτος τέθαλε
τωτ...(.)ριννοις ἄνθεσιν, αἰ <δ'> ἄηται
μέλλιχα πν<έ>οισιν [
_   [   ]   12
ἔνθα δὴ σὺ δός μ' ἐ<θέ>λοισα, Κύπρι,
χρυσίαισιν ἐν κυλίκεσσιν ἄβρως
<ὀ>μ<με>μείχμενον θαλίαισι νέκταρ
οἰνοχόαισα[ι.   16

1 δεῦρύ μ' ἐ<κ> Κρήτας Theander: δευρυμμεκρητασ ostr. πρ[οσίκαν'] supplevi]ἔναυλον
Pfeiffer:] εναυγον ostr.;]ε ναῦον Lobel   2 τοι] Page   8 κὰτ ἴρον scripsi coll. F 94.25 (κὰτ
ἴρρον iam Norsa): κατιρρον ostr., κατερρεῖ Hermog., κατέρρει Sitzler, κατάγρει Bergk   10 init.
λωτίνοις<ιν> Schubart, ἠρίνοισ<ιν> Vogliano   13 δός μ' ἐ<θέ>λοισα post Schubart (1938) et
Turyn (1942) legit et suppl. Malnati   16 οἰνοχόαισα[ι supplevi

---

on the matter)—both Malnati's supplement ἐ<θέ>λοισα at l. 13 and my οἰνοχόαισα[ι at l. 16
are almost unavoidable (a fact ignored by Di Benedetto 2006: 13–16. It also escapes his attention that the imperative of ἰκάνω that I have supplemented at l. 1 is not unattested: cf. Quint.
Smyrn. 10.324 ἀλλά μοι ἔρρε δόμοιο καὶ εἰς Ἑλένην ἀφίκανε). Furthermore, the words following οἰνοχοοῦσα in Athenaeus' text (11.463c–e), that is, τούτοισι τοῖς ἑταίροις ἐμοῖς γε καὶ
σοῖς must not be understood as the (corrupt) beginning of a new Sapphic stanza but rather
as Athenaeus' contextual adaptation of Sappho's quote to the actual banquet of the deipno-
sophists, according to a practice well attested in the erudite writer of Naucratis (see Nicosia
1976: 93–99). That this is the case is confirmed also by the fact that at the lower margin of the
ostrakon the scribe has left a certain amount of blank space which he would no doubt have
filled in if Sappho's original ode did not end at l. 16. Finally, and even leaving aside questions
of dialectal normalization, the participle οἰνοχοοῦσα transmitted by Athenaeus does not guarantee that οινοχοαισα[of the ostrakon must be likewise interpreted as a participial form (i.e.,
οἰνοχόαισα). Erasure of final letters in the right margin is not an isolated phenomenon in our
ostrakon: οινοχοαισα[at l. 16 might similarly conceal the aorist infinitive οἰνοχόαισα[ι. In fact
Athenaeus' οἰνοχοοῦσα seems to be the result of the dislocation of the verb of motion with
which the goddess is addressed from the incipit of l. 1 of the ostrakon (πρ[οσίκαν']) to the beginning of l. 13 (where Athenaeus' tradition has ἐλθὲ Κύπρι against ἔνθα δὴ σύ of the ostrakon).

[Come] here to me from Crete to this holy
setting³ whe[re are your] graceful grove
of apple[-trees] and your altars smoking
  with frankincense.   4

And in it cold water sounds through
apple branches and the whole place
is shadowed with roses and as the leaves are shaken
  sleep comes over the precinct.   8

And in it a meadow, where horses graze, blossoms
with [spring] flowers and breezes
like honey breath
  [   ]   12

In this place, Cypris, grant of your will
that I may delicately pour in golden cups
nectar mingled with
  festivities.   16

The "graceful grove of apple-trees" of ll. 2 ff. echoes the "grove" of F 94.27 and the whole poem unfolds as a celebration of a rite that envisages the epiphany of Aphrodite. The goddess is arriving from Crete⁴ to a sacred space gladdened by the vegetation dear to her (apple-trees, roses, perhaps spring flowers), while altars are smoking with incense and an impression of deep sleep descends on the place.

This space *en plein air*⁵ is about to welcome the goddess Aphrodite, probably within the context of a "theoxeny."⁶ For Sappho Aphrodite certainly represent-

---

3 In favor of ἔναυλον (Pfeiffer) cf. Eur. *Ba.* 121 ff. ζάθεοί τε Κρήτας | Διογενέτορες ἔναυλοι and see also Yatromanolakis 2003.

4 Pugliese Carratelli 1990: 73–75 has argued that F 35 ἤ σε Κύπρος καὶ Πάφος ἤ Πάνορμος might also belong to another invocation to Aphrodite as a goddess honored at Paphos in Cyprus and at Panormos in Crete (to be identified with the harbor of Apollonia, now Hagia Pelagia).

5 Alc. F 296b refers to a spring feast in honor of Aphrodite by "the lovely olive-trees" (l. 2) (for the lacuna at the beginning of the line one could think of ἐναύλω]ι as in Sapph. F 2.1).

6 See Vetta 1999: 127: given the presence of several altars (l. 3) Vetta posits a reference to an ancient joint cult of Aphrodite, Peitho, and Hermes at Lesbos, as attested in *IG* 12.2.73.

Di Benedetto's hypothesis—according to which the sacred grove should be located at Ortygia

ed, not only the Olympic deity and daughter of Zeus of the *Ode to Aphrodite* (F 1), but also the patron of seafaring[7] and the goddess of vegetation, honored as Aphrodite ἐν κήποις in various Greek places, including Attica, where a grove by the river Kephisos was consecrated to her.[8]

The religious and cultic context explains the presence of fresh water, gentle breezes and roses seen both in Sappho's F 2 and in the third stasimon of Euripides' *Medea* (ll. 835–45), where the chorus evokes the tradition according to which Cypris, drawing on the beautiful streams of the Kephisos, breathes a mild breeze upon the land of Erechtheus' descendants and where the goddess, with her hair ever-encircled by a crown of roses, sends off the Erotes, "companions of Sophia, fellow-workers in every virtue."

As for the role of Aphrodite in Cretan religious culture, G. Pugliese Carratelli[9] has called attention both to the discovery of a sanctuary of Aphrodite and Hermes Kedritas at Kato Simi, in the Viannos area (western Crete), which testifies to the continuity of the cult from the Minoan and Mycenean era up to the Roman period, and to Minoan and Mycenean gems representing epiphanies of a goddess in a tree-lined sanctuary in front of female worshippers.[10] Furthermore, one can add that the Cretans considered Aphrodite to be a native deity of their own land (cf. Diod. 5.77.5), that the Delians believed that Aphrodite came from Crete and that her cult had been founded by Theseus on the way back with Ariadne from his victorious expedition against the Minotaur,[11] and also that at Amatunte (Cyprus), Aphrodite was identified with Ariadne and honored in a sacred grove (Plut. *Thes.* 20.7). After all, in our poem itself the apple-trees that constitute the sacred grove are quince-trees, the Κυδώνιαι μηλίδες of Ibycus (fr. 286.1 f. *PMGF*), which derived their name from Kydonia (now Chania), the major Minoan site of western Crete, and seem thus to be an homage to Cretan Aphrodite.

---

close to Ephesos on the basis of Strabo's description of a grove at 14.1.20 (Di Benedetto 2006, 16)—is unlikely. It is difficult to imagine that Sappho would not mention the place of the epiphany if this happened to be outside Lesbos (an island still rich in vegetation and pleasant spots today).

7   Paus. 1.1.3 and 2.34.11 mention the epithets Εὔπλοια, Ποντία, and Λιμηνία (cf. also Posid. 39.2 A.-B. Εὐπλοίαι ... Ἀρσινόηι and Philodem. *A.P.* 10.21.1 Κύπρι γαληναίη: see Sider 1997: 92). It is within this context that the ode of F 5 begins with an apostrophe to Cypris and the Nereids.

8   See Nilsson 1967: 521 and 526 ff.

9   Pugliese Carratelli 1990: 59–72.

10   See Nilsson 1950: 266–88 and plates 131–32, 139, 140, and 158.

11   Cf. Call. *Del.* 307–9, Plut. *Thes.* 21.1, Paus. 9.40.3–4.

§2 The Nectar of Poetry

On the other hand, unlike the standard interpretation, it is not Aphrodite who performs the offices of Sappho's wine pourer. Rather, Sappho herself takes on this role and asks the goddess for the privilege of pouring into golden cups nectar mingled with festivities (ll. 13–16).[12]

The poem does not contain any specific reference to poetic or musical performances, but Sappho cannot but address this prayer to Aphrodite while singing and playing (perhaps to the accompaniment of dance movements by her pupils). The poet introduces here the traditional act of mixing water with wine (the task of the "wine pourer") by using the adverb ἄβρως, which expresses an essential value of Sappho's ideology (see V, § 5), and substitutes respectively wine for "nectar" on the model of the Homeric scenes of divine symposia,[13] and replaces water with a word (θαλίαισι) denoting the joys of the feast.[14]

Such a play of substitution hints at the symbolic tension with which the nectar is charged, with reference to Sappho's role as wine-pourer. Since Sappho is playing and singing, she does not so much want to distribute wine among her audience of persons participating in the rite as to dispense the nectar of poetry according to a metaphor that will be frequently employed by Pindar (cf. *O*. 7.7 νέκταρ χυτόν, Μοισᾶν δόσιν)[15] and other poets.

Aphrodite is thus not only the goddess to whom the actual feast is consecrated. Thanks to a play of mirroring and reciprocity that, within the privileged time of the rite, reduces the divide between mortals and immortals, the goddess—together with the values she is advocating—benignly supports Sappho in her role of poet and director of the rite.

12 The fact that in F 96.26–28 Aphrodite herself seems to pour nectar does not prove anything in favor of the traditional interpretation: the scene might well be circumscribed to the divine sphere, as is the case for Hermes as "steward" at F 141.

13 Cf. Hom. *Il*. 1.598 οἰνοχόει γλυκὺ νέκταρ ἀπὸ κρητῆρος ἀφύσσων and 4.2 f. πότνια Ἥβη | νέκταρ ἐοινοχόει.

14 There is a parallel in Xenoph. B 1.4 D.-K. κρητὴρ δ᾽ ἕστηκεν μεστὸς εὐφροσύνης, in the context of a programmatic elegy, similarly composed for performance not in a private house but within a sanctuary, as clearly shown by the presence of an altar (l. 11) and a table loaded with sacrificial offerings (bread, cheese, and honey: l. 9 ff.): see Vetta 1999: 237 ff.

15 Cf. also *O*. 6.91, *N*. 3.79 πόμ᾽ ἀοίδιμον, *I*. 6.2 ff., Dionys. Chalc. fr. 1.1 ff. and 4.1 W.², *Carm. Conv*. 917 (b).1, Mel. *A.P*. 4.1.35 ff. and see Ferrari 1988: 190–92. Furthermore from Aelius Aristides (*Or*. 49.57) we discover that in a poem that included our F 194 M. Pindar called his own poetry νέκταρ.

§3   The Return of Charaxos

F 5, a poem addressed to Aphrodite and the Nereids for the return from Egypt of Charaxos, Sappho's brother, also refers to the sacred space of a temple, place of worship and supplication:[16]

Κύπρι κα̣[ὶ] Νηρήιδες ἀβλάβη[ν μοι
τὸν κασί]γνητον δ[ό]τε τυίδ᾽ ἴκεσθα[ι
κὤσσα ϝ]ο̣ι θύμω<ι> κε θέληι γένεσθαι
_ πάντα τε]λέσθην,   4
ὄσσα δὲ πρ]όσθ᾽ ἄμβροτε πάντα λῦσα[ι
καὶ φίλοισ]ι ϝοῖσι χάραν γένεσθαι
.... ἔ]χθροισι, γένοιτο δ᾽ ἄμμι
_ ......μ]ηδ᾽ εἶς·   8
τὰν κασιγ]νήταν δὲ θέλοι πόησθα̣ι
        ] τίμας, [ὀν]ίαν δὲ λύγραν
        ]ο τοῖσι π[ά]ροιθ᾽ ἀχεύων
_   ].να   12
        ].εισαΐω[ν] τὸ κέγχρω
        ]λ᾽ ἐπαγ[ορί]αι πολίταν
        ]λλωσ̣[...]νηκε δ᾽ αὖτ᾽ οὐ
_   ]κρω[ ]   16
        ]ον αἴ κ[ε θ]έο[ι θέλω]σι
        ]..[.]ν· σὺ [δ]ὲ̣ Κύπ̣[ρι]..[..(.)]να
        ]θεμ[έν]α κάκαν [
        ]ι.   20

1 Κύπρι καὶ ex P.Mich. inv. 3498ʳ, col. III   7 init. κὠνίαν Blass   10 ἔμμορον] Wilamowitz   11 παρλύοιτ]ο τοῖσι Di Benedetto   12 init. θῦμον Bücherer   ἐδά]μνα Blass   13 τό κ᾽ ἐγ χρῶι Blass   14 ἐπαγ[ορί]αι Lobel   15 ἀ]λλ᾽ ὡς[ἐσύ]νηκε δαῦτ᾽ (δηῦτ᾽) Lobel   17 supplevi   18 fin. τέ[ρπ]να Page

O Cypris and Nereids, unharmed [to me]
grant that my brother arrive here,

---

16 On Charaxos and Sappho's poems about him, see Cavallini 1990.

[and all that] in his heart he wants to happen
        [all] be accomplished.   4

And all the wrong [that] he did before, undo it.
Make him a joy to his [friends],
[a pain] to his enemies, and let there be for us
        not one [   ]   8

May he wish to give [his si]ster
[her portion] of honor and [release] from painful anxieties
those [whose heart] he himself suffering in the past
        [subdued]   12

[   ] listening to what in the flesh (?)
[   ] the bla[me] of his fellow citizens
[   ] but now that he has understood again
        [   ]   16

[   ] if the g[ods] may be [willing]
[   ] and you [lovely] Cypris
[   ] the evil one [   ]
        [   ]   20

Unfortunately we do not have any explicit indication as to the specific occasion of the ode. Yet the information provided by Myrsilus of Methymna
(*FGrHist* 477 fr. 14), that a cult to the Nereids and Poseidon had been dedicated
at Lesbos in a harbor of the gulf of Pyrrha where the first Greek colonists of
the island had arrived, supports the hypothesis[17] that Aphrodite, patron of sea-
faring, shared that temple with the Nereids and that our poem must have been
performed in this very same temple in front of a large audience.

The speaking "I" presents itself from the very outset as a first-person voice,[18]
which later on merges into a plurality of φίλοι (l. 6 ff.). The prayer, with its
apostrophe to the divinity at the beginning and at the end of the ode, is meant
to include in its wish not only the *philoi* but the entire civic community (l. 14).[19]

17 See Lasserre 1989: 190–93.
18 The supplement ἀβλάβη[ν μοι at the end of line 1 is virtually unavoidable.
19 For ἐπαγ[ορί]αι "blame" cf. Pind. fr. 122.6 M. ἄνευθ᾽ ἐπαγορίας.

There does not seem to be any reference in the poem to a choral performance also because only Sappho herself could speak of her brother in the first person (the symmetry between τὸν κασί]γνητον at l. 2 and τὰν κασιγ]νήταν at l. 9, both at the beginning of the hendecasyllable, is noteworthy).

Whether or not the ode was accompanied by a dancing chorus, it is anyway a poem subjectively oriented, as acknowledged also by Lardinois.[20] The same must have been true for a twin ode (F 15) too,[21] also addressed to Cypris but devised as a wish not of returning home but of a safe landing at Naucratis for Charaxos, without rekindling the flame of passion for Doricha:

b
]α μάκαι[ρ
]ευπλο.·[
a   ].ατοσκα[
       ]   4
ὄσσα δὲ πρ]όσθ᾽ [ἄμ]βροτε κῆ[να λῦσαι
]αταισ.νεμ[
].ύχαι λι.ενοσκλ[
       ].[8
Κύ]πρι κα[ί σ]ε πι[κροτ᾽..]αν ἐπεύρ[οι
μη]δὲ καυχάσ[α]ιτο τόδ᾽ ἐννέ[ποισα
Δ]ωρίχα τὸ δεύ[τ]ερον ὡς ποθε[
..]ερον ἦλθε.   12

1 μάκαι[ρα Hunt, μάκαι[ραι Lasserre 5 ὄσσα δὲ Fränkel πρ]όσθ᾽ [ἄμ]βροτε Hunt κῆ[να λῦσαι Diehl 6 ναυβ]άταισ[ι] νέμ᾽ [αἰθρίαν Theander, ναυβ]άταισ᾽ [ἀ]νέμ[Fränkel, [ἀ]νέμ[ων ἀήταις Lasserre 7 σὺν] τύχαι λίμενος Fränkel 9 πι[κροτέρ]αν Wilamowitz, πι[κροτάτ]αν Lobel 11 πόθε[ννος Diehl, πόθε[ννον Edmonds (πόθε[ινον iam Hunt), ποθέ[σσαις Voigt 12 ἄψ]ερον Diehl, εἰς] ἔρον Hunt

] blessed[22] [
] good sea-faring [
[   ]
[   ]   4

20 Lardinois 1996: 170: "she sang while a chorus of young women danced."
21 Particularly remarkable is the coincidence between F 15.5 and F 5.5.
22 Perhaps, as suggested by Lasserre 1989: 198 ff., the beginning of the ode picked up the association between Nereids and Aphrodite of F 5.1.

tho[se wrongs] he [did] in the past he [redeemed them]
   to the sea]farers [the gusts] of winds [
    by good] luck [to reach] the harbor [
    [   ]   8

Cypris, and may he find you [more bitter]
nor Doricha ever boast say[ing
that for the second time he came back
long[ed for].[23]   12

Finally, F 7 must also have been concerned with the adventures of Charaxos, at least as far as it is possible to infer from the reference to Doricha at l. 1 (Δωρί]χας) and to arrogance at l. 4 (ἀγερωχία[).[24]

---

23   In the *editio princeps* of P.Oxy. 1231 Hunt supplemented πόθε[ινον | εἰς] ἔρον (πόθεννον later Edmonds, more correctly), but the collocation πόθεννον ἔρον seems redundant and artificial. Diehl (1917) suggested πόθε[ννος | ἄψ]ερον, and πόθε[ννος finds a parallel in Posidipp. 118.25 f. A.-B. ἐπὶ Ῥαδάμυνθυν ἱκοίμην | δήμωι καὶ λαῶι παντὶ ποθεινὸς ἐών. One could object that Doricha could rightly have boasted (καυχάσαιτο 10) that Charaxos had longed for her, but not that she herself had longed for his return (*LSJ* s.v. ποθεινός "full of longing" is an *ad hoc* solution), and certainly Voigt must have thought so when suggesting in the apparatus the supplement ποθέ[σσαις (with ἄψ]ερον). But more likely πόθεννος presupposes that Charaxos could answer to the summons of the hetaera, who, just as the speaking "I" of F 48.1 ἦλθες, καὶ (εὖ δ᾽ Lobel) ἐπόησας, ἔγω δέ σ᾽ ἐμαιόμαν, would have obtained what she wished.

24   See Treu 1954: 172. F 20 refers to a dangerous sea journey: cf. especially F 20.4 τ]ύχαι σὺν ἔσλαι with F 15.7 σὺν] τύχαι, F 20.5 λί]μενος with F 15.7 λίμενος, F 20.8 ναῦται with F 15.6 ναυβ]άταισ(ι).

XIII To Aphrodite

§1 Rite and Subjectivity

One can also find a subjectively marked "I" within a cultic context of supplication in the very famous *Ode to Aphrodite* that opened Sappho's Alexandrian edition (F 1):

Ποι̣κιλόθρο̣ν᾽ ἀθανάτ Ἀφρόδιτα,
παῖ̣ Δ̣ί̣ος δολ̣όπλοκε, λίσσομαί σε,
μή μ᾽̣ ἄσαισι ̣μηδ᾽ ὀνίαισι δάμνα,
_ πότν̣ια, θῦ̣μον,   4
ἀλλ̣ὰ τυίδ᾽ ἔλ̣θ᾽ αἴ ποτα κἀτέρωτα
τὰ̣ς ἔμας αὔ̣δας ἀίοισα πήλοι
ἔκ̣λυες, πάτρο̣ς δὲ δόμον λίποισα
_ χ̣ρύσιον ἦλθ̣ες   8
ἄρ̣ μ᾽ ὐπασδε̣ύξαισα· κάλοι δέ σ᾽ ἆγον
ὤ̣κεες στροῦ̣θοι περὶ γᾶς μελαίνας
πύ̣κνα δίν̣νεντες πτέρ᾽ ἀπ᾽ ὠράνω ἴθε-
_ ρο̣ς διὰ μέσσω·   12
αἶ̣ψα δ᾽ ἐξίκο̣ντο· σὺ δ᾽, ὦ μάκαιρα,
μειδιαί̣σαισ᾽ ἀθανάτωι προσώπωι
ἤ̣ρε᾽ ὄττ̣ι δηὖτε πέπονθα κὤττι
_ δη̣ὖτε κ̣άλ̣η̣μμι   16
κ̣ὤττι ̣μοι μάλιστα θέλω γένεσθαι
μ̣αινόλαι ̣θύμωι· τίνα δηὖτε πείθω
̣.. ἄγην ̣ἐς σὰν φιλότατα; τίς σ᾽, ὦ

      Ψά‿πφ᾽, ‿ἀδίκησι;   20
    κα‿ὶ γ‿ὰρ αἰ φεύγει, ταχέως διώξει,
    αἰ δὲ δῶρα μὴ δέκετ᾽, ἀλλὰ δώσει,
    αἰ δὲ μὴ φίλει, ταχέως φιλήσει
      κωὐκ ἐθέλοισα.   24
    ἔλθε μοι καὶ νῦν, χαλέπαν δὲ λῦσον
    ἐκ μερίμναν, ὄσσα δέ μοι τέλεσσαι
    θῦμος ἰμέρρει, τέλεσον, σὺ δ᾽ αὔτα
      σύμμαχος ἔσσο.   28

19 init. ἄ‿ψ σ᾽ Lobel, ἄ‿ψ {σ} Di Benedetto

You who sit upon an artfully wrought throne, divine Aphrodite,
daughter of Zeus, weaver of wiles, I beseech you:
do not subdue with pains and torments,
        o lady, my heart   4

but come here, if ever at another time
on hearing my voice from afar
you rose up, left your father's house
        and came in a golden   8

chariot you had yoked. And fine sparrows led you,
quick over the black earth
beating their thick wings down from the sky
        through midair.   12

And they arrived immediately, and you, o blessed one,
smiling in your deathless face
asked me what now again I suffered and why
        now again I called upon you   16

and what I wanted to happen most of all
in my mad heart. Whom this time am I to persuade

to come back (?)[1] to your love? Who, o
    Sappho, wrongs you?   20

For if she flees, soon she will pursue.
If she does not accept gifts, rather will she give them.
If she does not love, soon she will love
    even unwilling.   24

Come to me now and loose me from hard
anxiety and all my heart longs
to accomplish, accomplish. You yourself
    be my ally.   28

The ode displays the typical features of a cultic hymn. We have a preamble with the invocation of the deity defined by her traditional epithets, followed by a central section where the reference to a favor previously accorded represents the guarantee for the fulfillment of a new request, and finally an entreaty for help. Sappho works this traditional frame, well attested in the Homeric epic (cf. e.g. *Il.* 1.37–42 and 16.233–48, *Od.* 9.528–35), into a ring composition: ἔλθε of l. 25 echoes ἔλθ᾽ of l. 5, θῦμος of l. 27 repeats θῦμον of l. 4, χαλέπαν δὲ λῦσον | ἐκ μερίμναν of l. 25 ff. echoes with variation μή μ᾽ ἄσαισι μηδ᾽ ὀνίαισι δάμνα of l. 3.

The intersection between these two structural patterns is at the same time an intersection between cultic dimension and personal suffering (underlined

---

1 In the *editio princeps* of P.Oxy. 2288 Lobel suggested reading ἄ̣ψ̣ σ̣᾽ ἄγην and correcting the following σὰν to ϝὰν (an emendation already proposed by Edmonds 1920). The sense would then be "whom am I to persuade this time to bring you back to her love?" but one would expect Sappho to bring the fugitive to her own love and not vice versa. F. Blass had proposed πείθω|μαί σ(οι) but, with the exception of the particular case of δέ in F 31.9 (omitted, by the way, in the tradition of Plut. *Prof. in virt.* 81d), we do not have other instances of such a breach of the synapheia and hence elision between Sapphic hendecasyllables. Furthermore the scribe, according to common writing practice, would have carried on in the next line writing πείθω-|μ᾽ and not πειθωμ᾽|. Another hypothesis advanced by Lobel himself (mentioned by Turner 1973: 25) consists in preserving σάν by interpreting σ᾽ not as σ(ε) but as σ(οι) and in taking ἄγην (= Att. ἀγῆναι) as an aorist passive infinitive from ἄγνυμι with the metaphorical sense (a metaphorical use of ἄγνυμι is present also in F 31.9 γλῶσσα ἔαγε) "to be bent," cf. Eur. *Hipp.* 766 οὐχ ὁσίων ἐρώ-|των δειναῖ φρένας Ἀφροδί-|τας νόσωι κατεκλάσθη, Call. *Del.* 107 οὐδὲ κατεκλάσθης. Yet the expression ἐς σὰν φιλότατα more naturally leads one to interpret ἄγην as "to lead." Perhaps one could think of ἄψ {σ} (so Di Benedetto, but he also reads πείθωμ᾽|) and understand ἄγην as intransitive, however problematic this may be (cf. e.g. Xen. *Cyr.* 3.3.46).

also by the presence of the personal pronoun μοι at ll. 17, 25, and 26 and by the apostrophe ὦ | Ψάπφ' at l. 19 ff.), conventions and actual experience.

§2   The Beginning

The cultic dimension comes to the fore not only in the liturgical scheme of the cletic hymn but also in the very first word of the text: the epithet ποικιλόθρονε suggests the very presence of Aphrodite's statue and thus of a precise sacred space within the temple (the statue's niche).[2] Similarly, the skillfully wrought gold adorning the wooden image of Aphrodite in the Locrian temple of the goddess in Nossis *A.P.* 9.332.1 f. (= 4 G.-P.) performs a clearly deictic function:

> Ἐλθοῖσαι ποτὶ ναὸν ἰδώμεθα τᾶς Ἀφροδίτας
> τὸ βρέτας, ὡς χρυσῶι δαιδαλόεν τελέθει.

> Let us go to the temple to see the statue
> of Aphrodite, how skillfully wrought in gold it is.

Whether we should interpret ποικιλόθρονε of l. 1 as "sitting on a skillfully wrought throne" or "of the dress sprinkled with variegated flowers"[3] is a hotly debated issue. On either reading the adjectival compound (a *hapax* perhaps coined for the present occasion) suggests a deictic value linked to the actual performance of the poem.[4]

---

2   See Aloni 1997: xi ff.

3   In favor of the former hypothesis see Privitera 1974: 31 ff., Burzacchini 1977: 125 ff. and 2005: 16; for the latter, based on Hom. *Il.* 22.441 ἐν δὲ θρόνα ποικίλ' ἔπασσεν (first suggested by G. Wustmann, 1868), see Lasserre 1989: 205–14. The reading ποικιλόφρον' (MR) or ποικιλόφρων (DK) preserved by part of the manuscript tradition of the epitome of D.H. *Comp.* 23 seems to be a banalization. Finally, Winkler 1990: 172–75 too thinks of a possible derivation from θρόνα, but with the sense of "herbs for magical purpose," "spells" (cf. Theocr. 2.59, Nic. *Ther.* 493, Lyc. 674). Winkler's interpretation might seem to be supported by the anonymous entry in *Suda* s.v. πολύθρονος· πολυφάρμακος (= Call. *Hec.* fr. 3 Hollis) and Nonn. *Dion.* 13.530 ff. Κίρκη, | σύγγονος Αἰήταο πολύθρονος, but this sense of θρόνα (or compound with θρόνα) is unattested before the Alexandrinian period and is therefore suspect.

4   According to Page 1955: 5 the text does not refer to "any particular cult-divinity with cult-statue in a shrine on earth" but to "the Olympian goddess seated at home in heaven" as is the case in several representations of throned gods in sixth-century BC vase-paintings (e.g., Zeus and Hera on the François vase). However the two interpretations are not mutually exclusive: the

The comparison adduced by Bonanno[5] with the scene (*Od.* 1.130–32) in which Telemachos introduces Athena/Mentes into Odysseus' house at Ithaca, and where the two elements of the compound occur separately at short distance, strongly favors the interpretation of an Aphrodite sitting on her throne just like the Amyclean Apollo (cf. Paus. 3.18):

αὐτὴν δ᾽ ἐς θρόνον εἷσεν ἄγων, ὑπὸ λῖτα πετάσσας,
καλὸν δαιδάλεον· ὑπὸ δὲ θρῆνυς ποσὶν ἦεν.
πὰρ δ᾽ αὐτὸς κλισμὸν θέτο ποικίλον

He led her and seated her on a throne, spreading underneath a fine
    cloth;
it was a fine, skillfully wrought throne. Beneath there was a stool for
    her feet.
He himself drew up an elaborately decorated seat…

§3   Neurotic Symptoms?

The adoption of nontraditional epithets like ποικιλόθρονε and δολόπλοκε at l. 2 alongside "divine" and "daughter of Zeus" shows that in Sappho the rite is not an inert, fossilized relic: both its actions and accompanying words are reshaped and re-focalized. Different too is the way in which Sappho defines the reasons of her own supplication.

These reasons may be traced back to a situation that must have been typical and occurred quite frequently in the relationship between the leading figure of the group and her followers. The texts themselves reveal how strongly erotically charged these relations could be.

Later on I shall dwell at greater length on the manifestations of such a form of homoeroticism. It is clear in any case that both from a historical and anthropological perspective this does not stand in need of any kind of explanation (or even less justification), and that this does not deny but rather confirms the paideutic nature of the vertical relationship between teacher and pupil (complementary to the horizontal one between pupil and pupil). What I want to pay

---

statue in the temple may well have represented the goddess as imagined sitting on Olympus.
5   Bonanno 1997: 53–55.

closer attention to here is rather the *form* that the grief assumes at the abandonment of the beloved.

To suggest that the emphasis on one's own suffering is a conventional way of enhancing, by contrast, the value of the person who has caused grief and the importance of the bond that has been severed, is in itself correct. It probably also provides an adequate explanation for the "I would truly like to be dead" motif of F 94.1: it is a confession that is at the same time as much emphatic as generic, an idiomatic expression that we can find also in Anacr. fr. 411a *PMG* ἀπό μοι θανεῖν γένοιτ'.[6] But as soon as we read l. 3 of the first stanza of the *Ode to Aphrodite* this kind of explanation turns out to be entirely insufficient: Sappho's prayer not "to be overpowered with pains and torments" (ll.3–4) confronts us with an expression (the joint mention of ἄσαι and ὄνιαι) that finds a precise parallel only in a medical treatise on epileptic attacks.

In *De morbo sacro* (15.1–5 Grensemann = 6.388 Littré) ascribed to Hippocrates we read:[7]

> The corruption of the brain arises from phlegm and bile. You will recognize both in this way. Those who are mad because of the phlegm are quiet and do not yell or shout. Those who are mad because of the bile are noisy, malignant, and are not able to keep quiet but are always doing something improper: if their madness is thus constant this happens for these reasons. If dreads and fears assail them, this happens because of a change in the brain: the brain changes because it is heated and it heats because of the bile moving towards the brain through the blood vessels from the trunk of the body. The fear remains until the bile returns to the veins and trunk and then stops. The patient feels pain and sickness [ἀνιᾶται ... καὶ ἀσᾶται] if the brain becomes unseasonably colder and condenses more than usual. This happens because of the phlegm; and because of this same affection he loses also his memory. He shouts and yells during the night when the brain is suddenly heated

---

6 On the *topos* of love and death see Lanata 1966: 72 ff.

7 On the passage see Pigeaud 1981: 39, who refers also to *Morb. Sac.* 17.3, where we are told that when someone feels an unexpected surge of joy or grief, his φρένες jump up (πηδῶσι) and cause nausea (ἄσην) because they are thin and represent the most tense part of the body, and Plat. *Tim.* 71c λύπας καὶ ἄσας παρέχοι (the pathology of the liver when it is "frightened" by the intellect). The connection ἀνίη / ἄση emerges otherwise only in Hippocr. *Ep.* 19.16 ἀνιῆται δὲ καὶ ἀσῆται καὶ ἐπιλήθεται, παρὰ καιρὸν ψυχομένου τοῦ ἐγκεφάλου ὑπὸ φλέγματος καὶ ξυνισταμένου παρὰ τὸ ἔθος.

(this happens to the bilious, not to the phlegmatic); the brain over-heats when the blood reaches the brain in great quantity and seethes.

The author of the treatise contrasts the "phlegmatic" condition typical of those who "are mad while remaining quiet" and for that reason experience pain and nausea, to the case of fears that are instead provoked by the overheating of the brain because of the bile.[8]

From the text of F 1 one deduces that the condition that prompts nausea and pain coincides with χάλεπαι ... μέριμναι (l. 25 ff.). Accordingly, a "clinical" reading of the ode ought thus to acknowledge the outline of an anxious-depressive phase experienced by a subject who recognizes herself as usually vulnerable to impulses and emotional imbalance (cf. l. 18 μαινόλαι θύμωι).[9] It is thanks to Aphrodite's intervention that this subject would like to escape the frustration caused by the rejection on the part of the beloved.

Within this picture the nausea[10] represents, according to the Hippocratic medicine, the physical realization of an obsessive behavior named φροντίς—fixed thought, obsession[11]—as we can see in a passage of the Hippocratic *De morbis* (2.72):

The obsession [φροντίς] is a disease difficult to cure: the patient has the impression that he has in his bowels something like a thorn and that this is stinging him. He is seized by nausea and avoids light and men while loving darkness. He is seized by fear and his diaphragm swells internally and he feels pain at being touched. He is scared and suffers from terrible visions and nightmares and at times sees persons who are dead. This illness seizes the majority of the patients in springtime.

We can find a link between nausea and intense psychomotor seizure, accompanied at times by visual and acoustic hallucinations, also noted in other

---

8 On the mechanisms linked to the relationship between bile and phlegm see Di Benedetto 1986: 42 ff.

9 For μαινόλαι cf. Archil. fr. 196.20 W.² μαινόλις γυνή (referring to Neobule) and A. *Supp.* 107 διάνοιαν μαινόλιν with reference also to the sexual aggressiveness of the sons of Aegyptus). See Privitera 1974: 60 and Di Benedetto 1987: 17.

10 In Sappho the etymon is attested also in F 3.7 ἄσαιο (probably referring to Charaxos), F 91 ἀσαροτέρας (referring to Eirene); for Alcaeus cf. F 39.11 ἄσαις and 335.2 ἀσάμενοι. For ὀνία cf. F 5.10 [ὀν]ίαν δὲ λύγραν, 63.3 ἢ δεῖν' ὀνίας μ[, 88.19 ὀνίαρ[ο]ς and see Broger 1996: 37.

11 On φροντίς see Simon 1978: 234 and Di Benedetto 1986: 35–38.

Hippocratic passages.[12] Furthermore in the works of Aretaeus of Cappadocia (second century AD; he is also the author, among other things, of the treatise *De causis et signis acutorum morborum*), nausea opens an asyndetic series of symptoms completed by "disorientation, obfuscated sight, humming ears, headache and numbed limbs."[13]

§4   Between Disease and Passion

We could further this clinical reading of Sappho, or, better, of the fictionalized *persona* bearing her name in F 1,[14] but we must immediately ask ourselves what is the meaning of this identity of symptoms of grief between "Sappho" and the Hippocratic treatise *De morbo sacro*.

We must in fact take into account that Sappho, while speaking of her anxieties and torments, invokes Aphrodite as the only possible cure for her disease. On the other hand, the author of the treatise (composed perhaps in the second half of the fifth century BC) is engaged in an acrimonious controversy against a tradition (embodied by "conjurors, purificators, mountebanks and charlatans": 1.10, cf. 18.6) that had made epilepsy a "sacred disease" by ascribing to it a divine character and a status completely different from that of any other pathology, and this on the basis of both its extraordinary nature and the consequent human inability to interpret its genesis.

However, this "scientific" approach does not go beyond some therapeutic instructions linked to climate and diet: its premise is that the unleashing of the disease depends on a change of winds and the consequent flooding of the brain by the phlegm (11.1–2).

Sappho, on the other hand, not only positions herself, historically speaking, outside these and similar medical theorizations, but does not even speak of νόσος (as indeed Sophocles does insistently when referring to Ajax' fits of madness that obfuscate his mind).[15] What Sappho does instead is to limit herself to recording occasional symptoms within a personality admittedly inclined to μανία.

---

12 Cf. *Int.* 35 and *Epid.* 3.17 and 7.1.
13 Aret. *SA* 2.6.3 (cf. 2.9.15).
14 For further details see Ferrari 2001.
15 Cf. Soph. *Aj.* 59, 66, 86, 271, 274, and 452.

This of course does not rule out what is already well known, namely that the phraseology of Hippocratic medicine, just like that of the Pre-Socratic philosophers, slowly and gradually developed towards an autonomous and more specialized direction, taking its move from common language. From this perspective one may think that Sappho uses words and expressions that were common currency in her own day to express a discomfort and a suffering that in their turn went back to the conventions of love.

The similarities with several lines of Theognis (ll.1323–26) would seem to confirm this:

Κυπρογένη, παῦσόν με πόνων, σκέδασον δὲ μερίμνας
    θυμοβόρους, στρέψον δ᾽ αὖθις ἐς εὐφροσύνας·
μερμήρας δ᾽ ἀπόπαυε κακάς, δὸς δ᾽ εὔφρονι θυμῶι
    μέτρ᾽ ἥβης τελέσαντ᾽ ἔργματα σωφροσύνης.

Free me, Cypris, from toil and dispel the anxieties
    that devour my heart, and restore me to joy,
put an end to my sad concerns and with benign mind
    grant me a wise life once the measure of my youth is over.

The two texts share both the entreaty to Aphrodite to be released from suffering and the reference to "anxieties" (μέριμναι), although it is difficult to say whether these items occur independently from each other or because "Theognis" is reshaping Sappho. The way in which this longed-for freedom is envisaged is, however, different: in Sappho no alternative is offered to the goal of regaining the beloved, whereas in "Theognis" the wished-for aim is the warrant of σωφροσύνη once youth is over.

Further, we do not find in "Theognis" the "Hippocratic" joint mention of ἄσαι and ὄνιαι, as in Sapph. F 1.3: it is as if the two Theognidean elegiac couplets, consciously or not, set forth to normalize the extreme peaks of Sappho's pathology and bring them back to the traditional track of love didactics that is so characteristic of archaic elegy.

Sappho instead, it would seem, exploits traditional poetical patterns alongside elements drawn on common everyday language. She depicts a portrait of her own condition which, though moving from a conventional situation, expands on its existential value.

It is difficult to establish to what extent the poet is drawing on her own personal experience for this thematic and linguistic experiment, or, to put it another way, to what extent the forms of content and style depend on Sappho recognizing some of her own history in these forms. Obviously Sappho must have shared the emotional confusion of her experience with a communal audience within a cultic and festive scenario: hence, both the conceptual articulations of her songs and their forms of expression must have granted her a successful communication with her audience.

XIV "Pathography" 1: Panic

§1 F 31

In Sappho's extant fragments it is possible to find a moment (and in one of her most famous poems, often named the *Ode of Jealousy*, F 31) where one is peremptorily confronted with an accurate clinical pathography articulated in a series of paratactic expressions:

Φαίνεταί μοι κῆνος ἴσος θέοισιν
ἔμμεν᾽ ὤνηρ, ὄττις ἐνάντιός τοι
ἰσδάνει καὶ πλάσιον ἆδυ φωνεί-
_ σας ὐπακούει   4
καὶ γελαίσας ἰμέροεν, τό μ᾽ ἦ μὰν
καρδίαν ἐν στήθεσιν ἐπτόαισεν·
ὡς γὰρ <ἔϲ> σ᾽ ἴδω βρόχε᾽ ὤς με φώναι-
_ σ᾽ οὐδὲν ἔτ᾽ εἴκει,   8
ἀλλὰ κὰμ μὲν γλῶσσα ἔαγε, λέπτον δ᾽
αὔτικα χρῶι πῦρ ὐπαδεδρόμηκεν,
ὀππάτεσσι δ᾽ οὐδὲν ὄρημμ᾽, ἐπιρρόμ-
_ βεισι δ᾽ ἄκουαι,   12
ἀ δέ μ᾽ ἴδρως κακχέεται, τρόμος δὲ
παῖσαν ἄγρει, χλωροτέρα δὲ ποίας
ἔμμι, τεθνάκην δ᾽ ὀλίγω 'πιδεύην
_ φαίνομ᾽ ἔμ᾽ αὔται.   16
ἀλλὰ πὰν τόλματον, ἐπεὶ †καὶ πένητα†

9 δ᾽ om. Plut. *Prof. in virt.* 81d   11–12 ἐπιρομβεῖσι [Longin.], def. Prauscello coll. Sapph.

T 213 B.1–2: ἐπιβρόμεισι Bergk, Lobel-Page, Voigt   13 ἀ δέ μ' Bergk: ἀδεμ' *Epim. An. Ox.*
1.208.13 ff., ἔκαδε μ' [Longin.]

That man seems to me equal to gods
whoever sits across from you
and nearby attends you
sweetly speaking   4

and desirously laughing, which makes
truly the heart in my breast flutter.
For when I look upon you for but a moment
then no longer can I speak   8

but my tongue is broken, a subtle
fire straightway runs below my skin
with my eyes I see nothing, my ears hum   12

the sweat pours down me, and trembling
seizes me all through, I am more pale
than grass, and I seem to myself to be little
short of dying   16

but all can be borne, for even the poor man (?)

§2   Panic Disorder (PD)

The syndrome as recorded in the text consists of the following symptoms:

- heart palpitations (ll. 5–6)
- aphasia (ll. 7–9)
- hot flashes (ll. 9–10)
- blurred vision (l. 11)
- dizziness and disorientation (ll. 11–12)
- sweating (l. 13)
- trembling (ll. 13–14)
- pallor and sense of dying (ll. 14–16)

The panic attack disorder (PD) is in its turn a phase of intense anxiety and alienation during which some of the following symptoms suddenly arise. Usually they reach their climax within perhaps ten minutes:[1]

- heart palpitations
- sweating
- trembling or convulsions
- shortness of breath
- sensations of choking
- chest pain
- nausea or abdominal pain
- dizziness, instability, estrangement, or faintness
- alienation (sense of unreality) or de-personalization (sense of detachment from one's own body/world)
- fear of losing control or going mad
- fear of dying
- paresthesia (tingling sensations)
- hot or cold flashes

Can these two series of symptoms be somehow related to each other? It is of course only right and proper to emphasize the historical and anthropological differences related to both the sociology of the phenomenon itself and the cultural awareness, age, biological sex, or any other characteristic of the observer. Yet one has to bear in mind that in our contemporary world panic disorder is a pathology affecting between 3% and 4% of the global population; further, no meaningful statistical difference linked to different social conditions or different political and cultural areas may be observed. In short, it seems to be a pathology whose diffusion is wide enough to be immediately recognized as such by any audience but at the same time its circumscribed nature assures that it cannot be traced back to a general "human" condition.

As far as the overall interpretation of the syndrome described in F 31 is concerned, scholars have often seen in F 31 either an "ode of jealousy" or a declaration of love (or of the process of falling in love). This has mainly been determined on the basis of the indirect witness of [Longinus], who quotes

---

1 The defining criteria of panic attacks have been established with wide consensus in *DSM-III*, that is, the *Diagnostic and Statistical Manual of Mental Disorder* (3rd ed., Washington, 1980), published by the American Psychiatric Association and slightly modified in its fourth edition (1994).

our poem.[2] Nevertheless one must not lose sight of a fundamental distinction. Erotic excitement, inasmuch as it *is* a destabilizing drive, can indeed trigger in the subject a phobic reaction, as Plato[3] knew very well, and as is apparent already in Egyptian love lyrics dating to the age of Rhamses.[4] Yet the neurological profile of fear is substantially different from that of eros: the former triggers mechanisms of alarm and defense by increasing the levels of substances predisposing the organism to face danger (like adrenaline), whereas the latter generates the secretion of sexual hormones.

Discrete moments of F 31 have lent themselves, starting at least from Catullus 51 onwards, to be reinterpreted as love poetry or expressions of a hyperbolic emotional involvement (it is not by chance that Catullus exploits them with reference to his first contact with Lesbia).[5] Yet the difference between eros and phobia cannot be eliminated.[6] On the contrary, the very comparison with Catullus 51, a "translation" of the first three stanzas of F 31 with the significant omission of the fourth[7] (thus cancelling Sappho's symptoms 6–8: sweating, trembling, pallor, sense of impending death, all of them present in the modern diagnosis of PD) highlights such a distinction. Once reduced to the symptoms of the first three stanzas (heart palpitations, aphasia, hot flashes, blurred vision,

---

2   [Longinus] (ch. 10) introduces the ode, saying that Sappho describes in it the sufferings associated with the follies of love (τὰ συμβαίνοντα ταῖς ἐρωτικαῖς μανίαις παθήματα). After quoting the poem and explaining its tangle of passions, [Longinus] restates that "all this happens to those who love" but that it is "the choice of the most intense moments and their connection" that "has produced the resulting excellence."

3   Cf. *Phdr.* 251a-b where, within the discussion of the fourth "type of madness," a person who sees a divine face or some ideal bodily form is said to experience in quick succession shivering (φρίκη), sweating, and an unusual heat.

4   Particularly suggestive is the comparison adduced by Sofia 2006: 63 with P.Chester Beatty 1.5, C 2.9–10: "swiftly flees my heart when I think of the love I have for you: / it does not allow me to walk as a man but runs away from its place."

5   For other "erotic" imitations see Burzacchini 1977: 143 ff.

6   Differently Snyder 1997: 33, according to whom even the sense of impending death may assume an erotic nuance since " 'death' and orgasm often become one and the same in the Western literary imagination" and "the expression 'more moist than grass' is left to the hearer's imagination—whether Sappho means sweat, tears, or vaginal secretion." The caricature of Devereux 1971's essay by Parker 1993 is in itself justified ("... Devereux' now infamous picture of Sappho waking up one morning, realizing she has no penis, and dashing off fr. 31 in a (literally) hysterical seizure") yet it should not make one forget that it was Devereux who recognized the core of the Sapphic syndrome, giving it the name of "anxiety attack."

7   This is not the place to rediscuss the never-ending question (irrelevant for our purposes) whether the last stanza of Catullus 51 is the actual end of the ode, or instead an autonomous poem (or its beginning) glued to the previous stanzas only because of an accident of the manuscript tradition.

dizziness) Sappho's F 31 could still be made consistent, in Catullus' adaptation, with the perspective of a strong emotional tension without at the same time assuming the devastating outline of a PD.

Most significant in this respect is Theocritus' echo of Sappho F 31 in his second *Idyll, The Sorceress*. At l. 82 Theocritus describes Simaetha's love at first sight via an overt allusion to Sappho F 31.7:

χὣς ἴδον, ὣς ἐμάνην, ὣς μοι πυρὶ θυμὸς ἰάφθη

and as I saw, so I went mad, so my soul was burned

and later on declines the symptoms of sweating, aphasia, and paresthesia to express, this time, the *fear* of love[8] experienced by Simaetha when Delphis crosses the threshold accompanied by Simaetha's maidservant, Thestylis (ll. 106–10):

πᾶσα μὲν ἐψύχθην χιόνος πλέον, ἐκ δὲ μετώπω
ἱδρὼς μὲν κοχύδεσκεν ἴσον νοτίαισιν ἐέρσαις,
οὐδέ τι φωνᾶσαι δυνάμαν, οὐδ᾽ ὅσσον ἐν ὕπνωι
κνυζεῦνται φωνεῦντα φίλαν ποτὶ ματέρα τέκνα·
ἀλλ᾽ ἐπάγην δαγῦδι καλὸν χρόα πάντοθεν ἴσα.

All through I turned cold, more than snow, and from my forehead
sweat flowed down, like wet drops of dew,
nor did I succeed in speaking, not so much as in sleep
children make sounds whimpering to their dear mothers,
but all my lovely body became rigid, like a wax doll.

Furthermore, when in Lucretius (3.152–60) all of Sappho's symptoms resurface within a single context, they are clearly presented in a phobic perspective within a broader discussion of the relationships between *animus* (the hegemonic function located in the heart, center of *consilium* but also of fear and joy) and *anima* (scattered in the organism and regulated by the *animus*):[9]

Verum ubi vementi magis est commota metu mens,
consentire animam totam per membra videmus

---

8   See Pretagostini 1984: 105–17.
9   For other terms of comparison in Latin, see Neri-Citti 2005.

sudoresque ita palloremque existere toto
corpore et infringi linguam vocemque aboriri,   155
caligare oculos, sonere auris, succidere artus,
denique concidere ex animi terrore videmus
saepe homines; facile ut quivis hinc noscere possit
esse animam cum animo coniunctam, quae cum animi <vi>
percussast, exim corpus propellit et icit.   160

Indeed when the mind is moved by a stronger fear,
we see the whole spirit throughout the limbs sharing this feeling,
sweating and pallor coming on all over the body,
the tongue being broken and the voice fading away,   155
the eyes darkening, the ears resounding, the limbs failing,
in short we often see men grow faint because of the mind's terror
so one may easily recognize that the spirit is linked with the mind,
and when spirit is struck by the power of the mind,
it then drives and propels the body.   160

§3   Phlegm or Bile?

Di Benedetto[10] has observed the similarity, both on the level of expression and of specific symptoms, between F 31 and the description of one of the so-called thick illnesses in Hipp. *Affect. Int.* 49:

> Sometimes the pain reaches suddenly the head too, so that the patient cannot hear with his ears or keep his eyelids up because of the heaviness. A profusion of bad-smelling sweat floods the patient, especially when the pain diminishes and at night. The complexion of the patient becomes almost entirely jaundiced. This disease is less fatal than the previous one.

The medical record reduces to a biological alteration a series of symptoms whose psychological context has not been handed down to us. It is, however, certain that the physician is proceeding by comparison/contrast with the previ-

10   Di Benedetto 1985 and 1987: 27–29.

ous medical record of ch. 48 ("this disease is less fatal than the previous one").
There we find described a "thick illness" caused not by the phlegm but by the
bile and that triggered aggressive reactions (physical attacks, threats) alternat-
ing with depressive states.[11]

Furthermore, the medical record of ch. 49 is articulated in two sections: the
first describes the effects of the corruption of phlegm in the abdominal area,
whereas in the second section that opens with "sometimes" we find the sudden
manifestation of symptoms that can be connected to those of Sappho F 31.

On the other hand, the lack of indications about the phobic nature of this pathology and the qualification that the sweating goes on even when (and especially
at night) there is a remission of the pain rules out the possibility that in *Affect. Int.*
48 we have a panic attack. On the contrary, the fear is instead traced back, just as
in *Morb. Sac.* 15.1–3, to an alteration of the brain by the bile, not by the phlegm.

In fact the pathology triggered by the phlegm in *Affect. Int.* 49[12] is closely
paralleled by that of *Morb. Sac.* 11.6 (where as a consequence of an inundation
by the phlegm the body shivers and the patient becomes aphasic and is not
able to breathe in the air but the brain becomes compressed and the blood is
clogged). The pathology described is thus exactly that of the "sacred disease"
or epilepsy,[13] usually preceded by anticipatory anxiety and agoraphobia (cf.
Morb. Sac. 12.1–2: "those who are already accustomed to the disease perceive
in advance when the onset of the illness is about to seize them and flee from
crowded places"), but not so much accompanied by phobic manifestations as
by spasms and convulsions.

The partial convergence between *Affect. Int.* 49 (from the acute onset onwards)
and the modern diagnosis of PD can be explained in terms of:

> a vast area of symptomatic overlap between PD and epilepsy of the tem-
> poral lobe. Now, the very fact that "neurotic" symptoms characteristic
> of panic/agoraphobia are largely present also in a neurological disease
> caused by a lesion of the temporal lobe allows us to formulate new hy-

---

11 Such a description finds significant analogies in the hallucinatory νόσος experienced by
Ajax in Sophocles' homonymic tragedy: cf. especially Athena's words in the prologue at l. 51 ff.: ἐγώ
σφ' ἀπείργω, δυσφόρους ἐπ᾽ ὄμμασι | γνώμας βαλοῦσα τῆς ἀνηκέστου χαρᾶς. The alternation
between hallucinatory states and phases of lucidity, motor excitement and prostration, threatening
cries and silence, corresponds to what Tecmessa recalls in Soph. *Aj.* 257 ff. and 305 ff.

12 Cf. the symptomatology of *Mul.* 151 and also Plat. *Tim.* 83 d–e.

13 On ancient epilepsy, corresponding to what is today defined as "essential epilepsy," see
Pigeaud 1987: 48–63.

potheses on an illness long believed to be of a "psychological" nature. We can say that in PD the temporal lobe is very often involved. Of course we must not confuse PD and epilepsy: they are two radically different diseases.[14]

However, if our closest term of comparison with F 31 on the level of expression is not relevant to the syndrome described, we are nevertheless able to recognize or at least suspect "real" panic attacks in some other medical records that, though much shorter and lacunose, are reliable enough as far as phobic symptoms are concerned.

Two textbook cases for the transparency of the triggering events are those of Nicanor and Democles in *Epid.* 5.81–82:

"Whenever [Nicanor] goes for a drink with his companions, [he] is seized by a fear of the flautist. As soon as he hears the first notes of the aulos during the symposium he is overwhelmed by disturbance brought on by fear, and if it happens at night he can hardly restrain himself, but if it happens in daylight he remains quiet."

Democles instead "believes that his sight is blurred and to be about to faint and is not able to pass by a cliff or across a bridge nor can he cross even the shallowest ditch."[15]

Aretaeus mentions another similar case (*SD* 1.6.6):

Also this story is told. There was once a carpenter who was very skilled at his work in measuring, cutting, planing, nailing, fitting together pieces of wood, bringing to completion buildings in a state of sobriety, getting on well with his employers and dealing with them to get paid a fair wage. He was always balanced on the place of work. But when he went to the market place or to the baths or in whatever other place it was necessary, he started weeping as soon as he was putting down his tools and until he put them on his shoulders on the way back. And when he was far away from the sight of the laborers, work or construction-site, he was seized by total madness. When he went back to his work he immediately became balanced again.

14 Cassano 1993: 210.
15 Ciani 1983: 23–25, has rightly identified in the two medical records two rare cases of "'pure' mental disorder not dependent on somatic influences."

§4 Phlegm and Bile

One can see then a contrast between the clues offered by the *Ode to Aphrodite* and those of F 31. At least to the mind of a Hippocratic physician of the fifth or fourth century BC, the former belonged to a phlegmatic temperament, whereas the second belonged to a bilious one, and this is in contrast with the usual classification of an individual within a single temperamental profile.

On the other hand such a disposition to alternate obsessive states of φροντίς and aggressive manic fits, anxious depression and hypertimia, belongs to a precise clinical case history, which is nowadays defined as "bipolar disorder." It manifests itself when the mental balance of an individual seems to be significantly threatened by disorders consisting alternatively in an excessive rising (hypertimia) and plummeting (hypotimia) of the mood. The resulting instability is such that it may be able to drag the patient's personality towards the territory of psychosis proper, especially when the same symptoms are reiterated as in Sappho. Such a form of psychosis had already been adumbrated in Sappho, even if *in malam partem,* by those ancient readers who, according to a Peripatetic source, censured the poet as "turbulent in temper."[16]

The onset of a new hypertimic phase can be seen with particular intensity in F 130.1–2:

Ἔρος δηὖτέ μ' ὁ λυσιμέλης δόνει,
γλυκύπικρον ἀμάχανον ὄρπετον.

Limb-loosening Eros again assails me,
sweet-bitter creeping thing that knows no remedy.

Eros is said to be "limb-loosening"[17] (compare the heart and knees that "are loosened" in the formulaic expression λύτο γούνατα καὶ φίλον ἦτορ, attested two times in the *Iliad* and seven times in the *Odyssey*) since it disjoins those limbs whose cohesion and integrity normally guarantee the solidity and agility

---

16 P.Oxy. 1800, fr. 1 = Chamael. fr. 27 Wehrli: ἄτακτος ... τὸν τρόπον.
17 Cf. Hes. *Th.* 120 ff. and 910 ff., *Carm. Pop.* 873.3 ff. *PMG*, Archil. fr. 196 W.^{2}, Alcm. fr. 3.61 *PMGF* λυσιμελεῖ τε πόσωι and Andò 2005: 189.

of the person himself. In the upset caused by the sexual impulse, the "I" finds itself vulnerable and dismayed, helpless.[18]

But the paralyzing fear induced by eros lets us also catch an immediate glimpse, beyond the initial shock, of the triggering of a new trajectory of passion: we do not find here a lasting frustration but, juxtaposed by asyndeton to ἀμάχανον, we find a sensation of "bittersweet" (γλυκύπικρον)[19] that, as Galen will observe,[20] carries with it a culinary resonance by presenting eros as a kind of appetizer.

Yet the initial sense of dismay is such as to produce an hallucinatory vision, that ὄρπετον that has been interpreted in the sense of a generic "terrestrial animal" (as in Hom. *Od.* 4.417 ff., Alcm. fr. 89.3 *PMGF*, A. R. 4.1240) or "reptile" (as in Pind. *P.* 1.25, Eur. *Andr.* 269 ff., Aristoph. *Av.* 1069).

If the chronological spread of the occurrences of the word would induce one to prefer the meaning of "animal," the stronger icastic value of the signifier is in favor of "reptile" or "serpent." Likewise, in A. *Supp.* 895 ff. the chorus of the Danaids, terrified by the announcement of the arrival at Argos of their cousins, sons of Egypt, who want to possess them even by force, envisage as an objective correlative of their sex-phobic panic a δίπους ὄφις and an ἔχιδνα that are approaching threateningly.

At the opposite end of the spectrum we can assume as representative of a depressive phase those cases where an impulse of death comes to the fore, and this notwithstanding the fact that according to Aristotle (*Rh.* 1398b = Sapph. T 201) Sappho herself had once declared in a lost poem that τὸ ἀποθνήισκειν κακόν· οἱ θεοὶ γὰρ οὕτω κεκρίκασιν· ἀπέθνηισκον γὰρ ἄν.

§5   The Banks of Acheron

The famous jump from the cliff of Leucas (Sapph. T 211),[21] the mythical sea cliff from which one threw oneself to forget his/her own losses in love (cf. Anacr. fr. 376.1 *PMG*, Men. *Leuc.* 40–47 Arnott), and the "I'd truly like to be dead" motif

18 For ἀμάχανον cf. Hom. *H.Merc.* 434 ἔρος ἀμήχανος.

19 This compound (on which see Broger 1996: 121 ff.) does not occur again before Sophron (*PSI* 1214d.2) and the Hellenistic epigram (Posid. *A.P.* 5.134.4, Mel. *A.P.* 12.109.3); but cf. already Theogn. 1353 ff. πικρὸς καὶ γλυκύς ἐστι καὶ ἁρπαλέος καὶ ἀπηνής, | ὄφρα τέλειος ἔηι, Κύρνε, νέοισιν ἔρως.

20 11.586 K.: εἰ γὰρ ἀναμίξας ἀκριβῶς ἴσον ἀψινθίου καὶ μέλιτος ὄγκον ἐπιθείης τῆι γλώττηι, γλυκύπικρον, ὥσπερ οἱ ποιηταὶ τὸν ἔρωτα προσαγορεύουσι, φανεῖταί σοι τὸ μικτὸν ἐξ ἀμφοῖν.

21 See Nagy 1973 (later in Greene 1996a: 5–57).

of F 94.1 clearly repeat traditional forms. F 95 allows us to catch a glimpse of a more precise personal stance in a dialogue with Hermes:

```
_.ου[
ἦρ’ ἀ[
δηρατ.[
_Γογγυλα.[                                    4
ἦ τι σᾶμ’ ἐθε.[
παισι μάλιστα.[
_μας γ’ εἴσηλθ’ ἐπ.[                          7
εἶπον· ὦ δέσποτ’, ἐπ.[
ο]ὐ μὰ γὰρ μάκαιραν [
_ο]ὐδὲν ἄδομ’ ἔπαρθ’ ἀγα[                     10
κατθάνην δ’ ἴμερός τις [ἔχει με καὶ
λωτίνοις δροσόεντας [ ὄ-
_χ[θ]οις ἴδην Ἀχερ[                           13
.]..δεσαιδ’.[
.].νδετο.[
_μητισε                                       16
```

5 ἐθέσ[πισδε Diehl   6–7 Ἔρ-|μας Blass, Ἔρ-|μαις Lobel-Page   8 e.g. ἔπλ[εό μοι φίλος (cf. Alc. fr. 71.1 φίλος μὲν ἦσθα)   9 fin. ἔγωγ’ Edmonds   10 ἄγα[ν Schubart   ἔπαρθα γᾶ[ς ἔοισα West   fin. πόθοισι suppleverim; ἄσαισι Di Benedetto   13 Ἀχέρ[οντος Lobel, Ἀχερ[οισίοις Fränkel (cf. A. A. 1160 f. Ἀχερουσίους | ὄχθους)

...

Gongyla   4

indeed, a sign foretold [...]
[...] most [... Her-]
mes[22] came [...]   7

I said: "Lord, [you have been my friend.]
No, by the blessed goddess, [I][23]

---

22   For a defense of the form Ἔρμας against Lobel-Page's emendation Ἔρμαις see Hooker 1977: 30–34.
23   At l. 9, just as at l. 6, there must have been an anaclastic form of the glyconic: we can

do not like to let myself be raised too much [by desires,]   10

[but I have] a wish to die [and]
to see the dewy banks of
Acheron covered with lotus blossoms ["   13

...

Sappho—or at least the fictionalized persona called Sappho staged by the poet—is fantasizing about landing at the shores of the Underworld as if it were an immersion into a fairy scenario, where dew and lotus take the place of the asphodels of Hom. *Od.* 24.13 (cf. 11.539 and 573) in keeping with F 96 ll. 12–14 and already the Διὸς ἀπάτη (Hom. *Il.* 14.348 λωτόν θ' ἐρσήεντα).

To recover the line of thought of the lyric discourse on the basis of the extant data is very arduous. Yet the epiphany of Hermes *psychopomp*, his own words, and the oath by Persephone may lead one to envisage a situation (perhaps only dreamed of or narrated to Gongyla) where a sign (σᾶμα) has announced to the speaking "I" an impending death; perhaps the poet has seen Hermes appearing before her eyes and she has immediately declared to him that she longs to land at the flowered banks of the Acheron.[24]

Since the passive form of the verb ἐπαίρω (ἔπαρθ(αι) l. 10) in relation to emotional states of mind normally qualifies an attitude inclining towards exaltation or at least confidence,[25] the speaking "I," faced with the prospect of death, must have said that she did not want to yield to delusions or empty hopes. Since after ἄγα[v there is room only for the dative of a bacchic-shaped noun (‿ - -) linked to ἔπαρθ', we must therefore posit a reference in the lacuna to a consolatory element that was either thought of as vain and inadequate or as dangerous and potentially deceitful, depending on wheth-er the phrase was in contrast with the following formulation of the desire to

---

hence posit in the lacuna at line end a sequence ‿ - in order to obtain a series interpretable as choriambic dimeter B (cf. F 96.7 -κεσσιν ὡς ποτ' ἀελίω). Since it is difficult to envisage the name, in the accusative, of a female deity beginning with a vowel and having the shape of ‿ -, one can think to supplement [ἔγωγ' (Edmonds) and identify in μάκαιραν an allusion to Persephone.

24 I do not believe that in the lacuna of the second part of l. 8 Sappho wanted to declare so much that she was not at all afraid (ἔπτ[ακον οὐδάμως Di Benedetto) as rather that the god's arrival was pleasant or unexpected to her.

25 Cf. Hdt. 1.120.3 εὐτυχίαι ἐπαίρεσθαι, 5. 81.2 εὐδαιμονίηι ... μεγάληι ἐπαρθέντες, Xen. *Cyr.* 1.6.21 δώροις ἐπαίρεσθαι, Plut. *Mor.* 32d μηδ' ἐπαίρεσθαι τοῖς παρὰ τῶν πολλῶν ἐπαίνοις.

die ("I do not delude myself that I shall survive") or instead prepared it as a kind of praeteritio ("I do not delude myself that dying is beautiful").[26]

On either reading, the desire to die and the fancy for the Underworld as an idyllic place imply, apart from the mystic beliefs that we have already tracked down in *Against Andromeda* (see V § 3), an attraction that is insidiously antithetical to erotic drives.

§6   F 31: The Occasion

But let us go back to F 31 and its communicative *Sitz im Leben*. As far as our evidence goes the ode seems to be organized along the opposition drawn between φαίνεταί μοι ... ἔμμεν᾽ of l. 1 ff.[27] and φαίνομ᾽ ἔμ᾽ αὔται of l. 16: to the initial deixis κῆνος ... ὤνηρ corresponds a monologic retreat at the end of the description of the pathological symptoms.

It has often been asked whether "that man" is to be envisaged as present or not at the moment of the actual performance: this question is strictly linked to the longstanding issue whether ἴσος θέοισιν at l. 1 represents the formulaic expression of a nuptial wish.

We can try to answer these questions starting from the acknowledgment of an inner tension within the lyric discourse. Whereas the indicative mood of φαίνεται (l. 1), ἰσδάνει (l. 3) and ὐπακούει (l. 4) itself implies an actual dimension, the demonstrative κῆνος and the indefinite pronoun ὄττις ("whoever may be that")[28] distance the man, blurring his outlines into an evanescent symbolic figure: as observed by Aloni,[29] " 'that man' is defined by his distance."[30]

---

26   Especially according to the latter interpretation, dew and lotus are not "decorative details" (Page 1955: 86), but rather essential elements for presenting the journey in the Underworld as desirable. Arriving in a landscape covered by trees where one can sing while reclining on the blooming meadows can be found in Simon. F. 22 W.^{2} (= 9 G.-P.); for its utopian dimension see Mace 1996.

27   Although A.D. *Pron.* 1.82.14 ff. (= Sapph. F 165) mentions the presence of the expression φαίνεταί ϝοι somewhere in Sappho's poetry, φαίνεταί μοι transmitted by [Longinus] must be kept. Furthermore the same Apollonius Dyscolus (*ibid.* 1.59.9 ff.) elsewhere quotes the beginning of our poem as φαίνεταί μοι.

28   See Page 1955: 20 ff.

29   Aloni 1997: 63. One can compare the function of κῆνος in Alc. F 68.4; 70.6; 72.7; 129.14.

30   See also Latacz 1985: 83: "der Mann, von dem die Rede ist, hat vor dem Augenblick des Sprechakts noch keine Existenz."

The parallel adduced by Winkler[31] with Hom. *Od.* 6.158 ff. (Odysseus is addressing Nausicaa), where κεῖνος identifies a hypothetical, future spouse of the girl, is enlightening in this respect:

κεῖνος δ᾿ αὖ περὶ κῆρι μακάρτατος ἔξοχον ἄλλων,
ὅς κέ σ᾿ ἐέδνοισι βρίσας οἴκόνδ᾿ ἀγάγηται

But happier in his heart than all others will be that man, who,
prevailing in the contest of wedding gifts, will conduct you to his
home

Also, Sappho elsewhere calls the groom (or the spouses) "godlike" and compares him to a specific deity (F 44.21 and 34 and F 111.5). Yet in this case the comparison with Odysseus' praise of the man who will have Nausicaa as his bride, whereas it confirms the nuptial overtone of the *incipit* of the poem (as already claimed by Wilamowitz and then Snell),[32] at the same time contrasts with an epithalamian contextualization of the ode as a whole.[33]

As a point of fact the scene cannot refer either to the wedding procession (groom and bride proceeding side by side on foot or on a wagon) or to the banquet at the bride's paternal house before the actual departure of the nuptial party, since during such an occasion the couple did not sit in front of each other but separately, the tables of the men being distinct from those of the women (in the Ἀνακαλυπτομένη of the comic poet Evangelus we are even told the number of the tables, cf. F 1.1 f. K.-A.).

The intimacy evoked by man and woman sitting in front of each other is instead consistent with a context of courtship: from the Cologne *Epode* of Archilochus (frr. 196A.14–16 and also 28–30 W.²) to the *Ephesian Tales* of Xenophon (1.3) and up to Musaeus' epyllion *Hero and Leander*, wooing generally takes place within the space of a sanctuary during a religious festival. This context represented "one of the few places where it was possible, given the constraints of Greek society, for affairs, initial overtures between adolescents, and proposals of marriage to occur":[34] it is exactly

31 Winkler 1990: 178–80.
32 See Wilamowitz 1913: 56–9, and Snell 1931.
33 Against this contextualization see Snyder 1997: 29 ff., who however does not explain the role played by the man of the *incipit*.
34 Gentili 1988: 187 (on the Cologne *Epode* of Archilochus).

within such a context that Sappho could express the feelings described in the poem.

But how do we account then for the explosion of the panic attack syndrome? The text explains it clearly: the man (the wooer) who sits in front of you while you sweetly talk to him and lovingly laugh at him seems to me to be godlike and that causes in me this anxiety. . .

It has been long debated whether τό at l. 5 (corresponding to Catullus' *quod*) refers to the two indicatives ("is sitting" and "is listening") or to the two participles (the girl's sweet talk and lovely laughter). However, even if formally it is the "lovingly laughing" that is in the foreground, as suggested by the enjambment at the beginning of both line and stanza, the reaction of the "I" is triggered by the sight of the girl's laughter and words, inasmuch as this laughter and these words are embedded within the communicative context of the girl herself and the man sitting in front of her.

Within such a web of relationships the panic attack occupying the center of the ode can only be interpreted as a phobic anticipation of an event inscribed in the ordinary history of the group: the symbolic frame set up in the first stanza announces to the "I," as in a sort of premonition, that that girl is already ready for marriage and will soon wed and abandon those habits ingrained and integrated within her when she was only an unripe *pais*,[35] with all the emotional implications that we have observed in F 94 and F 96.

Hence we can understand the sense of quasi-death, which has telling precedents in Andromache's fear for her husband in Hom. *Il.* 22.452–54 and 460–74.[36] Andromache first speaks of her throbbing heart, her loosening knees, her terror lest Hector may have been cut off outside the city gates. The poet then describes the darkness of night falling on her eyes and adds that from her head she cast the diadem, the net, the ribbon, and the veil that had been given to her as bridal gifts. Finally the sequence closes with the image of Andromache seized by a distress (l. 474 ἀτυζομένην) dragging her to the threshold of death.

§7   Eros and Poverty

The erotic dimension is anything but absent from the poem. Yet it does not so much represent its substance as rather its premises: the anxiety for detach-

35 See Williamson 1995: 154–60, esp. 159: "all the singer's actions—complimenting the man, praising the girl, expressing grief at separation—can be linked with the situation of a girl's approaching marriage."

36 See Di Benedetto 1987: 29 ff.

ment bursts in because the departure of the girl will break a long-cherished bond.

Yet what triggers the series of symptoms described by Sappho is not eros but the deep sensation of dismay conveyed by the aorist ἐπτόαισεν.[37] In this context the meaning of the word goes well beyond the state of bewildered astonishment attested in the alleged parallels that have been adduced in relation to the erotic specialization of the verb.[38] In those passages the connection between the verb and the phobic symptoms that is so fundamental for the inner structure of F 31 is totally missing.

We can instead find a reference to sweat (ἄσπετος ἰδρώς), the immediacy of the phenomenon (αὐτίκα), the use of the verb πτοιῶμαι in conjunction with the act of looking (ἐσορῶν) in Mimnermus fr. 5.1–5 W.[2] (= "Theognis" 1017–21):[39]

> αὐτίκα μοι κατὰ μὲν χροιὴν ῥέει ἄσπετος ἰδρώς,
>   πτοιῶμαι δ᾽ ἐσορῶν ἄνθος ὁμηλικίης
> τερπνὸν ὁμῶς καὶ καλόν· ἐπὶ πλέον ὤφελεν εἶναι·
>   ἀλλ᾽ ὀλιγοχρόνιον γίνεται ὥσπερ ὄναρ
> ἥβη τιμήεσσα ...   5

> ... straightway down along my skin flows unstopping sweat,
>   and I am confused as I look at the flower of my age-mates,
> pleasurable and beautiful at once. If only it lasted longer!
>   But precious youth is of little duration
> as a dream...   5

What is described here is certainly not a state of being enamored but rather the deep dismay that seizes the speaking "I" when, confronted with its usual

---

37 Inasmuch as it is correlated to a protasis marked by ὡς + subjunctive (ὡς ἴδω), the function of this aorist indicative is not only "ingressive" but also "anticipatory."

38 See Lanata 1966: 77 and Burzacchini 1977: 142–43, with the reference to F 22.13–14 ἁ γὰρ κατάγωγις αὔτα[ν | ἐπτόαισ᾽ ἴδοισαν, Alc. F 283.3 ff. κἀλένας ἐν στήθ[ε]σιν [ἐ]πτ[όαισεν | θῦμον Ἀργείας, Anacr. fr. 346, fr. 1.11 f. *PMG* πολλοὶ | πολ]ιητέων φρένας ἐπτοέαται (yet Anacreon also uses the verb to denote the fear of the abandoned fawn at fr. 408.3 *PMG*), but also the precise notes of Privitera 1974: 107–8, who also mentions two Homeric passages related to panic (*Od.* 18.340 ὡς εἰπὼν ἐπέεσσι διεπτοίησε γυναῖκας and 22.298 τῶν δὲ φρένες ἐπτοίηθεν).

39 I.e., in a text earlier than Sappho, if we accept the "early" chronology of Mimnermus, tied to the testimony of the *Suda* (3.397.20 Adler) = T 1 G.-P. (at his height in 632 BC) and the identification of the solar eclipse that the poet mentions (fr. 20 W.[2] = 20 G.-P.) with that of 648 BC.

object of desire ("the contemporary," subsumed in the collective singular of Homeric reminiscence ὁμηλικίη), it anxiously reflects on the brevity of youth. Furthermore, if F 31 were really to represent the effects of love at first sight, the expression πὰν τόλματον in the admittedly most problematic last (to us) line of the ode (l. 17) would make no sense. What can be endured is not eros but anxiety, perhaps comforted by a line of thought that West,[40] on the basis of ἐπεὶ {καὶ} πένητα, has identified in the confidence (or at least hope) that sooner or later things will change, just as a poor man may suddenly become rich through the gods' favor.

The link between an oppressive state of mind and a reference to poverty finds a precise parallel in an elegy of the Theognidean sylloge (ll. 657–66):

> Μηδὲν ἄγαν χαλεποῖσιν ἀσῶ φρένα μηδ᾽ ἀγαθοῖσιν
>   χαῖρ᾽, ἐπεὶ ἔστ᾽ ἀνδρὸς πάντα φέρειν ἀγαθοῦ.
> Οὐδ᾽ ὀμόσαι χρὴ τοῦτο· τί; μήποτε πρᾶγμα τόδ᾽ ἔσται;
>   θεοὶ γάρ τοι νεμεσῶσ᾽, οἷσιν ἔπεστι τέλος·   660
> †καιπρηξαι† μέντοι τι· καὶ ἐκ κακοῦ ἐσθλὸν ἔγεντο
>   καὶ κακὸν ἐξ ἀγαθοῦ. καί τε πενιχρὸς ἀνήρ
> αἶψα μάλ᾽ ἐπλούτησε καὶ ὃς μάλα πολλὰ πέπαται
>   ἐξαπίνης ἀπό τ(οι) οὖν ὤλεσε νυκτὶ μιῆι.
> καὶ σώφρων ἥμαρτε, καὶ ἄφρονι πολλάκι δόξα   665
>   ἕσπετο, καὶ τιμῆς καὶ κακὸς ὢν ἔλαχεν.

Do not load down your spirit too much with burdens, nor rejoice too
    much at good fortune, since it is the lot of a good man to endure all.
Nor need you swear saying: "What? This will never be."
The gods, on whom the outcome depends, might be angered.   660
[...] and it happens that from evil arises good,
    and from good evil: a poor man
unexpectedly becomes rich, one who possesses much
    at one stroke loses all in a single night.
A prudent man errs and often fortune accompanies   665
    the fool, who gains honor even if he is unworthy.

West has observed that, according to this interpretation, the closure of F 31 could well express the same optimism (the same confidence in a future suc-

40 West 1970: 312–13.

cess) as that present in the closure of the *Ode to Aphrodite,* and he has linked
the possibility of a change in the future to "that man" ("the man who appeared
ἴσος θέοισιν, and was displaced from our attention almost at once by his companion, is sharply recalled by the warning that prosperity may collapse if God
so wills. The tables may be turned."). But, as West himself observes, after the
first stanza we entirely lose sight of the man, and, in addition, the link between
the invitation to endure and the appeal to the law of change that is evoked by
the prior mention of the poor who may become rich (not of the rich who may
become poor) suggests a more immediate reference to the speaking "I."

Beyond the crisis caused by the anticipation of the future departure of the
beloved, the text must have envisaged the possibility of a restored emotional
balance and joy of life, in keeping with the therapeutic function of the crisis
from a panic attack. Once the pathological syndrome has exhausted itself, the
afflicted person recognizes herself as free from the anxieties that the crisis had
brought to light.

§8   The Context

We have seen so far that F 31 does not offer any "stage" directions referring to
external scenarios/perspectives that fall within the perception of the audience.
The only "external" reference we can find in F 31 is to a space where a man,
unknown to us, is sitting in front of an equally anonymous girl. On the other
hand, a reference to the actual performance can be seen in F 22,[41] a poem that
shares with F 31 the motif of "fear induced by sight" (compare here again the
use of the same verb πτόαμι):

> .].ε.[....].[...κ]έλομαι σ.[9
> ..].γυλα.[...]ανθι λάβοισα.α.[
> πᾶ]κτιν, ἄς σε δηὖτε πόθος τέ[ουτος
> _   ἀμφιπόταται   12
> τὰν κάλαν· ἀ γὰρ κατάγωγις αὔτα[ν
> ἐπτόαισ᾽ ἴδοισαν, ἔγω δὲ χαίρω,
> ____ καὶ γὰρ αὔτα δή πο[τ᾽] ἐμεμφ[

41   In fact line 9 is the first line of fr. 15 of P.Oxy. 1231: its join with another fragment (fr.
12), suggested by Lobel in his 1925 edition and accepted by Voigt, has been called into doubt by
Yatromanolakis 1999b.

  _ Κ]υπρογέν[ηα   16
 ὡς ἄραμα[ι
 τοῦτο τῶ[
 β]όλλομα[ι

9 σ᾽ ἀ[είδην West 10 Γο]γγύλα Wilamowitz, Γο]γγύλαν multi [Ἄβ]ανθι Lobel-Page,
[Μέλ]ανθι vel [Κλέ]ανθι Di Benedetto; fort. [ὦ Ἄβ]ανθι λάβοισαν Theander 11 τέ[ουτος
supplevi 13 αὖτα[ν Diehl 15 fort. ἐμέμφ[ετ᾽ (Hunt) ἄμμι (Milne)

... I call on you [to sing of]   9
Gongyla, [Ab]anthis, taking [...]
the harp until anew [a like] charm
    fly about you   12

who are beautiful, because this cloak frightened her
upon seeing it, and I am pleased,
and in fact once the very goddess
    native of Cyprus faulted us   16

as I pray [...]
this ...
I desire ...

    A girl, probably named Abanthis,[42] is invited at once to take the pektis and
to praise in song the same Gongyla whom we have already encountered as a
runaway to Gorgo's group in T 213 (cf. VII § 7) and whom the *Suda* (Σ 107)
mentions as a "pupil" from Colophon. Abanthis must sing until[43] the charm of
desire once again flies around her: for the sight of Abanthis' dress has excited
Gongyla and Sappho is pleased about it, especially since, as far as one can infer

---

    42 The sequence [...]ανθι was completed as Ἄβ]ανθι by Lobel-Page on the basis of com-
parison with *Inc. Auct.* 35.8, as Κλέ]ανθι or Μέλ]ανθι by Di Benedetto 1986: 22. To get
around the brevity of the supplement Ἄβ]ανθι one might consider [ὦ Ἄβ]ανθι with synalephe, cf. Alc. F 130b.4 ὠγεσιλαΐδα. 307a.1 ὦναξ, 365.2 ὦ Αἰσιμίδα and see Hamm 1958: § 80.
    43 With ἆς (= ἕως) at l. 11, cf. F 4.5, 9.6, 25.3, 45 and 88.15; cf. Di Benedetto 1987: 60–64.
For the image of charm flying about, cf. Catul. 68.133 ff. *quam circumcursans hinc illinc saepe
Cupido / fulgebat,* Hor. *Carm.* 1.2.33–34 *Erycina ridens, / quam Iocus circumvolat et Cupido,*
Quint. Sm. 5.71 τὴν δ᾽ Ἵμερος ἀμφεποτᾶτο, for the supplement τέ[ουτος F 56.2–3 and 113.1–2.

from the last extant words, Aphrodite had once faulted Abanthis' dress, extending her reproach to Sappho herself.[44]

The turn of phrase may cause surprise: one would expect that it is the girl who is praised (Gongyla) who should wear the charming dress. In this case Sappho would be almost dictating to Abanthis the theme to pursue in the song, namely praising her friend. Several ineffectual attempts have thus been made to reconcile the text with this interpretation.[45]

But if it is Abanthis who is wearing the dress, and Gongyla remains troubled by its recall, this means that Sappho does not intend to instruct Abanthis on the theme of the song that she ought shortly to sing. She wants rather to suggest to her that she should choose the occasion to sing for Gongyla, taking advantage of the astonishment that her own garment has just aroused in her friend. This Abanthis should do while this charm surrounds her and highlights her beauty. In other words, music and song should combine with beauty of figure and elegance of the cloak as instruments of seduction.

Even if Sappho's direction, at the moment in which an exemplary situation of internal relations of the group occurs, moves in a triangle figured of herself, Abanthis, and Gongyla, this does not imply that the performative scenario is of a private character. What rather suggests the opposite is the object that constitutes the scene's visual focus, namely the garment called κατάγωγις at line 13. This κατάγωγις—as far as we can deduce from Hesychius[46] and its etymology suggests—was a long-sleeved cloak that came down to the feet, an expensive himation suitable for a young girl to wear in public, a young girl who knew how to sing and play the pektis. The habitual costume of musicians playing the cithara and the aulos on Attic black-figure ceramics of the sixth century BC consists of a richly adorned chiton and himation. And the Parcae, who dance and sing at the wedding of Peleus and Thetis at Catul. 64.305–6, are clothed in a white garment with a purple hem that falls all the way to the feet: *his corpus*

---

44   See Gentili 1988: 86 n. 71.

45   In particular, it has been suggested restoring at the end of line 13 not αὔτα[ν (Diehl) but αὔτα[ς σ' (West), with the reference of τὰν κάλαν of line 13 being as much Abanthis as Gongyla (see Stehle 1997: 304: "because it stands at the beginning of the line and has the same metrical shape as Γογγύλαν two lines above, it could be heard as applying to Gongyla also and epitomizing what Abanthis should sing about her"). But with αὔτα[ς σ' the elision would violate the block of synapheia without respecting the verse pause between the first and second hendecasyllable of the Sapphic strophe (furthermore the copyist would have written σ' at the beginning of the following line); also, τὰν κάλαν is clearly linked, with emphatic hyperbaton, to σε of line 11.

46   Hesych. Κ 1043 καταγωγίς· ἱμάτιον ποιόν, παράπηχυ γυναικεῖον.

tremulum complectens undique vestis / candida purpurea talos incinxerat ora. And in Theocritus' *Pharmaceutria,* Simaetha, who has put on a tunic of fine linen to take part in a procession to Artemis' sanctuary, at the moment of leaving the house, wraps herself in a cloak—a ξυστίς, again a long refined garment descending to the feet—borrowed from Clearista.[47]

This display of the κατάγωγις recurs in the parodic echo that we find in Euripides' *Cyclops* when, imitating precisely Sapph. F 22 (but with collusion with F 16),[48] the coryphaeus of satyrs imagines that Helen abandoned Menelaus after being overwhelmed by the vision of the multicolored trousers Paris wore, as well as the large chain hanging from his neck (ll. 182–86):

> τὴν προδότιν, ἣ τοὺς θυλάκους τοὺς ποικίλους
> περὶ τοῖν σκελοῖν ἰδοῦσα καὶ τὸν χρύσεον
> κλωιὸν φοροῦντα περὶ μέσον τὸν αὐχένα
> ἐξεπτοήθη, Μενέλεων ἀνθρώπιον
> λῷστον λιποῦσα.

... the traitress! When she saw him put on a pair of multicolored trousers, and wear a large chain of gold around his neck, she stayed open-mouthed and abandoned Menelaus, that brave little man.

F 21,[49] where the same type of invitation to sing as that of F 23 reappears, and F 160 can also confidently be placed in a context of songs performed in succession during a festival:

> τάδε νῦν ἑταίραις
> ταῖσ᾽ ἔμαισι τέρπνα κάλως ἀείσω.

2 ἔμαισι Seidler: ἐμαῖς Athen. 13, 571c-d (cod. A)

... now these delightful words
shall I artfully sing for my companions.

---

47   Theocr. 2.74 κἀμφιστειλαμένα τὰν ξυστίδα τὰν Κλεαρίστας.
48   See Di Marco 1980 and Napolitano 2003: 112.
49   On this fragment see XV, § 5.

If we accept this, the most economical of the proposed solutions[50] for restoring what seems to be part of a Sapphic strophe, the phrase ταὶς ἔμαισι ... κάλως ἀείσω seems to correspond to the ἄεισον ἄμμι of F 21.12. The only difference is that, considering that Sappho did not refer to her pupils with the term ἔταιραι (which denotes a familiar rapport between age-mates, cf. F 142 and F 126), the *persona loquens* here must be one of the girls of the group.

---

50   That is Seidler's ἔμαισι. For the legitimate combination of the "short" dative ἐταίραις and the "long" ἔμαισι cf. F 81.4 ἐράταις φόβαισιν (Voigt accepts Fick's emendation ἐράτοις), Alc. F 130b.15 συνόδοισί μ᾽ αὔταις (v. l. ταύταις). In general, for the presence of "short" datives in Aeolic lyric, cf. also Sapph. F 44.21 and 55.3 (Voigt accepts Fick's emendation δόμωι).

XV "Pathography" 2: Old Age

§1   The New Sappho of Cologne

We have seen that a minute delineation of symptoms of fear occupies the central stanzas of F 31. Similarly, a description of symptoms of old age is the central theme of a poem that a recent papyrus find has allowed us to recover almost in its entirety. In what follows, to avoid confusion in line numbers between F 58 Voigt and the new Cologne papyrus (P.Köln VII, 429), we shall call this poem the "Old Age Poem."

Recovered from mummy cartonnage, P.Köln Inv. 21351 was first published by Gronewald and Daniel in the summer of 2004,[1] and shortly after the first editors added another piece (Inv. 21376) belonging to the same papyrus roll.[2] They have subsequently published the last extant part of the papyrus (fr. 2, col. II ll. 9–21)[3] that preserves a lyric poem composed in a language and meter surely non-Sapphic and that has been copied by a different, though contemporary, hand. It is thus legitimate to infer that the papyrus roll, or at least part of it, contained a lyric anthology.

The handwriting of both the Sapphic and non-Sapphic poems is characteristic of the first decades of the third century BC: the Cologne roll is therefore our oldest known papyrus of Sappho, earlier even than the poem (F 2) preserved by the so-called Florentine ostrakon and that on the headband for Cleis (F 98) preserved by the Copenhagen and Milan papyri.

The text of the Cologne papyrus partly overlaps with that transmitted by P.Oxy. 1787, fr. 1 (= F 58), a papyrus dating to the end of the second century

1   Gronewald-Daniel 2004a.
2   Gronewald-Daniel 2004b.
3   Gronewald-Daniel 2005.

AD (see II, § 3). An interesting surprise offered by the Cologne papyrus is that the remnants of the poems preceding and following the twelve lines of the "Old Age Poem" are not the same as those transmitted by P.Oxy. 1787.

The lack of correspondence between the text of the Cologne papyrus and what in P.Oxy. 1787 fr. 1 precedes line 11 has confirmed Gallavotti's hypothesis that line 11, with its address to a group of young girls (and not line 13, as supposed by others), represents the very beginning of the "Old Age Poem."[4] On the other hand the absence in the new papyrus of the two distichs that were recovered on the basis of P.Oxy. 1787, fr. 1.23–25 and fr. 2.1 and the quotation from Clearch. fr. 41 Wehrli, and that had so far been considered as the end of Sappho's "Old Age Poem" (cf. V, § 5), has shown that this very same poem came to an early closure that emphasized the theme of old age without any explicitly consolatory elements in it.

§2   Old Age Poem

We have already treated both the poem that in the Cologne papyrus precedes the poem on old age (see V, § 4) and the one that follows it in the Oxyrhynchus papyrus (that is, F 58.23–26: see V, § 5). Let us now turn to the "Old Age Poem" itself:

> x - ˘ ˘ - - - ἰ]οκ[ό]λπων κάλα δῶρα, παῖδες,
> _x - ˘ ˘ - -]. φιλάοιδον λιγύραν χελύνναν   2
> x - ˘ ˘ - -] ποτ᾽ [ἔ]οντα χρόα γῆρας ἤδη
> _x - ˘ ˘ λεῦκαι δ᾽ ἐγ]ένοντο τρίχες ἐκ μελαίναν,   4
> βάρυς δέ μ᾽ ὁ [θ]ῦμος πεπόηται, γόνα δ᾽ οὐ φέροισι,
> _τὰ δή ποτα λαίψηρ᾽ ἔον ὄρχησθ᾽ ἴσα νεβρίοισιν.   6
> τα<ῦτα> στεναχίσδω θαμέως, ἀλλὰ τί κεν ποείην;
> _ἀγήραον ἄνθρωπον ἔοντ᾽ οὐ δύνατον γένεσθαι·   8
> καὶ γὰρ π[ο]τα Τίθωνον ἔφαντο βροδόπαχυν Αὔων
> _ἔρωι ...α.εισαν βάμεν᾽ εἰς ἔσχατα γᾶς φέροισα[ν   10
> ἔοντα [κ]άλον καὶ νέον, ἀλλ᾽ αὖτον ὔμως ἔμαρψε
> _χρόνωι πόλιον γῆρας ἔχ[ο]ντ᾽ ἀθανάταν ἄκοιτιν.   12

1 init. Ὕμμες πεδὰ Μοίσαν West (Μοίσαν iam Stiebitz), Ὕμμιν φίλα Μοίσαν Di Benedetto; fort. Αἰ στέργετε Μοίσαν   2 init. χορεύσατε (olim Di Benedetto) vel ἐλίσσετε κὰτ τὰ]ν sup-

---

4 See Di Benedetto 1985: 147.

pleverim: σπουδάσδετε καὶ τὰ]ν West (τὰ]μ [l. τὰν] iam Gronewald-Daniel), πρέπει δὲ λάβην τὰ]ν Di Benedetto   3 init. ἔμοι μὲν ἔκαρψεν] Snell, ἔμοι δ᾽ ἄπαλον (hoc iam Gronewald-Daniel) πρίν] Di Benedetto   4 init. ἐπέλλαβε West, διώλεσε Di Benedetto   λεῦκαι et ἐγ]ένοντο Hunt δ᾽ Lobel   7–12 suppl. Gronewald-Daniel   10 ἔρωι <ἴ>φι δάμεισαν βάμεν᾽ possis: ἔρωι δέπας εἰσανβάμεν (εἰσομβάμεν) Gronewald-Daniel, ἔρωι φ..αθεισαν βάμεν᾽ West, ἔρωι λα[λ]άγεισαν βάμεν᾽ Janko

[If you love,] o girls, the beautiful gifts [of the Muses] of the violet
   bosom,
[dance to the tune of this] melodious lyre that loves the song,   2
[but my body], once [tender], old age already
has seized,] and my hair has turned white from black,   4
and my heart has become heavy, my knees do not support me,
that once a time were nimble in dancing as fawns.   6
I often bewail this: but what could I do?
Being mortal you cannot escape old age   8
for they said that once rose-armed Dawn,
conquered by the force of her passion,[5] carried off Tithonus,   10
who was handsome and young, to the world's end,
but him too, who had an immortal wife, gray age seized in time.   12

The first editors of the Cologne papyrus have already adduced a series of passages that attest to the conventional character of this symptomatology of old age at least since Archilochus fr. 188.1–2 W.[2]:[6]

Οὐκέθ᾽ ὁμῶς θάλλεις ἁπαλὸν χρόα· κάρφεται γὰρ ἤδη
   ὀγμοῖς, κακοῦ δὲ γήραος καθαιρεῖ ...

You are no longer blooming thus in your gentle flesh: it has already
   withered
   with wrinkles, and [the dooming lot] of the ugly old age is seizing you.

___
5 In P.Köln what precedes the sure ειcαν must have been μ, not αc (Gronewald-Daniel) nor ΑΓ (Janko). At the beginning of the line immediately after ερωι, the reading φ, already suggested by West, seems plausible (the first editors read δ) above all because of the extant traces of a vertical bar in the central area of the letter. Line 10 might then have begun with ἔρωι (or Ἔρωι) <ἴ>φι δάμεισα: this expression has precise parallel in F 102.2 πόθωι δάμεισα and Theogn. 1350 καλοῦ παιδὸς ἔρωτι δαμείς. For the juxtaposition of the dative of agency and ἶφι cf. Hom. Il. 19.416–17 ἀλλὰ σοὶ αὐτῶι μόρσιμόν ἐστι θεῶι τε καὶ ἀνέρι ἶφι δαμῆναι; for the synalephe between -ω and ἶ- cf. F 1.11 ὠράνω αἴθερος, 55.1 κείσηι οὐδέ, Soph. Ph. 446 ἐπεὶ οὐδέν and see West 1982: 13–14, Martinelli 1997: 48–49.
6 Gronewald-Daniel 2005: 3.

Mimnermus (frr. 1.5–10 and 2.10–15 W.²) enumerates the miserable consequences of old age "that makes even a handsome man ugly" and in fr. 4, just
as Sappho, he recalls the story of Tithonus "to whom (Zeus) gave old age as an
everlasting evil, which is even more terrible than horrible death."

Particularly close to Sappho's poem is the catalogue of symptoms of old age
listed in Anacreon fr. 395.1–8 *PMG*. We find there the same paratactic articulation; also, Anacreon's symptoms end with a verb (ἀνασταλύζω 7) denoting
the sobbing of the speaking "I" just as in Sappho's "Old Age Poem" at line 7
(στεναχίσδω):

Πολιοὶ μὲν ἡμὶν ἤδη
κρόταφοι κάρη τε λευκόν,
χαρίεσσα δ᾽ οὐκέτ᾽ ἤβη
πάρα, γηραλέοι δ᾽ ὀδόντες,
γλυκεροῦ δ᾽ οὐκέτι πολλὸς
_ βιότου χρόνος λέλειπται·   6
διὰ ταῦτ᾽ ἀνασταλύζω
θαμὰ Τάρταρον δεδοικώς·

My temples are already gray
and my head is white,
graceful youth is no more
by me, my teeth are old,
and a long span of sweet life
is left to me no longer.   6
For these reasons I often
weep fearing Tartarus.

One could also add, as a sarcastic exposition of this motif, the portrait of
the aged lover (perhaps the same as in *Ep.* 12) of *Ep.* 8.1–10 of Horace.

We know that Archilochus, Mimnermus, and Anacreon performed their
poems to the lyre or aulos at the symposia of aristocrats or tyrants, whereas
the fictional persona of Horace addresses a hated woman via the written me-
dium of his book (which in itself does not rule out the possibility of private
readings in front of few selected friends). But what was the context of Sappho's performance?

§3   Roles

According to the first editors of the Cologne papyrus, in the first two lines Sappho would be saying to the young girls whom she is addressing (παῖδες) that she herself will bring the gifts of the Muses by taking up the lyre again.[7] West has reconstructed a rather vague exhortation that they should attend with zest to the gifts of the Muses and the lyre,[8] as if it were normal practice for a chorus of young girls to dance and play the lyre simultaneously. Likewise, Janko has suggested that the beginning of the poem is characterized by the contrast between the singing and dancing of the young girls and the incapacity of the lyric "I" to join in their steps of dance.[9]

The new papyrus has confirmed the presence, already suspected by Edmonds, of the verb ὄρχησθ(αι) at line 6: the enumeration of the symptoms of old age clearly culminates in the impossibility of dancing on the part of the speaking voice. We can then understand that Sappho must have been inviting the young girls of her group not to listen or play but to dance, just as Abanthis was invited to dance in *Inc. Auct.* 35.8:].ιν ὄρχησθ[᾽ ἐρό]εσσ᾽ Ἄβανθι.

Old age prevents the poet from leading the dances of the chorus as she once used to do, as is attested by an anonymous epigram of Hellenistic age[10] (*A.P.* 9.189 = anon. 38 *FGE*):

Ἔλθετε πρὸς τέμενος ταυρώπιδος ἀγλαὸν Ἥρης,
   Λεσβίδες, ἁβρὰ ποδῶν βήμαθ᾽ ἑλισσόμεναι·
ἔνθα καλὸν στήσασθε θεῆι χορόν· ὕμμι δ᾽ ἀπάρξει
   Σαπφὼ χρυσείην χερσὶν ἔχουσα λύρην.
ὄλβιαι ὀρχηθμοῦ πολυγηθέος· ἦ γλυκὺν ὕμνον
   εἰσαΐειν αὐτῆς δόξετε Καλλιόπης.

---

7   Gronewald-Daniel 2005: 5: "[Ich bringe hier] der purpurgegürten [Musen] schöne Gaben" on the basis of the editors' conjecture for the beginning of the line φέρω (vel ἔχω) τάδε.

8   West 2005: 5: Ὕμμες πεδὰ Μοίσαν ... | σπουδάσδετε καὶ τὰ]ν φιλάοιδον λιγύραν χελύνναν: "[You for] the fragrant-bosomed Muses' lovely gifts / [be zealous,] girls, [and the] clear melodious lyre."

9   Janko 2005: 19.

10   See Page 1981: 338: "The epigram is manifestly Alexandrian in style and spirit."

Come to the splendid sanctuary of ox-eyed Hera,
   girls of Lesbos, whirling the delicate steps of your feet.
Form there a beautiful chorus in honor of the goddess. Sappho
   will lead you with the golden lyre in her hands.
Blessed you in the joy of your dance: surely you will
   believe you are listening to the sweet song of Calliope herself.

The temple of Hera was the heart of the federal sanctuary dedicated to Zeus, Hera (the central deity), and Dionysus at Messa.[11] It is at this sanctuary that the hetaireia of Alcaeus invokes the punishment of Pittacus in F 129 and where Alcaeus himself is the spectator of the beauty contest of F 130b.[12]

Because of the limits imposed on her by old age, Sappho can sing but cannot join in the dance: her young pupils are thus invited to celebrate the gifts of the Muses by accompanying the music and songs of their teacher (presumably in a sitting posture, as in the above-mentioned hydria from Vari—see VIII § 3—or on the obverse of a coin from Mytilene dating to c. 150 AD and now at the British Museum).[13] Sappho's poem on old age does thus replicate in its basic structure the situation presupposed by Alcman's famous lines on the cerylus and halcyons (fr. 26 *PMGF*).[14] But whereas Alcman's poem in dactylic hexameters must have been part of a kitharodic "proem," which led the way to a parthenion sung and danced by the very same maidens addressed by the poet in the proem, in Sappho's ode the chorus of girls limits itself to dancing.[15]

§4   Aphrodite and Anchises

The narrative of Eos and Tithonus that occupies the final part of the "Old Age Poem" finds its nearest antecedent (perhaps only some decades earlier) in the Homeric *Hymn to Aphrodite*.

11   See Robert 1969: 801–31 and Liberman 1999: I.61 n. 127. Ruins of a late fourth-century BC temple survive in this area. Alcaeus F 130a.15 τεῖχος βασιλήϊον (see also the scholium τὸ τῆς Ἥρας) seems to testify to the presence of a boundary wall surrounding the shrine rather than to the wall of the temple. Sappho refers to this very same sanctuary in F 17 where Hera, Zeus protector of the suppliants, and Dionysus are mentioned.

12   That this was the location of the καλλιστεῖα is attested in Schol. DA in Hom. *Il.* 9.129 παρὰ Λεσβίοις ἀγὼν ἄγεται κάλλους γυναικῶν ἐν τῶι τῆς Ἥρας τεμένει, λεγόμενος καλλιστεῖα.

13   See Bernouilli 1901: 62 ff.

14   On the contextual affinity between Sappho's and Alcman's odes on old age see Lardinois 1996: 169, Ferrari 2003: 72–76, Hardie 2005: 27 ff.

15   For a similar nostalgia for lost youth, see the Athenian Stranger's words in Plat. *Lg.* 657d.

Anchises is terrified at the thought of having united himself with a goddess, and prays Aphrodite not to let him live among the mortals. The goddess replies by exhorting Anchises to be brave and announces that he will have from her a son (Aeneas), destined to rule over the Trojans. At this point Aphrodite mentions to him the story of Eos and Tithonus (ll. 225–38):

τὸν δ᾽ ἦ τοι εἵως μὲν ἔχεν πολυήρατος ἥβη,   225
Ἠοῖ τερπόμενος χρυσοθρόνωι ἠριγενείηι
ναῖε παρ᾽ Ὠκεανοῖο ῥοῇις ἐπὶ πείρασι γαίης·
αὐτὰρ ἐπεὶ πρῶται πολιαὶ κατέχυντο ἔθειραι
καλῆς ἐκ κεφαλῆς εὐηγενέος τε γενείου,
τοῦ δ᾽ ἦ τοι εὐνῆς μὲν ἀπείχετο πότνια Ἠώς,   230
αὐτὸν δ᾽ αὖτ᾽ ἀτίταλλεν ἐνὶ μεγάροισιν ἔχουσα
σίτωι τ᾽ ἀμβροσίηι τε καὶ εἵματα καλὰ διδοῦσα.
ἀλλ᾽ ὅτε δὴ πάμπαν στυγερὸν κατὰ γῆρας ἔπειγεν
οὐδέ τι κινῆσαι μελέων δύνατ᾽ οὐδ᾽ ἀναεῖραι,
ἥδε δέ οἱ κατὰ θυμὸν ἀρίστη φαίνετο βουλή·   235
ἐν θαλάμωι κατέθηκε, θύρας δ᾽ ἐπέθηκε φαεινάς.
τοῦ δ᾽ ἦ τοι φωνὴ ῥεῖ ἄσπετος, οὐδέ τι κῖκυς
ἔσθ᾽ οἵη πάρος ἔσκεν ἐνὶ γναμπτοῖσι μέλεσσιν.

In truth for so long as he was in the period of lovely youth,   225
and gave pleasure to early-born Dawn of golden throne,
he dwelt by the currents of Ocean, at the ends of the earth.
But when the first gray hairs came forth
from his fair head and noble chin,
him did lady Dawn keep away from her bed   230
though yet keeping him in her halls she fed him
with ambrosial food and gave him beautiful clothes.
But when hateful old age weighed him down entirely
and he could no longer move nor raise his limbs,
this seemed to her heart the best decision.   235
She cast him in a bed-chamber, and closed the shining doors
    upon him.

His voice flows forth without end,[16] but his strength
is not that which before existed in his agile limbs.

As many have observed,[17] Aphrodite could have avoided repeating the fatal
forgetfulness of Eos by asking Zeus to bestow on her beloved not only immortality but also eternal youth. Yet this possibility is not even acknowledged,
and the more so because Aphrodite, as she herself immediately adds (247 ff.),
will already have enough trouble in ignoring the other gods' disapproval of her
union with a mortal. Nor does the myth meet with better fortune in the various
tests of immortality that Calypso makes Odysseus undergo, or Demeter the little
Demophon, or Selene Endymion. Anchises himself is well aware that "whoever
will join with immortal goddesses will not have a flourishing life" (189–90).

The "correct" reaction is Sappho's reply "but what can I do?" This is almost a
later version of "but everything can be endured" from F 31, where such awareness stops the enumeration of the pathological symptoms. In both cases the
reference to lived experience results in a recognition of necessity, and giving up
a bond that cannot continue, or a utopia of eternal youth that becomes a cue for
singing, and a wisdom to share that made the poet also a teacher of life. For
a sensible examination of the reference to Tithonus' myth and of the message
the lyric "I" aims to convey to its audience (especially the idea that the Muses'
gifts can remain while sprightliness and beauty do not), see Rawles 2006.

If the most beautiful thing for men is not power or force, whose emblems are
the Lydian chariots and infantry in full armor, but rather to obtain that which
one desires (F 16), then, in a case where this is not possible, its renunciation
—whether through acceptance of institutionalized conditions (departure of a
beloved girl) or biological ones (old age)—becomes the best substitute.

In the case of old age, if one accepts the inevitable decline of one's limbs, the
consolation (but a consolation completely implicit in the text) can come, for a
poet like Sappho, in the joy of still being able to instruct a chorus of adolescent
girls in music and song or in being able to hear the song of a pupil whom the poet
herself has patiently instructed. This last eventuality we find among the frac-
tures of another poem in which the motif of old age occurs, and with the pure
coincidence, in two different metrical patterns, of the same verbal sequence
(χρόα γῆρας ἤδη).

---

16 The reference is to the final metamorphosis of Tithonus into a cicada, according to a tradition already known by Hellanicus of Lesbos (*FGrHist* 4 fr. 140).

17 Strauss Clay 1989: 186 ff.

§5 "Sing for Us"

The fragment in question is F 21, recovered (but with large lacunae) from P.Oxy. 1231. Here too the invitation that the *persona loquens* expresses is tied to the reality of old age—trembling knees (l. 4), dry skin (l. 6), sadness (?) that envelops the mind (l. 7), vanished charm (l. 8), directed here not to a choral group, but rather to a single figure, and concerning not dancing but singing (l. 12):

```
]
].επαβοληϲ[
]ανδ᾽ ὄλοφυν [....]ε.
] τρομέροιϲ π.[..]αλλα
]                                                5
] χρόα γῆραϲ ἤδη
]ν ἀμφιβάϲκει
]ϲ πέταται διώκων
]                                                9
]ταϲ ἀγαύαϲ
]εα, λάβοιϲα
] ἄειϲον ἄμμι
τὰν ἰόκολπον                                      13
]ρων μάλιϲτα
]αϲ π[λ]άναται
```

6 πάντα μοι κάρφει] Snell   7 κώνία ... νόο]ν Snell   8 Ἔρω]ϲ vel Ἴμερο]ϲ Wilamowitz, πόθ]οϲ Di Benedetto   14 fort. μακά]ρων

...

... to be competent[18] ...
... lament ...

---

18 For].επαβοληϲ[Voigt rightly notes: "neque χα]λέπα (Wil. ap. Hunt) placet propter ᾽βόληϲ[ε, neque ἐπάβολ᾽ (Hunt) propter vocat." This must have been a form of the verb ἐπαβόλημ(μ)ι = ἐπηβολέω "to be in charge of (competent)" (cf. Pind. *Pae.* 6.181 ff. (= fr. 52f M.) Μοιϲᾶν | ἐπαβολέοντ[α] ... | ἐννόμων ἐ[νοπ]ᾶν).

... trembling ...

...   5

now old age [desiccates all my] skin
[and sorrow] surrounds [my mind]
[... and longing] flies away in pursuit

...   9

... of the noble
... after taking
[the lyre ...] sing for us
        who has the violet bosom,   13

[...] especially [among the blessed]
... goes wandering ...

Along with this communicative setting, the lyric "I" appears, in an immediate future that will be bound with the music and dance of the addressee, as
though part of a group (ἄμμι of l. 12).

Given the lacunae it is not easy to reconstruct the train of thought, but there
is clearly a relation between something that moves around (line 7) and something that "flies in pursuit" (l. 8). A negative mental disposition (sadness, anxiety) envelops the mind of the subject[19] while a longing (or Pothos)[20] flies far off
in search of other young figures.

These lines and the following invitation to take up the lyre and sing certainly introduce the performance of a song in honor of the figure of the violet
bosom.[21] If the passage concerns violet-bosomed Aphrodite,[22] the general sense
would seem to be that the condition in which Sappho actually finds herself

---

19 Snell (*ap.* Voigt) supplemented κώνία at the beginning of line 7, recalling Hom. *Il.* 6.355
ἐπεί σε ... πόνος φρένας ἀμφιβέβηκεν.

20 For the divinity Pothos cf., e.g., A. *Supp.* 1039 and Posidipp. 129.4 and 137.1 A.-B.

21 The reading τὰν ἰόκολπον (line 13) was recovered from codex A of A.D. *Pron.* 1.97. The
epithet is also attested in F 30.4 ff. νύμ-|φας ἰοκόλπω, in F 103.3 παῖδα Κρονίδα τὰν ἰόκ[ολπ]ον
(Aphrodite?) and 4 ἰόκ[ολ]πος α[and in the "Old Age Poem" 1.

22 See Treu 1954: 189. Also ἀγαύας of line 10 would suit Aphrodite (Homer occasionally
uses the adjective for gods and especially Persephone, cf. *Od.* 11.213, 226 and 635 and also *H.Cer.*
348), but we cannot exclude the possibility that it refers to a *parthenos* (cf. Noss. *A.P.* 6.265.3 ff.
ἀγαυὰ ... Θευφιλίς).

keeps her from celebrating the goddess of love. This is not because her age deters her from playing and singing as she is now doing, but because the years and perhaps also a woeful event (l. 4)[23] distract her from themes dear to the goddess. She nevertheless wishes that the celebration take place, and so invites one of her pupils to dedicate in turn a song to the figure "of the violet bosom."[24]

§6 Premonitions

The work of E. Puglia has given us a happy combination of two scraps of P.Oxy. 1787—namely fr. 3, col. II 15–24 (= F 63) and fr. XXI 2166 (d) 3 = F 87 (13) LP (Voigt does not record this last fragment). This combination shows us that the theme of old age was also delineated in another composition (F 63):

Ὄνοιρε μελαινα[˘ ˘ - - - ˘ - ˘ - -
_φ[ο]ίταις ὄτα τ' Ὕπνος [˘ ˘ - - - ˘ - ˘ - -
γλύκυς θ[έ]ος, ἦ δεῖν' ὀνίας μ[ανύματ' - ˘ - -
_ζὰ χῶρις ἔχην τὰν δύναμ[ιν - ˘ - ˘ - -
ἔλπις δέ μ' ἔχει μὴ πεδέχη[ν - ˘ ˘ - ˘]ησθα.   5
_μηδὲν μακάρων ἔλ[πομ' ἔχην δὶς πολύκα]ρπον ἄβαν·
οὐ̣ γάρ κ' ἔον οὔτω [˘ ˘ - - - ˘ - - ˘ ὤστε
_ἀθύρματα καὶ [- ˘ - - - ˘ - -˘]εσθαι·
γένοιτο δέ μοι [
_τοὶς πάντα [10

1 μελαίνα[ς διὰ νύκτος vel μελαίνα[ις πτερύγεσσιν Hunt, μέλαινα[ν κατὰ νύκτ' ὃς Snell 2 [καταχεύηι βλεφάροισι λάθαν Hunt, [κατέχηι μ(ε) Latte 3 μ[ανύματ' supplevi: μ[νάματ' Diehl fin. e.g. ἄμμι φαίνηις vel φέρηις 4 δύναμ[ιν Diehl fin. e.g. ὔμμιν ἀμάχανον δή 5 πεδέχη[ν Hunt φέρ]ησθα Puglia 6 ἔλ[πομ' Schadewaldt ἔχην δὶς supplevi πολύκα]ρπον Puglia 7 fin. ὤστε Puglia 8 fort. μά]εσθαι 9 fort. [γήρας

O Dream, [through] the dark [night ...]
you wander[25] while Sleep you [...]
sweet god, [you show us] terrible [presentiments] of anguish.
[It is truly impossible] to keep [your] power apart,

---

23 For ὄλοφυν at line 3 cf. Hesych. Ο 641 ὄλοφυς· οἶκτος, ἔλεος, θρῆνος.
24 See Tsomis 2001: 252.
25 Cf. A. Pr. 657 νυκτίφοιτ' ὀνείρατα.

but the hope of not having part [of the pain you bring]   5
comforts me.
No, I do not hope [to enjoy twice²⁶] the fecund youth of the blessed,
for I could not be so [foolish ... as to]
[still long for the] toys and [...],
but may mine be [an old age free of ills ...]
those that everything [10

The dream, personified, is apostrophized directly as at Hom. *Il.* 2.8 βάσκ᾽ ἴθι, οὖλε Ὄνειρε, θοὰς ἐπὶ νῆας Ἀχαιῶν and is almost reproached for having shown or brought expectations (premonitions) of anguish, in contrast to sleep. Hypnos is defined as "sweet god" at the beginning of l. 3.

In general it is understood that Oneiros arouses or sends "recollections" (μ[νάματ᾽ of Diehl) of anguish, but now that we know that the poem revolves around the antithesis of youth and old age we can exclude the possibility that Oneiros sends "recollections," much less recollections of anguish. The malignant deity must rather have revealed to the sleeping woman expectations or presentiments (μ[ανύματ᾽, cf. "Orph." *Hymn.* 86.16 ἀλλά, μάκαρ, λίτομαί σε θεῶν μηνύματα φράζειν precisely in the context of an apostrophe to Oneiros) connected to old age that the "I" is not in a condition to avert, except with the hope (ἔλπις at line 5) of not suffering its most painful consequences.²⁷

Therefore the recognition of the separation between the conditions of the gods, who enjoy a perpetual youth "full of blessings,"²⁸ and of the human impossibility of continuing to take pleasure in youthful playthings and diversions of youth (ἀθύρματα 8), does not result in depression, but in the prayer for a serene decline that keeps for the speaker the restorative power of sleep, without the anxiety of dreams.

26 Cf. Theogn. 1009 ff. οὐ γὰρ ἀνηβᾶν | δὶς πέλεται πρὸς θεῶν, .
27 For the declaration of line 4 Schadewaldt suggested comparing Pind. *N.* 6.1 ff. ἓν ἀνδρῶν, ἓν θεῶν γένος· ἐκ μιᾶς δὲ πνέομεν | ματρὸς ἀμφότεροι· διείργει δὲ πᾶσα κεκριμένα | δύναμις, ὡς τὸ μὲν οὐδέν, ὁ δὲ | χάλκεος ἀσφαλὲς αἰὲν ἕδος | μένει οὐρανός, but, as Puglia notes, this does not seem to concern the difference in terms of ability between men and gods (a motif that emerges however at line 6), but the impossibility of breaking the synergy between the power (cheering) of Hypnos—the νήδυμος Ὕπνος of Hom. *Il.* 14.242 and 354 (cf. Soph. *Ph.* 828 Ὕπν᾽ ὀδύνας ἀδαής, Ὕπνε δ᾽ ἀλγέων)—and that (anxiety bearing) of Oneiros.
28 The adjective πολύκαρπος recurs in the *Odyssey* in a literal sense of a vine or garden (7.122 and 24.221; cf. Eur. *Ph.* 230), but close to πολύκα]ρπον ἄβαν is the combination πολυάνθεμος ὥρη, which in Mimn. 2.1 W.² refers both to spring and, metaphorically, to youth (cf. line 3 ἄνθεσιν ἥβης and fr. 1.4 W.² ἥβης ἄνθεα, Hom. *Il.* 13.484 ἥβης ἄνθος, Tyrt. fr. 10.28 W.² ἥβης ἀγλαὸν ἄνθος).

Bibliography

Alexiou, M. *The Ritual Lament in Greek Tradition*. Cambridge, 1974.

Aloni, A. *Cantare glorie di eroi. Comunicazione e performance poetica nella Grecia arcaica*. Turin, 1998.

Aloni, A., ed. *Saffo. Frammenti*. Florence, 1997.

Andò, V. *L'ape che tesse. Saperi femminili nella Grecia antica*. Rome, 2005.

Andrisiano, A. "Sapph. fr. 67. Una rivale priva di stile." *MCr* 32–35 (1997–2000): 7–24.

Bartol, K. "Saffo e Dika (Sapph. 91 V.)." *QuadUrb* ns 56 (1997): 75–80.

Battezzato, L. *Saffo, Kleis e i Kleanaktidai*. Forthcoming.

Battezzato, L. "Song, Performance, and Text in the New Posidippus." *ZPE* 145 (2003): 31–43.

Bernouilli, J.J. *Griechische Ikonographie I*. Munich, 1901.

Bernsdorff, H. "Offene Gedichtsschlüsse." *ZPE* 153 (2005): 1–6.

Bonanno, M.G. "Saffo, fr. 1.1 (ποικιλόθρονος)." In *Mousa. Scritti in onore di Giuseppe Morelli*, 53–55. Bologna, 1997.

Brand, H. *Griechische Musikanten im Kult von der Frühzeit bis zum Beginn der Spätklassik*. Würzburg, 2000.

Bravo, B. *Pannychis e simposio. Feste private notturne di donne e uomini nei testi letterari e nel culto*. Pisa-Rome, 1997.

Broger, A. *Das Epitheton bei Sappho und Alkaios*. Innsbruck, 1996.

Brown, C. "Anactoria and the Χαρίτων ἀμαρύγματα: Sappho fr. 16, 18 Voigt." *Quad Urb* ns 32 (1989): 7–15.

Burnett, A.P. *Three Archaic Poets: Archilochus, Alcaeus, Sappho*. London, 1983.

Burzacchini, G. "Fenomenologia innodica nella poesia di Saffo." *Eikasmos* 16 (2005): 11–39.

Burzacchini, G. *Lirica arcaica (I)*. In *La Vecchiaia nel mondo antico, I, Grecia*, ed. U. Mattioli, 69–124. Bologna, 1995.

Burzacchini, G. *Saffo*. In *Lirici greci. Antologia*, ed. E. Degani and G. Burzacchini. Florence, 1977.

Calame, C., ed. *Alcman. Fragmenta*. Rome, 1983.

Calame, C. *Lex choeurs de jeunes filles en Grèce archaïque*. 2 vols. Rome, 1977.

Canfora, L. *Il papiro di Dongo*. Milan, 2005.

Cannatà Fera, M., ed. *Pindarus, Threnorum fragmenta*. Rome, 1990.

Cassano, G.B., in collaboration with S. Zoli. *E liberaci dal male oscuro*. Milan, 1993.

Catenacci, C. *Il tiranno e l'eroe: per un'archeologia del potere nella Grecia antica*. Milan, 1996.

Cavallini, E. "Due poetesse greche, I: Testimonianze antiche e versi di Saffo: alcune testimonianze a confronto." In *Rose di Pieria*, ed. F. De Martino, 99–116. Bari, 1990.

Cavallini, E. "Lesbo, Mileto, la Lidia: Sapph. frr. 16 e 96 Voigt." In *I luoghi e la poesia nella grecia antica*, ed. M. Vetta and C. Catenacci, 145–58. Alexandria, 2006.

Cavallini, E. *Presenza di Saffo e Alceo nella poesia greca fino ad Aristofane*. Ferrara, 1984.

Cerri, G. "Il significati di *sphregis* in Teognide e la salvaguardia dell'autenticità testuale nel mondo antico." *QS* 17 (1991): 21–40.

Ciani, M.G. *Psicosi e creatività nella scienza antica*. Padua, 1983.

Contiades Tsitsoni, E. *Hymenaios und Epithalamion. Das Hochzeitslied in der frühgriechischen Lyrik*. Stuttgart, 1990.

Cucchiarelli, A., ed. *La veglia di Venere*. Milan, 2003.

D'Alessio, G.B. "Tra gli dei ad Apollo, e tra gli uomini ad Echecrate. P. Louvre E 7734+7733 (*Pind. fr. dub. 333 S-M.*)." In *Poesia e religione in Grecia. Studi in onore di G.A. Privitera*, ed. M. Cannatà Fera and S. Grandolini, 233–61. Naples, 2000.

Davies, M. "Monody, Choral Lyric, and the Tyranny of the Handbook." *CQ* ns 38 (1988): 52–64.

Devereux, G. "The Nature of Sappho's Seizure in fr. 31 LP as Evidence of Her Inversion." *CQ* 20 (1970): 17–31.

Di Benedetto, V. "Contributi al testo di Saffo." *RFIC* 10 (1982): 5–21.

Di Benedetto, V. *Il medico e la malattia. La scienza di Ippocrate*. Turin, 1986.

Di Benedetto, V. "Il tema della vecchiaia e il fr. 58 di Saffo." *QuadUrb* ns 19 (1985): 145–63.

Di Benedetto, V. "Il tetrastico di Saffo e tre postille." *ZPE* 155 (2006): 5–18.

Di Benedetto, V. "Integrazioni al P. Oxy. 1231 di Saffo (frr. 27 e 22 V.). *QuadUrb* ns 24 (1986): 19–25.

Di Benedetto, V. "Intorno al linguaggio amoroso di Saffo." *Hermes* 113 (1985): 145–56.

Di Benedetto, V. "Introduzione." In *Saffo, Poesie*, ed. V. Di Benedetto and F. Ferrari, 5–78. Milan, 1987.

Di Benedetto, V. "La nuova Saffo e dintorni." *ZPE* 153 (2005): 7–20.

Di Benedetto, V. "Osservazioni sul nuovo papiro di Saffo." *ZPE* 149 (2004): 5–6.

Di Marco, M. "Una parodia di Saffo in Euripide (*Cycl.* 182–86)." *QuadUrb* ns 5 (1980), 39–45.

Dover, K.J. *Greek Homosexuality*. London, 1978.

Esposito, E., ed. *Il fragmentum Grenfellianum (P. Dryton 50)*. Bologna, 2005.

Fassino, M. and L. Prauscello. "Memoria ritmica e memoria poetica: Saffo e Alceo in Teocrito Idilli 28–30 tra ἀρχαιολογία metrica e innovazione alessandrina." *MD* 46 (2001): 9–37.

Ferrari, F. "Contro Andromeda: recupero di un'ode di Saffo." *MD* 55 (2005): 13–30.

Ferrari, F. "Due note al testo del fr. 2 di Saffo." *APapyrol* 12 (2000): 37–44.

Ferrari, F. "Formule saffiche e formule omeriche." *ASNP* s. III, 16 (1986): 441–47.

Ferrari, F. " 'Hai fatto la tua scelta': due storie di diserzione attraverso i papiri di Saffo." In *I papiri di Saffo e di Alceo*. Atti del Convegno Internazionale di Studi: Firenze, 8–9 giugno 2006, ed. G. Bastianini and A. Casanova, 17–29. Florence, 2007.

Ferrari, F. "Il pubblico di Saffo." *SIFC* s. IV, 1 (2003): 42–89.

Ferrari, F. "Il tempo del sonno: Saffo, fr 168B." *CivClCr* 4 (1983): 329–32.

Ferrari, F. "*P. Berol. inv. 13270*: i canti di Elefantina." *SCO* 38 (1988): 181–227.

Ferrari, F. "Per il testo di Posidippo." *MD* 54 (2005): 185–212.

Ferrari, F. "Saffo: Nevrosi e poesia." *SIFC* s. III, 19 (2001): 3–31.

Ferrari, F., ed. *Teognide, Elegie.* Milan, 1989.

Fraenkel, E. "An Epodic Poem of Hipponax." *CQ* 36 (1942): 54–56. Later published in *Kleine Beiträge zur klassischen Philologie I.* Rome, 1964.

Fränkel, H. *Dichtung und Philosophie des frühen Griechentums.* Munich, 1969.

Fränkel, H. Review of *The Fragments of the Lyrical Poems of Sappho* and *The Fragments of the Lyrical Poems of Alcaeus*, both ed. Edgar Lobel. *GGA* 1928: 258–78.

Friis Johansen, H. "Alcaeus and the Kottabos-Game." In *Studies in Honour of T.B.L. Webster*, ed. J.H. Betts, J.T. Hooker, and J.R. Green. 2 vols. 1: 93–101. Bristol, 1985.

Funghi, M.S. and G. Messeri Savorelli. "Lo scriba di Pindaro e le biblioteche di Ossirinco." *SCO* 42 (1992): 43–62.

Gentili, B. "Alceo, fr. 249 Voigt." *Sileno* 10 (1984): 241–43.

Gentili, B. *Poetry and Its Public in Ancient Greece from Homer to the Fifth Century.* Trans. A.T. Cole. Baltimore, 1988.

Gentili, B. et al., eds. *Pindaro. Le Pitiche.* Milan, 1995.

Gianotti, G.F. "Nota di lessicografia: Esichio B 1047 L." *QuadUrb* ns 9 (1981): 163–68.

Gossel-Raeck, B. "Komos-Bürger ziehen durch die Nacht." In *Kunst der Schale, Kultur des Trinkens*, ed. K. Vierneisel and B. Kaeser, 293–98. Munich, 1992.

Gostoli, A., ed. *Terpander.* Rome, 1990.

Grandolini, S. "Forme rituali e coscienza religiosa nel tiaso di Saffo." In *Poesia e religione in Grecia. Studi in onore di G.A. Privitera*, ed. M. Cannatà Fera and S. Grandolini, 353–65. Naples, 2000.

Greene, E., ed. *Reading Sappho. Contemporary Approaches.* Berkeley, CA,1996a.

Greene, E., ed. *Re-Reading Sappho. Reception and Transmission.* Berkeley, CA,1996b.

Greene, E. "Sappho, Foucault and Women's Erotics." *Arethusa* 29 (1996c): 1–14.

Gronewald, M. and R. Daniel, "Ein neuer Sappho-Papyrus." *ZPE* 147 (2004a): 1–8.

Gronewald, M. and R. Daniel, "Lyrischer Text (Sappho-Papyrus)." *ZPE* 154 (2005): 7–12.

Gronewald, M. and R. Daniel, "Nachtrag zum neuen Sappho-Papyrus." *ZPE* 149 (2004b): 1–4.

Hamm, E.M. (= E.M. Voigt). *Grammatik zu Sappho und Alkaios.* Berlin, 1958.

Hardie, A. "Sappho, the Muses and the Life after Death." *ZPE* 155 (2005): 13–32.

Henderson, J. *The Maculate Muse. Obscene Language in Attic Comedy.* 2nd ed. New Haven, 1991.

Hooker, J.T. *The Language and Text of the Lesbian Poets.* Innsbruck, 1977.

Hutchinson, G.O. *Greek Lyric Poetry. A Commentary on Selected Larger Pieces.* Oxford, 2001.

Janko, R. "Sappho Revisited." *Times Literary Supplement,* December 23 and 30, 2005.

Johnson, W.A. *Bookrolls and Scribes in Oxyrhynchus.* Toronto, 2004.

Kakridis, J.T. "Zu Sappho 44 LP." *WS* 79 (1966): 21–26.

Kirk, G.S. "A Fragment of Sappho Reinterpreted." *CQ* 13 (1963): 51–52.

Kurke, L. "The Politics of ἀβροσύνη in Archaic Greece." *CA* II (1992): 91–120.

Lanata, G. "L'ostracon fiorentino con versi di Saffo. Note paleografiche ed esegetiche." *SIFC* 31 (1959): 64–90.

Lanata, G. "Sui linguaggio amororo di Saffo." *QuadUrb* ns 2 (1966): 64–90. Published in English in *Reading Sappho, Contemporary Approaches,* ed. E. Greene, 11–25. Berkeley, CA, 1996.

Lapini, W. *Elementi biografici di Pittaco nei frammenti alcaici.* In *I papiri di Saffo e di Alceo.* Atti del Convegno Internazionale di Studi: Firenze, 8–9 giugno 2006, ed. G. Bastianini and A. Casanova, 167–75. Florence, 2007.

Lardinois, A. "Subject and Circumstance in Sappho's Poetry." *TAPA* 124 (1994): 57–84.

Lardinois, A. "Who Sang Sappho's Songs?" In *Re-Reading Sappho. Reception and Transmission,* ed. E. Greene, 150–72. Berkeley, CA, 1996b.

Lasserre, F. *Sappho: une autre lecture.* Padua, 1989.

Latacz, J. "Realität und Imagination." *Mus Helv* 42 (1985): 67–94.

Lavecchia, S., ed. *Pindari dithyramborum fragmenta.* Rome-Pisa, 2000.

Lefkowitz, M. *The Lives of Greek Poets.* London, 1981.

Lentini, G. "I simposi del tiranno: sui frr. 70–72 V. di Alceo." *ZPE* 139 (2002): 3–18.

Lentini, G. "Pittaco erede degli Atridi: il fr. 70 V. di Alceo." *SIFC* S. III, 18 (2000): 3–14.

Lesky, A. *History of Greek Literature.* London, 1966.

Liberman, G., ed. *Alcée. Fragments.* 2 vols. Paris, 1999.

Lissarrague, F. *Aesthetics of the Greek Banquet: Images of Wine and Rituals.* Trans. A. Szegedy-Maszak. Princeton, NJ, 1990.

Livrea, E. "Critica testuale ed esegesi del nuovo Posidippo." In *Il papiro di Posidippo un anno dopo,* ed. G. Bastianini and A. Casanova, 61–77. Florence, 2002.

Lloyd, A.B., ed. *Erodoto, Le Storie, vol. II, Libro II: L'Egitto.* Trans. A. Fraschetti. Milan, 1989.

Lobel, E. ΣΑΠΦΟΥΣ ΜΕΛΗ. *The Fragments of the Lyrical Poems of Sappho.* Oxford, 1925.

Lobel, E. and D. Page, eds. *Poetarum Lesbiorum fragmenta.* Oxford, 1955.

Luppe, W. "Überlegungen zur Gedicht-Anordnung im neuen Sappho-Papyrus." *ZPE* 149 (2004): 7–9.

Lyghounis, M.G. "Elementi tradizionali nella poesia nuziale greca." *MD* 27 (1991): 159–98.

Maas, P. *Kleine Schriften.* Munich, 1973.

Mace, S. "Utopian and Erotic Fusion in a New Elegy by Simonides (22 W^2)." *ZPE* 113 (1996): 233–47.

Malnati, A. "Revisione dell'ostrakon fiorentino di Saffo." *APapyrol* 5 (1993): 21–22.

Martinelli, M.C. *Gli strumenti del poeta. Elementi di metrica greca.* Bologna, 1991.

Marzullo, B. *Il problema omerico.* 2nd ed. Naples, 1970.

Marzullo, B. *Studi di poesia eolica.* Florence, 1958.

Mazzarino, S. *Fra Oriente e Occidente. Ricerche di storia greeca arcaica* (1947). Milan, 1989.

Mazzarino, S. "Per la storia di Lesbo nel VI secolo a.C." *Athenaeum* 21 (1943): 38–78.

Merkelbach, R. "Sappho und ihr Kreis." *Philologus* 101 (1957): 1–29.

Merkelbach, R. "Wartetext 11: Sappho?" *ZPE* 13 (1974): 214.

Muth, R. "Hymenaios und Epithalamion." *WS* 67 (1954): 47–58.

Nagy, G. "Phaethon, Sappho's Phaon, and the White Rock of Leukas." *HSCP* 77 (1973): 137–77.

Nagy, G. *Pindar's Homer. The Lyric Possession of an Epic Past.* Baltimore, MD, 1990.

Napolitano, G., ed. *Euripide, Ciclope.* Venice, 2003.

Neri, C., ed. *Erinna. Testimonianze e Frammenti.* Bologna, 2003.

Neri, C. and F. Citti. "Sudore freddo e tremore." *Eikasmos* 16 (2005): 52–62.

Nicosia, S. *Tradizione testuale diretta e indiretta dei poeti di Lesbo.* Rome, 1976.

Nilsson, M.P. *Geschichte der griechischen Religion.* Vol. 1. 3rd ed. Munich, 1967.

Nilsson, M.P. *The Minoan-Mycenaean Religion and Its Survival in Greek Religion.* 2nd ed. Lund, 1950.

Norsa, M. "Dai Papiri della Societa Italiana: Elezione del κεφαλαιωτής di una corporazione del V sec. d.C.; Versi di Saffo in un ostrakon del sec. II a. C." *ASNP*, s. 11, 6 (1937): 1–15 (8–15).

Noussia, M., ed. *Solone. Frammenti dell'opera poetica.* Trans. M. Fantuzzi. Milan, 2001.

Page, D., ed. *Further Greek Epigrams.* Cambridge, 1981.

Page, D. *Sappho and Alcaeus. An Introduction to the Study of Ancient Lesbian Poetry.* Oxford, 1955.

Palmisciano, R. "È mai esistita la poesia popolare nella Grecia antica?" In ΡΥΣ-ΜΟΣ. *Studi di poesia, metrica e musica greca offerti dagli allievi a Luigi Enrico Rossi per i suoi settant' anni*, ed. R. Nicolai, 151–71. Rome, 2003.

Palmisciano, R. "Lamento funebre, culto delle Muse e attese escatologiche in Saffo (con una verifica su Archiloco)." *SemRom* I (1998): 183–205.

Parker, H.N. "Sappho Schoolmistress." *TAPA* 123 (1993): 309–51.

Pernigotti, C. "Tempi del canto e pluralità di prospettive in Saffo, fr. 44 V." *ZPE* 135 (2001): 11–20.

Perrotta, G. *Saffo e Pindaro.* Bari, 1935.

Pigeaud, J. *Folie et cures de la folie chez les médecins de l' antiquité greco-romaine.* Paris, 1987.

Pigeaud, J. *La maladie de l'âme. Étude sur la relation de l'âme et du corps dans la tradition médico-philosophique antique.* Paris, 1981.

Pintaudi, R. "Ermeneutica *per epistulas*: l'ostrakon fiorentino di Saffo (PSI XIII 1300)." *APapyrol* 12 (2000): 45–62.

Pöhlmann, E. "Mündlichkeit und Schriftlichkeit Gestern und Heute." *WJ* 14 (1988): 7–20.

Porro, A. *Vetera Alcaica. L'esegesi di Alceo dagli Alessandrini all'età imperiale.* Milan, 1994.

Prauscello, L. *Singing Alexandria. Music between Practice and Textual Transmission.* Leiden-Boston, 2006.

Prauscello, L. and C. Pernigotti. " 'Spartiti musicali' nella Grecia ellenistica: pluralità delle occasioni del canto e discontinuità della tradizione." In *Mittelfest* 2001 —*Settore Musica a Arti visive, Grecia,* 29–37. Trieste, 2002.

Pretagostini, R. "Anacr. 33 Gent. 356 P.: due modalità simposiali a confronto." *Quad Urb* ns 10 (1982): 47–55.

Pretagostini, R. *Ricerche sulla poesia alessandrina*. Rome, 1984.

Privitera, G.A. *La rete di Afrodite. Studi su Saffo*. Palermo, 1974.

Puglia, E. "Per la ricomposizione del quarto libro dei canti di Saffo (POxy. 1787)." *SemRom* 10 (2007): 17–39.

Puglia, E. "P.Oxy. 2294 e la tradizione delle odi di Saffo." *ZPE* 166 (2008): 1–8.

Pugliese Carratelli, G. *Tra Cadmo e Orfeo. Contributi alla storia civile e religiosa d'Occidente*. Bologna, 1990.

Reitzenstein, R. *Epigramm und Skolion. Ein Beitrag zur Geschichte der alexandrinischen Dichtung*. Giessen, 1893.

Rissman, L. *Love as War: Homeric Allusion in the Poetry of Sappho*. Königstein, 1983.

Robbins, E. "Who's Dying in Sappho fr. 94?" *Phoenix* 44 (1990): 111–21.

Robert, L. *Opera minora selecta*. 2 vols., vol. 2. Amsterdam, 1969.

Rösler, W. *Dichter und Gruppe. Eine Untersuchung zu den Bedingungen und zur historischen Funktion früher griechischer Lyrik am Beispiel Alkaios*. Munich, 1980.

Schadewaldt, W. *Sappho, Welt und Dichtung*. Potsdam, 1950.

Schulze, W. *Quaestiones epicae*. Gütersloh, 1892.

Sider, D., ed. *The Epigrams of Philodemos*. Oxford, 1997.

Simon, B. *Mind and Madness in Ancient Greece. The Classical Roots of Modern Psychiatry*. Ithaca, NY, 1978.

Snell, B. "Der Anfang eines äolischen Gedichts." *Hermes* 81 (1953): 118–19.

Snell, B. "Sapphos Gedicht ΦΑΙΝΕΤΑΙ ΜΟΙ ΚΗΝΟΣ." *Hermes* 66 (1931): 71–90.

Snyder, J. McIntosh. *Lesbian Desire in the Lyrics of Sappho*. New York, 1997.

Sofia, A. "Nosside, Saffo e la lirica d'amore neoegizia." *ARF* 8 (2006): 53–70.

Stehle, E. *Performance and Gender in Ancient Greece. Nondramatic Poetry in Its Setting*. Princeton, NJ, 1997.

Strauss Clay, J. *The Politics of Olympos. Form and Meaning in the Major Homeric Hymns*. Princeton, NJ, 1989.

Tedeschi, G. *Saffo. Biografia e antologia di versi*. Trieste, 2005.

Tomsen, O. *Ritual and Desire: Catullus 61 and 62*. Aarhus, 1992.

Treu, M. "Neues über Sappho und Alkaios (P. Oxy. 2506)." *QuadUrb* ns 2 (1966): 9–36.

Treu, M. *Sappho*. 2nd ed. Munich, 1954.

Tsomis, G. *Zusammenschau der frühgriechischen monodischen Melik (Alkaios, Sappho, Anakreon)*. Stuttgart, 2001.

Turner, E.G. *Greek Papyri*. Oxford, 1968.

Turner, E.G. *The Papyrologist at Work*. Durham, NC, 1973.

Vetta, M., ed. *Aristofane, Le donne all'assemblea*. Trans. D. del Corno. Milan, 1989.

Vetta, M. *Symposion. Antologia dai lirici greci*. Naples, 1999.

Vetta, M., ed. *Theognis. Elegiarum liber secundus*. Rome, 1980.

Vogliano, A., ed. *Sappho: una nuova ode della poetessa*. Milan, 1941.

Voigt, E.-M., ed. *Sappho et Alcaeus*. Amsterdam, 1971.

West, M.L. "Alcmanica I. The Date of Alcman." *CQ* 15 (1965): 188–202.

West, M.L. *Ancient Greek Music.* Oxford, 1992.

West, M.L. "Burning Sappho." *Maia* 22 (1970): 307–30.

West, M.L., ed. *Hesiod. Works and Days.* Oxford, 1978.

West, M.L. "Notes on Sappho and Alcaeus." *ZPE* 80 (1990): 1–8.

West, M.L. "The New Sappho." *ZPE* 151 (2005): 1–9.

Wilamowitz-Moellendorff, U. von. "Neue lesbische Lyrik (Oxyrhynchus Papyri X)." *NJA* 33 (1914): 225–47. Later in *Kleine Schriften*, vol. 1, 384–414. Berlin, 1935.

Wilamowitz-Moellendorff, U. von. *Sappho und Simonides. Untersuchungen über griechische Lyriker.* Berlin, 1913.

Williamson, M. *Sappho's Immortal Daughters.* Cambridge, MA, 1995.

Winkler, J.J. *The Constraints of Desire. The Anthropology of Sex and Gender in Ancient Greece.* London, 1990.

Yatromanolakis, D. "Alexandrian Sappho Revisited." *HSCP* 99 (1999b): 179–95.

Yatromanolakis, D. "Contrapuntal Inscriptions." *ZPE* 152 (2005): 16–30.

Yatromanolakis, D. "Ritual Poetics in Archaic Lesbos: Contextualizing Genre in Sappho." In D. Yatromanolakis and P. Roilos, eds., 43–59. *Towards a Ritual Poetics.* Athens, 2003.

Yatromanolakis, D. "Visualizing Poetry: An Early Representation of Sappho." *CP* 96 (2001): 159–68.

Yatromanolakis, D. "When Two Fragments Meet: Sapph. fr. 22 V." *ZPE* 128 (1999a): 23–24.

Zellner, H. "Sappho's super-superlatives." *CQ* 56 (2006): 292–97.

Additional Bibliography to the English Edition

Bastianini, G. and Casanova, A., eds. *I papiri di Saffo e di Alceo. Atti del Convegno Internazionale di Studi: Firenze, 8–9 giugno 2006.* Florence, 2007.

Ferrari, F. "Due sequenze saffiche in *P.Oxy.* 1787: Esili e i tre carmi dell'ultima colonna." *SemRom* 10 (2007): 10–15.

Prauscello, L. "Le 'orecchie' di Saffo: qualche osservazione in margine a Sapph. 31.11–12 V. e alla sua ricezione antica." In G. Bastianini and A. Casanova, eds., 191–207 and plate vii. *I papiri di Saffo e di Alceo. Atti del convegno internazionale di studi, Firenze, 8–9 giugno 2006.* Florence 2007.

Puglia, E. "P.Oxy. 2294 e la tradizione delle odi di Saffo." *ZPE* 166 (2008): 1–8.

Rawles, R. "Notes on the Interpretation of the 'New Sappho'." *ZPE* 157 (2006): 1–7.

Rösler, W. "Ein Gedicht und sein Publikum. Überlegungen zu Sappho Fr. 44 Lobel-Page." *Hermes* 103 (1975): 275–85.

Yatromanolakis, D. *Sappho in the Making. The Early Reception.* Cambridge, MA, 2007.

Indices

Index Verborum